THEORIES OF DEVELOPMENT

THEORIES OF DEVELOPMENT

RICHARD PEET

with

ELAINE HARTWICK

THE GUILFORD PRESS
New York / London

© 1999 The Guilford Press
A Division of Guilford Publications, Inc.
72 Spring Street, New York, NY 10012
http://www.guilford.com

Printed in the United States of America

This book is printed on acid-free paper.

Last digit is print number: 9   8   7   6   5

Library of Congress Cataloging-in-Publication Data

Peet, Richard.
    Theories of development / Richard Peet with Elaine Hartwick.
      p. cm.
    Includes bibliographical references (p.   ) and index.
    ISBN 1-57230-489-8 (pbk.)
    1. Economic development.   2. Dependency.   3. Capitalism.
  4. Marxian economics.   I. Hartwick, Elaine R. (Elaine Rachel),
  1961– .   II. Title.
  HD72.P44   1999
  338.9—dc21   99-28968
                                                  CIP

For our parents,

Eileen Migala
Harold Wilfred Peet
Anna B. Hartwick
John A. Hartwick

ABOUT THE AUTHORS

Richard Peet holds a PhD from the University of California, Berkeley. He was editor of *Antipode: A Radical Journal of Geography* between 1969 and 1985 and coeditor of *Economic Geography* between 1992 and 1998. His research interests include the study of underdevelopment, global systems, and the geography of consciousness and rationality. He is presently a professor in the Graduate School of Geography, Clark University, Worcester, Massachusetts.

Elaine R. Hartwick received a PhD from the Graduate School of Geography, Clark University, Worcester, Massachusetts, in 1995. Her current research is concerned with a politics of consumption, using poststructural thought, "materialist deconstruction," and commodity chain analysis. She has taught at the University of Southern Maine, Central Connecticut State College, Clark University, and Keene State College.

PREFACE

This book began as a rewrite of *Global Capitalism*, published by
Routledge in 1991. But it quickly became far more than that.
Indeed, we retained only a few paragraphs from the earlier work.
There are four new chapters, while the other three now display only ves-
tiges of their former contents. The book is much more a critical survey of
the main theories of development than a geography of global capitalism,
although the intent remains one of explaining differences in the spatial
distribution of wealth and poverty. We wrote the book during a period
of transformation in the global economy, a period when the "new"
international division of labor entered middle-aged crisis, while the "certainties" of the past thirty years were becoming increasingly precarious,
when the economic "miracles" of East Asia and Latin America became
mirages almost overnight. During this time, the need for fundamental
understanding, the need for reexamining the great attitudinal paradigms
of development, took on new significance. This lent our work an
urgency which, we hope, spills over onto its pages, lending the contents
some semblance, at least, of the seriousness we felt in writing them.

Despite its somewhat strange designation of authorship, Richard
Peet *with* Elaine Hartwick, this book results from long collaboration
between what is now a wife and husband partnership. Specifically,
Elaine wrote most of Chapter 6, while Richard wrote most of the rest.
More generally the book results from many conversations and collabo-
rations stretching over spaces and times scattered across the last fifteen
years of our friendship. The designation "with" is the consequence of
Elaine's New England reticence for accepting "credit" for that which she
did not write directly. "Authorship" should actually include many others
for, as quickly becomes apparent, we draw on the work of dozens of
writers in a synthetic statement which tries to represent the finest ideas

in the field of development from the past two centuries and more—from Adam Smith, through Karl Marx, to contemporary feminist and post-structural thinkers. Most of the ideas that appear in the book "belonged" originally to others, and we take responsibility only for the way they are presented in this instance. Even so, we have not taken a passive attitude toward these ideas, content merely to present them accurately. Instead, each chapter concludes with a critique which tries to undercut the very foundation on which the ideas rest. Is this because we feel criticism to be the highest form of appreciation? Or does it result from a more pragmatic political conclusion that thinking about development needs rethinking, not only in the postdevelopmental sense of destabilizing modern certainty, but more in the critical modernist sense of replacement with something better? In answer we can only say that our intention has been to survey the past in order to stimulate a new discourse about development in the future, and that this entails criticism which delights in negative excess, but also criticism which aims eventually at positive replacement.

Both of us have taught the book several times—indeed, as we wrote it, dreams of past conversations with our students colored the grey matter of our theoretical memories. Elaine would like to thank students at SUNY Albany, Mount Holyoke College, the University of Southern Maine, Central Connecticut State College, Clark University, and Keene State College who participated in her courses dealing with many of the issues in this book. Elaine would also like to thank Susi Steinmann of Clark University for her friendship and conversations. Richard would like to thank his students in political economy and advanced development theory at Clark University, and also participants in courses taught at the University of Iowa, the University of California at Santa Barbara, and the University of the Witwatersrand in Johannesburg, South Africa. The Guilford Press had an earlier draft read by two reviewers, and the comments of one of these, Susan Roberts, of the University of Kentucky, proved useful in revising our earlier version—we thank Susan for her time, effort, and criticisms. The book is dedicated to our parents directly, for making our ideas possible, but also to all working-class peoples indirectly, for their labor that makes existence possible. As Marx said a hundred and fifty years ago, "The philosophers have only interpreted the world, in various ways; the point, however, is to change it."

RICHARD PEET
ELAINE HARTWICK
Leominster, Massachusetts

CONTENTS

Chapter 1

INTRODUCTION

Development is a founding belief of the modern world. Progress has long since replaced God as the icon of our age. In development, all the modern advances in science, technology, democracy, values, ethics, and social organization fuse into the single humanitarian project of producing a far better world. In its strong sense, development means using the productive resources of society to improve the living conditions of the poorest people. In its weaker sense, development means more of everything for everyone in the context of a lot more for a few. Even in this latter form, when development basically means economic growth led by an elite, faint echoes can be still be heard of the progressive notion of improving the material life conditions for many people—although the main mechanism by which this transfer is supposed to occur, through "trickle-down" from the rich to the poor, must arouse intense suspicion.

Development differs from economic growth in that it pays attention to the conditions of production, for example, the environments affected by economic activity, and to the social consequences, for example, income distribution and human welfare. Stemming from Enlightenment notions of the use of the modern, scientific mind for improving existence, development entails human emancipation in two senses: liberation from the vicissitudes of nature through advanced technology and self-emancipation, that is, control over social relations, conscious control over the conditions under which human nature is formed. In both senses, development entails economic, social, and cultural progress, including, in the latter sense, finer ethical ideals and higher moral values. Development means improvement in a complex of linked natural, economic, social, cultural, and political conditions. Developmentalism is the belief in the viability and desirability of this kind of economic progress.

1

Such self-congratulatory views of modern developmentism have been challenged several times—by romanticism, anarchism, and marxism in the nineteenth century; by existentialism in the early twentieth century; and by postmodernism and feminism in the late twentieth century. Critics say that Western modernism and developmentism, exactly by monopolizing dreams of progress, destroy alternative conceptions of the future based in the ancient cultures found in the world's regions other than Europe. Also, it is pointed out, progress generates its own breed of victims: peasants relegated to peripheries drained of their youth, "nimble-fingered" women assigned the most boring tasks in computer chip mills, colonized societies raided for resources, their people moved at random to satisfy the whims of corporate leaders, or manipulated as mass markets for goods, such as cigarettes, now deemed too dangerous for Western lungs. Then, too, progress leaves basic needs (like housing and food) unmet even in the citadels of modernity, in the inner cities of the United States, which are filled with the homeless, plagued by drug addiction (despite the incarceration of millions of addicts), let alone in the megacities at the fringes of the modern world teeming with desperate hordes of rural migrants. Modern Reason in its "Purityrannical" form drains experience of emotion so that people become machine-like workers. Modern advertising converts the previously discriminating into consumption drones running to buy "the latest thing" (as with Beanie Baby frenzies). What appear to be the finest developmental principles behind the best of modern existence are increasingly subject to intense skepticism. Modernity, reason, development, and consumption are no longer deemed automatically "good" by thinking beings.

Yet development, and the theories that explain it, have been lain to rest before, criticized for being at an impasse, outdated, moribund, or morally corrupt, only to rise again. When something is heavily criticized, yet persists, it probably has real content. Could it be that development embodies both the best and worst of human projects? Either way, as the finest ideal of an enlightened humanity, or as a strategy of modern mind control, development is too easily simplified, too quickly dismissed, and then too readily forgotten—especially by those who take its undoubted benefits for granted. This book argues that development is a complex, contradictory phenomenon, one reflective of the best of human aspirations and yet, exactly because great ideas form the basis of power, subject to the most intense manipulation and liable to be used for purposes that reverse its original ideal intent. Theories of development reach deep into culture and metaphilosophy for explanatory and persuasive power, while the end products of such deep thinking, together with the dedicated practices of millions of well-meaning people, are political tools with mass appeal. Developmentalism is a battle ground where contention rages between bureaucratic economists, Marxist revolutionaries, environmental activists, feminist critics, postmodern skeptics, radical democrats, and others. This is an area with profound significance for the interests of the world's most vulnerable people, an area where shifts in emphasis, for example, the World Bank's move from supporting basic needs in the 1970s to advocating structural adjustment in the 1990s, can result in the deaths of thousands of babies and make life far more miserable, desperate, and short for countless millions in countries distant from London, Geneva, or Washington, DC, where the decisions are made. Therefore we have to make clear the basic theoretical positions in the development debate through effective presentation and thorough critique. We have to survey fundamental criticisms of the whole development enterprise. And we must not let these criticisms rest easily on the assumption that because they are "the latest thing," they are the last, best word. From the critique of development might yet still come . . . another development?

The Geography of Development

Development theories differ according to the political positions of their adherents, their philosophical origins, and their place and time of construction. They differ also according to scientific orientation, that is, whether predominantly economic, sociological, anthropological, historical, or geographical. Social science looks at the human being as an individual; at the society as a collective of individuals organized into groups, like classes, genders, or races; at the interactions between individuals and collectivities; and at the world as a natural entity and a system of interacting societies. Societies and human individuals vary greatly from one time and place to another time and place, particularly in the social and economic type of their development process or, more generally, their historical dynamic, and in the consequences development entails in terms of life chances and material circumstances.

These variations in level of development are explored in this book mainly from a geographical perspective. The disciplinary specialization called "geography" looks at two aspects of life, which it claims are interrelated: the aspect of nature, that is, the relations between societies and environments, and the aspect of space, that is, the regional variations in societies, together with spatial relations between regionally differing societal types. The connection between the two types of geography is that regional variations are essentially produced by differing ways of socially transforming nature. For example, different types of economy, such as agriculture, industry, or services, or different complexes of social relations, such as kin-ordered societies or capitalist societies of various kinds, have different types and degrees of relations with natural environments; they are also bound together through various kinds of spatial relation, such as commodity chains, the communication of messages, or the flow of profits; and the entire complex of regional economic forms, tied together by spatial relations, makes up a whole way of life, a global totality composed from myriad local forms. This way of approaching the totality of existence goes through its regional and local parts.

The mode of the production of existence (the character of its main social forces, relations, institutions, and thought patterns) varies over space. Most significantly, the degree of material development, particularly the standard of living, is completely different in one place and society than in another. This entails different lifestyles and life chances for individuals born at various places on the earth's surface: for example, in some places children almost automatically survive their traumatic first moments, while in other places death follows quickly on birth so often as to be expected. An individual's life is experienced as having some fundamental similarities with the lives of all other people, indeed with all other natural organisms, but is also a definite version or, in the case of geography, a place-bound type, of this entire existence. In other words, life has universal qualities and particular characteristics. Real differences in the mode of life, differences that arise from spatial variations in the type and level of development, are what geographers try to understand as their specialized task in social science.

Measuring the Geography of Development

In capitalist societies development is conventionally measured in terms purely of the size of the economy, as the Gross National Product (GNP)—that is, the value of the "total final output of goods and services produced by an economy" (World Bank 1989: 291). Generally, the higher the GNP/capita ("per capita income"), the more "developed" a country or region is said to be. Economic growth is conventionally measured in terms of increase in the total size of the economy: the higher the annual growth of GNP/capita, the more rapidly a country is said to "develop." In the mid-1990s, the World Bank (1997: 214–215), the global institution that publishes much of the basic data on such matters, called 49 countries "low income" because GNP/capita averaged less than $730 a year; 58 countries were called "middle income" with GNP/capita in the $770–$8,210 range; and 25 countries were labeled "high income" with GNP/capita in the $9,700–$40,630 range. As shown by Table 1.1, 4.8 billion people live in low- and middle-income countries (the "Third World") where GNP/capita averages $1,090 a year. By comparison 0.9 billion people live in high-income countries (the "First World") where GNP/capita averages $24,930. Furthermore, high-income countries, for the last decade, had GNP/capita growth rates far higher (1.9% a year) than the low- and middle-income countries (0.4% a year). Without China's rapid GNP growth (8.3% a year), and GNP growth rates of 4–8% a year in a few industrializing and oil-exporting economies, conditions in the economies of the Third World countries, as measured by change in GNP/capita, have been getting worse. Other data frequently used to measure standard of living—poverty, life expectancy, calorie intake, infant mortality, population per physician, secondary education, and use of commercial energy and electricity—support conclusions apparent from the income tables: people in different kinds of places live at entirely dissimilar material levels.

An alternative measure that takes into account social and cultural variables more attuned to development than just economic growth alone is the "Human Development Index" (HDI) calculated by the United Nations Development Program (UNDP). Stemming from an alternative conception of development, "enlarging people's choices," especially in terms of increasing access to knowledge, nutrition and health services, security, leisure, political and cultural freedoms, the HDI measures "development" in terms of longevity (life expectancy at birth), knowledge (adult literacy and mean years of schooling), and income sufficiency (the proportion of people with sufficient resources to live a decent life). By comparing countries in terms of GNP/capita and HDI at the same time, the emphasis on the provision of basic social services to all people (HDI), relative to the economic ability for providing these services (GNP), emerges as a key indicator of level of development as "social progress." For example, Malaysia and Iraq have the same per capita GNP, but life expectancy in Malaysia is five years longer, adult literacy 17 percentage points higher, and infant mortality less than one-fourth that in Iraq (these figures predate the Gulf War). In 1998 the countries at the top of the HDI were Canada, France, Norway, the United States, Iceland, Finland, the Netherlands, Japan, New Zealand, and Sweden (United Nations Development Program 1998). The UNDP also calculates a "Human Freedom Index" that measures political participation, the rule of law, freedom of expression, and nondiscrimination because, as one commentator puts it, "life expectancy and literacy could be quite high in a well managed prison. Basic physical needs are well met in a zoo" (Streeten 1995: xiv). This index places countries like Sweden, Denmark, and the Netherlands in the high freedom range and those like

TABLE 1.1. Area, Population, and Income in 1995

Economies grouped by income level and region	Number of countries	Surface area (000 sq km)	Population (millions)	GDP ($000 millions)	GNP Per capita ($)	GNP Avg. annual growth, 1985–1995 (%)
Low income	49	40,600	3,180	1,352	430	3.8
Middle income	58	60,840	1,590	4,033	2,390	-0.7
Low and middle income	107	101,450	4,770	5,393	1,090	0.4
Sub-Saharan Africa	—	—	583	297	490	-1.1
East Asia and Pacific	—	—	1,706	1,341	800	7.2
South Asia	—	—	1,243	439	350	2.9
Europe and Central Asia	—	—	489	1,103	2,220	-3.5
Middle East and North Africa	—	—	272	—	1,780	-0.3
Latin America and Caribbean	—	—	478	1,688	3,320	0.3
High income	26	32,040	902	22,486	24,930	1.9
World	133	133,480	5,673	27,846	4,880	0.8

Source: World Bank (1997).

Haiti, Zambia, and Malaysia in the low freedom range. The idea behind this kind of work is to capture more, and different, aspects of the human condition in a redefinition of development (ul Haq 1995; United Nations Development Program 1991, 1998).

This notion of human development defends the project of intervening in the improvement of conditions in the "developing countries." So the United Nations's annual *Human Development Report* carries a balance sheet of "progress" over the last 30 years. In the developing countries average life expectancy increased by a third, to 63 years; the proportion of people with access to health services rose to 63%; adult literacy rates increased from 46% to 60%; mortality rates for children under five were halved; primary school enrollment for females increased from 79% to 87%; and the proportion of rural people with access to adequate sanitation doubled. Thus, for the UNDP (1991: 14), development "has succeeded beyond any reasonable expectation. . . . Developing countries have achieved in 30 years what it took industrial countries nearly a century to accomplish. . . . The overall policy conclusion is clear. The development process *does* work. International development cooperation *has* made a difference."

However the UNDP then shows that the gap between rich and poor countries widened so that the average household in Africa now consumes 20% less than it did a quarter-century ago, while Americans spend more on cosmetics than it would cost to provide basic education to the two billion people in the world who lack schools, and Europeans spend more on ice cream than it would cost to provide water and sanitation to those in need (UNDP 1998). The UNDP optimistically concludes that human development can be achieved by promoting more equitable economic growth and by using participatory, democratic political methods. The organization proposes that poor countries "leapfrog" over the Industrial Revolution to use modern, efficient technologies.

Critique—I

We should immediately note two kinds, or even levels, of deficiency associated with the official data and the conclusions drawn from them. At the first level of criticism, not only do the data vary greatly in reliability from country to country, but basic accuracy in measuring things like production, income, education, or the use of energy has to be treated with the deepest suspicion. National and international agencies report only that which can be measured using conventional accounting procedures. Whose "convention" is "conventional"? That of the First World market economies, of course! Thus "Gross Domestic Product" (GDP) measures that part of production sold for a price in a formal market. Note that GDP is usually defined as total personal consumption expenditures, plus gross domestic investment, plus government purchases of goods and services, plus or minus net exports of goods and services. But, products consumed within the family, or exchanged "informally," a major part of economic activity in many Third World countries, are ignored or underestimated. Much of this unreported product results from women's work (Rogers 1980: 61): 60–80% of the food produced in the "informal sector" and 70% of informal entrepreneurs are women (Snyder 1995: xv). All this literally does not count when measuring the economy. In Russia, a government survey of the 210 largest companies revealed that more than 70% of receipts are collected in nonmonetary forms (*New York Times* September 6, 1998: 6). Estimates made in France, generally considered to be a highly organized market economy, show informal exchanges of income, such as gifts, amounting to 75% of the official GNP (Insel 1993). The figure is much higher in Third World countries where far more economic activity takes place outside formal markets. Similarly, "education" is officially measured as enrollment in a "school" and thus excludes informal educational institutions; "energy consumption" excludes "traditional fuels" like firewood and dried animal excrement; and so on. Many critics conclude that GNP and GDP measure economic modernization in the prejudiced sense of how closely a country replicates the characteristics of the West, rather than development in a whole range of indigenous senses. Increases in GNP/capita, energy use, or education may merely reflect an increase in the proportion of activity occurring in the organized, taxed, market sector of an economy, rather than in the informal sector; total production, or commitment of resources to education or health services, could actually be declining. GDP may measure quantitative change in market production ("economic growth"), but it is a gross indicator when it comes to the qualities of domestic production.

Average figures like GDP/capita, or people per physician, hide so many differences between groups within countries, as between classes or genders, or between rural and urban populations, that the figure is often meaningless in terms of representing the real situation. Generally, Third World countries have more unequal income distributions than First World countries, inequality being measured in social terms, like class, and in spatial terms, like region. The poorest fifth of families receive 4.6% of national income in the 26 low- and middle-income countries for which data are available, while the poorest fifth receive 6.5% in 20 high-income countries (World Bank 1989: 222–223). The difference at the other end of the class spectrum is even wider, with the richest fifth of families receiving 56.3% of income in low- and middle-income countries and 40.4% in high-income countries. Some Third World countries have such distorted income and consumption distributions that social revolution (which often appears as crime and violence) is endemic: in Guatemala, the richest 20% of the population receive 63% of total income, while the poorest 20% receive 2.1%; in South Africa, the equivalent figures are 63% and 3.3%; in Brazil, the split is 67.5% and 2.1%, indicating that Brazil is the most unequal society in the world (World Bank 1997: 222–223). Looking at another key social indicator, the number of people per physician is 5,410 for all low-income countries, but 77,360 for Ethiopia where, in addition, most physicians practice in cities and towns—hence formally trained physicians are effectively unavailable in rural Ethiopia. In summary, the available data give only a poor and misleading indication of the level and movement of economic development, if by this term we basically mean the level of material standards of living for the majority of the population. However, it remains the case that differences in living standards between peoples with $300 a year (most of Africa) and those with $20,000 or more a year (much of Western Europe, North America, and Japan) are so profound, no matter how far the data are biased, that we can theorize about entirely different regional levels of development.

Accepting the critique that the available statistical data give but a poor representation of social and economic reality, we can proceed, with trepidation, to look at the broad patterns of development distributed across earth space. Looking at the data we can safely generate a simple statement: geographic inequality between countries in the global system is more extreme than social inequality between income groups in the world's most unequal country! Sixteen percent of the world's people living in 26 high income countries have 80.75% of the world's income, while 56% of the world's people living in 49 low-income countries have only 4.85% of the world's income. Again, this simple statement survives even serious problems with the data. Thus, by combining income with distribution and growth rate figures, we can see who uses the world's resources, and for what purpose. The answer is a few tens of millions of rich people satisfying their whims and desires, and not the billions of poor people trying to satisfy their needs: a mere 5% of the world's people have 50% of the world's income and consume an even higher proportion of its resources (perhaps as much as 75%) at a rate that is growing by 2 or 3% a year. As we said a little earlier, there are significant regional differences in the conditions of human existence and in relations with natural environments. These differences have drastic consequences.

The analogy between class and geography is not accidental according to some (critical) theories. Class processes yield dissimilar income levels within national populations because some people get their livelihoods at the expense of others. This is true also in terms of space: explaining the small sizes of the economies of countries in Latin America, Africa, and South Asia is impossible except in relation to the large sizes of the Western European and North American economies. In the radical view, income flows between classes *and* among regions, to the advantage of some and the disadvantage of others, while nation-states are political containers for the accumulation of economic wealth. The geography of trade is a massive spatial process of wealth transfer: trade does not equalize, but instead concentrates wealth. If satellites were used to record economic movements over space, the world would look like a giant wealth-accumulation system, with status, power, and income focused on (over)consumption in a few hundred privileged suburbs. Income and resources flow over space from poor to rich countries and then to the elite areas within these rich countries. Class, gender, race, and space interact in the causes of inequality.

Critique—II

Now, however, we move to the second, more profound level of criticism of the use of GNP and GDP data to measure development. Even when qualified by statements about the unreliability and insufficiency of the data, conclusions drawn from income figures are increasingly suspect to those theorists intensely skeptical about modernity, development, progress, and many similar notions previously taken for granted in the post-Enlightenment world. The argument is increasingly made that GNP/capita, and even more benign statistical devices like the HDI, have *nothing* to do with the quality of life. This applies to peasants on the margins of a supposedly good earth, but also to the richest people ensconced in the suburbs of Western cities, whose lives are impoverished by an abundance of gadgets and whose aspirations are limited merely to getting more. Statistical tables of GNP/capita are seen as instruments of power, rather than as neutral methods of measurement, because their very structures, as comparative series, implies a hierarchy that must be replicated for people to be said to be living well. High per capita GNP, reached through economic growth, becomes the objective of development, the economic and political methods used by the rich countries become development policy, and success is measured by changes in tabular ranking. Yet some theorists persist in saying that people are not statistics but living beings. And there is the underlying contradiction that as GNP increases, resource use and environmental damage increase even faster, with proven results like destruction of the protective ozone layer, or possible consequences like El Nino effects exaggerated by global warming. In discourses that transcend developmentalism (discourses in the "post-developmentalist" tradition) GNP/capita measures, if anything, cultural deprivation and environmental degradation.

Critical Modernist Development

Here we take a critical modernist view, one that hears and takes seriously objections to the modern enterprise of development, but finds still unrealized potentials in progress and modernity. According to this view, quantitative measures of GNP/capita and qualitative information on standards of living retain usefulness in pointing to the gross inequalities emerging from processes of modernization. Indeed, the data reveal poverty so horrendous that it is impossible for ethical people to conclude that the modern history of the West should ever be repeated in anything like the same form. Yet the data also reveal that forms of thought (like rationalism) and techniques of production (like mechanization) have been discovered, elaborated, and practiced that enable security of life for larger numbers of people than ever before. Modern economic growth underlies basic discoveries in medical science, while a sophisticated economic infrastructure enables hospitals to function. To give but one example: in regions where all childbirths are attended by a trained health professional, the maternal mortality rate is less than 25 per 100,000 births: but where only a third of births are professionally supervised, the maternal mortality rate is 400–600 per 100,000 births, and is over 1,000 in some countries (UNDP 1991: 28, 142–143). For a critical modernist these are important social indicators. They show the positive potential of modernity, what might be done under the right circumstances. For a critical modernist, therefore, development must involve growth in that part of a society's economy that serves the needs of poor people. The fact that growth for poor people has to "trickle down" from growth for rich people shows the degree to which the modern organization of growth needs changing. Critical modernism does not challenge economic growth in and of itself. A critical modernist wants to extend the benefits from economic growth to a world of people, starting with the poorest while, in the process, transforming social relations of control to democratize all aspects of existence, and rethinking relations with nature to ensure both continued livelihoods and the fecundity of nature. This is a tall order, even more difficult, theoretically and practically, than totally rejecting modernity or development. It deserves the finest efforts of our most committed theorists and social activists.

Ethics of Development

The discussion so far implies a significant ethical dimension to development. Why is it important that academic specializations, like geography, economics, anthropology, or sociology, yield insights into basic human processes like growth, development, and progress? The reason could simply be to understand life better in that idealistic, liberal Enlightenment tradition that regards greater understanding as the main goal in life, with education as its means. But for many academics, students, and policymakers the drive to understand derives from an ethical, political ideal beyond understanding for its own sake. Many of us are primarily motivated by a desire to change the activities that make life possible, or rather by an urge to improve them. Human beings are differentiated from the rest of nature mainly by self-consciousness, by which is meant the ability to contemplate existence, even to the point of trying to find its meaning. By applying thought to guiding the productive process in a beneficial way, humans have the potential to live well—that is, with material sufficiency and in social and natural harmony. But, as we argued previously, this modern potential is realized to differing degrees, is corrupted, or used as domination, depending on the power relations within which life is conducted. The purpose of a *critical* modernist developmentalism, to which this book aspires, involves examining the causes of material differences with a view to changing them, enabling more human potentials to be realized, especially for people whose life chances are restricted (or even eliminated) by the constant pressure of overwhelming need. This is merely a more precise version of the purpose of radical modern science in general: making the world a better place.

Arguments within Western Developmentalism

This book surveys some of the leading social and economic theories of development. The basic pattern of affluence and poverty that characterizes the contemporary geography of the world was already obvious in the nineteenth century, and immediately stimulated intense social scientific interest. However, scientific interest is hardly separable from the desire for social legitimation. A good theorist always pursues truth. But "truth" varies depending on the truth teller's proclivities. And the theorist's logical capacity is not located in a sphere separate from her empathy for others, his desire for self-justification, or one's wish to be of service to the dominant social order. The connections between science and values are especially evident when an issue like the development of some people at the expense of others rises reluctantly in the imagination. Theory easily diverts into ideology when the mind tries to comprehend scarcely comprehensible things like racism, imperialism, sexism, and exploitation, all of which are involved in unequal development.

With notions like these in mind, that is, ideology as partial and biased "truths," we first survey some system-supporting (politically conservative) theories of uneven growth and development. Chapter 2 isolates the economic aspect of development, the part designated as economic growth, and separates out the specialized study of this dimension, the discipline called economics, for particularly intensive examination. Anyone wishing to understand development theory must know the basic history of economic theories. Yet economic ideas cannot entirely be separated from their material and ideational contexts. So we delve into the philosophies on which classical economics was founded, especially notions of the modern, free individual, which form the basis of Adam Smith's and David Ricardo's economics, and then follow the continuing relations with broader social, cultural, and especially political ideas as economics moved through its various phases. The purpose of Chapter 2 is not merely to provide a quick introduction to economics, but to demonstrate that the dominant notion of development as a certain kind of economic growth founded on capitalist efficiency results from *one* interpretation of *one* aspect of *one* people's history. Yet this notion is universalized in contemporary neoliberalism as *the* proven solution to the social and economic problems of *all* countries. The chapter therefore concludes with a critique of economic theories of growth drawn mainly from institutional economics, leaving more radical criticisms of conventional economic discourse to the remainder of the book.

Chapter 3 discusses how the first modern (late-nineteenth-century) theories of societal development drew on evolutionary biology for explanatory power, essentially arguing that geographical differences in human achievement were the inevitable consequences of prior variations in natural environments. There were two versions of this idea: the strong (deterministic) thesis that nature creates people with unequal potentials, especially differing levels of intelligence; and the weak thesis that nature provides superior resource environments that permit easier or quicker development in some places rather than others. In concluding that the natural environment determines levels of development, both versions essentially say that nature chooses who should be successful and who should not; this is often extended into the notion that the strong have to exploit the weak in order to survive or, more benignly, to bring progress to the world. These are not ideas that have disappeared; indeed, today they are staging a comeback. There is a second tradition covered by Chapter 3 that sees development as a consequence largely of social rather than of natural events. In the tradition of Max Weber's sociology, the rationalization of the world, its disenchantment in natural and mystical terms, was the original mainspring for the rise of the West. Chapter 3 argues that structural functionalism, which became the leading sociological paradigm in the 1940s and 1950s, synthesized Weberian notions of rationalism with the theoretical results of Darwinian naturalism. Thus the main functions carried out by all organisms are replicated by the institutional subsystems of society, and these functions may be carried out in more or less rational ways. Developed societies carry out their social and economic functions in highly rationalized ways to achieve the rewards of development. Modernization theory applies this formulation to societal evolution, arguing that modern institutional organizations and rational forms of behavior first appeared in fifteenth- and sixteenth-century Europe, and that subsequent development took the form of the spread of rational action and efficient institutions. Modernization geography thus explains regional variations in development in terms of diffusion, from the originating cores, of modern institutions and rationalized practices. As these innovative cores happened to lie in Euro-America, modernization theory can be seen as continuing the ideological tradition of neoclassical economics. We subject these ideas to considerable criticism.

From this we move to Marxist and neo-Marxist theories of societal development in Chapter 4. The most powerful critique of modernization came from theorists schooled in the dependency perspective. Dependency theory argues, on a neo-Marxist basis, that contact with Europe may indeed bring modernization to some people in the societies of the Third World, but that modernity comes at the price of exploitation. For dependency theorists, the spread of European "civilization" to the rest of the world was accompanied by the extraction of raw materials, the draining of social resources, and the inhabitants' loss of control over the basic institutions of their society—hence the notion of "dependency," or at best "dependent development," in what rapidly became the periphery of a world system dominated by a European center. Instead of being "developed" by their connections with the center of the global capitalist order, peripheral societies were actively *under*developed. The political and ethical conclusions are catastrophic for European understanding.

Most versions of the dependency perspective draw on Marxism as their main philosophical and theoretical basis. Marxism is a materialist explanation of societal structures that sees workers as active agents transforming nature through the labor process and achieving development by building the productive forces. However, development takes place in class societies, so that the material benefits derived from hard work and increased productivity are unequally distributed. Class struggle forms the basis of the societal dynamic (including the economic development process), while profit and overconsumption drive environmental destruction. Marxism espouses a dialectical understanding of history, in which change stems from contradictions between human groups and between society and the natural world. Marxist structuralism sees new modes of production emerging from the contradictions in the old, maturing, spreading in space, bringing different types and levels of development to societies. The idea of articulations (interpenetrations, combinations) between modes of production is a way of understanding intersocietal relations that yields a richer version of the theory of underdevelopment than dependency alone. Criticisms of Marxism generally emphasize its functional and teleological excesses, linking totalization in theory with totalitarianism in politics. We reply to these criticisms from the perspective of our own socialist politics, which takes the form of radical democracy and critical modernism. We conclude that by listening to criticism and changing, Marxism remains capable of providing, still, a coherent, insightful critical theory of societal structures and dynamics as the basis for a liberatory politics.

Marxism comes in for more than its share of criticism: from neoliberalism and conservatism obviously, as a vision supposedly tried and abjectly failed in the Soviet Union and Eastern Europe; but also from poststructural and postmodern critics as one more (and sometimes the archetypical) modern theory. Poststructuralism criticizes all modern theories for their essentializing and totalizing pretensions, while postmodern theorists evidence the most extreme skepticism about the entire modern project of human emancipation. These criticisms intersect with new examinations of the experiences of the formerly colonial countries by postcolonial critics located often in hybrid positions combining societal types. Then, too, radical and liberal development practice goes through a phase of disillusionment and despair in an age of neoliberal triumphalism. These tendencies come together in the poststructural critique of modern developmentalism. What previously was seen as automatically good is now theorized as a political technique of modern power, effective exactly because it claims to serve the interests of humanity. A number of positions uneasily cohere in a growing "postdevelopmentalism," which entails the complete rejection of modern development rather than its modification or democratization, and the hesitant proposal of some new principles, like thinking locally rather than globally, living more simply in material terms, or seeking more spiritual lives rather than worshiping the latest fashion. Yet the criticisms of the postdevelopmentalists are so severe, so all-encompassing, that they too must be deconstructed—perhaps modernism is discarded too easily, without regard for modern discoveries like machines and hospitals, which have their beneficial uses. All these issues are extensively debated in Chapter 5.

Chapter 6 looks at feminist attempts at reformulating development theory. Women perform most of the work in many, if not most, societies. So why have women been excluded from development theory? What difference would it make if theory were to be reformulated to center on gender relations? For feminists, new aspects of development are brought into focus, for example, the informal and rural sectors of the economy, the reproductive sphere, or the relations between production and reproduction. This does not merely change development theory, but improves or transforms it. There are several different approaches in the interaction between feminist theory and development: Women in Development (WID); Women and Development (WAD); Gender and Development (GAD); Women, Environment, and Alternatives to Development (WED); and Postmodernism and Development (PAD). We survey these, present a brief criticism (brief because we agree with much that is said), and conclude that our own position is most similar to the WAD perspective.

Chapter 7 reconsiders development in the light of the postdevelopmental and feminist critiques. For the writers of this book, modernity, emancipation, and development are all fine principles that have been perverted by capitalism. A critical modernist developmentalism, we argue, learns from these critiques, but retains a belief in the radical potential of modernity. Development in this view entails increasing the economic capacity of the poorest people. Whereas this conventionally means entrepreneurial skills, here we mean capacity literally, that is, control over production and reproduction within a democratic politics quite different from either private ownership or state control. Finally, the authors' belief that theory is not made by the exercise of logic alone, but reflects the theorist's moral reaction to a world in crisis, culminates in a discussion of the ethics of development, liberation ecologies, and radical democracy. A radical proposal for guiding developmental efforts is presented more to stimulate discussion about alternatives than as a universal blueprint for developmental planning. Readers who think that democratic socialism is the dismal politics of social dinosaurs might peruse this last chapter first. You should know where we are going, and why we are going there, before the journey begins.

Chapter 2

ECONOMIC THEORIES
OF GROWTH
AND DEVELOPMENT

B asically, development means improving the conditions of life. Basically, economics is knowledge about the effective use of resources in producing the material basis of life. Therefore, development is fundamentally an economic process, economics has an abiding interest in development, and all theories of development have significant economic dimensions. In this chapter we separate out the economic aspect of development for particular attention. We also separate economics as a formal discipline from the rest of social science because it specializes more than most on developmental issues. Separations like these arise from purely intellectual exercises that simplify the complex whole of an interrelated social, cultural, political, and economic process, and the whole knowledge about it. This kind of specialization into academic disciplines has been the scholastic norm since the nineteenth century.

In particular, economics has been a highly specialized field of knowledge since at least the mid-nineteenth century. More than other forms of social knowledge, economics claims the status of "science" in terms of its logical rigor and mathematical sophistication. Economists, more than other academic practitioners, are experts listened to with respect because they are thought to speak the scientific truth about issues of vital concern. As a result of these and other factors, "economic" theories of growth, and to a lesser degree "economic" theories of development, have their own philosophical bases, their own histories, their own trajectories, their own typical kinds of practice, different from sociological theories, for instance, indeed often with only tangential relations to cognate fields. Specialization and intellectual isolation have resulted in a highly formulated discipline, with rigorous rules of academic and practical conduct—for example, very careful forms of expression using a closely defined set of terms. But we will argue that this highly specialized knowledge rests on a precarious philosophical base resulting from one particular reaction to the rise of modern market systems, yet universalized as the foundation of a scientifically true discourse valid for all situations. We speak here of that line of economic theories stemming from the classical tradition of Adam Smith and David Ricardo, outlined in the late eighteenth and early nineteenth centuries, continued in nineteenth-century neoclassical (marginalist) economics, modified by twentieth-century Keynesian economics, and resuscitated in the new classical economics of the late twentieth century. We follow the convention of dividing mainstream economic theory into historical periods or "epochs," but alter the usual system of designation (e.g., Dasgupta 1985) to look at developmental issues during five phases of economic thought: preclassical, classical, marginalist, Keynesian, and post-Keynesian theories.

Preclassical Beginnings

Seldom are ideas thought up anew in the sense that theorists suddenly think entirely new thoughts. Just as material structures rest on the base of earlier relics, even more are recent ideas formulated using earlier ideas as media (the thoughts we think with) and materials (the ingredients we think about). This additive, cumulative structure of knowledge is particularly the case when the relation between recent and previous ideas is compatible rather than critical, but obtains even when there are disagreements between schools of thought. Small wonder, therefore, that the French poststructuralist philosopher Michel Foucault (1972) called the historical recovery of the basis of ideas "archaeology." Thus, in the case of economic theory, many of the concepts of classical economics were continuations, in new forms, of earlier preoccupations. We begin with medieval Christianity.

Medieval thinkers found God active in all worldly processes. Medieval theorists always combined religion with economy; indeed, economics was thought through the medium of religion. Medieval (Catholic) Christianity emphasized duty to God rather than the rights of the individual; this duty entailed moral limitations on the economic actor. Furthermore, according to the medieval doctrine of "just price," every commodity had a true, absolute value. True value was determined by common estimation of the cost of production, which usually meant the amount of labor contained in a product. There was concern also that the price set by the market for a commodity should be just and equitable, a concern that went back to the Greek philosopher Aristotle, if not to earlier thinkers. For the leading lights of the medieval period, thinkers like Albertus Magnus (c. 1200–1280) or Thomas Aquinas (1225–1274), prices were matters of justice and the law had a duty to fix them and punish individuals who exceeded the just price (Haney 1949: 95–100).

The belief that communal economic justice reflected God's will began to erode with urbanization, monetization, secularization, and the Protestant Reformation, that is, with the onset of modernity, with its central belief that humans create their own destiny. In the case of attitudes toward work, classical antiquity had associated wage labor with slavery, while Augustinian Christianity defined work as punishment for Adam's disobedience of God. But in the late Middle Ages in Europe the notion began to emerge of labor as the virtuous source of wealth. The most radical version of this new idea is associated with the sixteenth-century Protestants. They wanted to glorify God not through prayer alone but more actively, by working hard, even at ordinary tasks. In Protestantism, the idea was that God worked his will through secondary means, principally the labors of individual men and women, rather than directly through miracles. According to Martin Luther (1483–1546), God might grant gifts to humans, but people had to lend a hand by working—people had to give God a mask behind which he could act. For John Calvin (1509–1564), the notion of predestination, the idea that entry to heaven had already been decided for each person, paradoxically meant that individuals were responsible for their own behavior. Calvinism was elaborated, by a series of Puritan theologians between 1580 and 1640, as an ethical code for the conduct of daily life, and as a set of institutions necessary for compelling obedience among the faithful. Protestants of a Puritanical, and especially a Calvinist, bent pursued their "calling" (the occupation to which God called male individuals, while taking their talents into account) with a rigorous discipline that despised idleness or shoddy craftsmanship as dishonoring God. Human acquisitiveness changed from being a sin in medieval Catholicism to being a service to the community under early modern Protestantism. In Calvinism the hope for salvation (going to heaven) was reinforced by an ethic of self-discipline (Innes 1995: Ch. 1, 3). Classical economics derives from the new, Protestant attitudes toward labor, wealth, and productive life.

Classical economics developed also in a conflictual relation with mercantilism. Lasting from the fifteenth to the early nineteenth centuries, mercantilism was a total system of ideas, politics, institutions, and economic practices. Mercantalist political policy aimed at increasing national power, symbolized by the political might of the state. National power, it was realized, rested on economic means, rather than the bravery of a country's citizenry or the spirit of its people. Production was understood in the modern way as the application of labor to natural resources. The aim of state policy was to increase national control over larger amounts of productive resources. Harsh methods were used to extract hard work—often from paupers, criminals, and slaves. Colonies were desired to enrich the mother country by providing raw materials for its businesses and markets for its manufactures. Under mercantilism, the European states granted trading monopolies over great stretches of the world's surface to joint stock companies, with the king and members of the court benefiting through stockholdings. In Great Britain, examples included the British Muscovy Company, the Virginia Company, the East India Company and, infamously, the Royal African Company. According to mercantilist ideology, a country was considered prosperous when it had a favorable balance of trade, specifically an increased inflow of bullion (gold and silver). To achieve this favorable balance, trade was controlled by the state. In an early statement about economic growth the mercantalist Philipp von Hornick said:

> Gold and silver once in the country . . . are under no circumstances to be taken out . . . but must always remain in circulation. . . . Under these conditions, it will be impossible for a country that has once acquired a considerable supply of cash . . . ever to sink into poverty; indeed it is impossible that it should not continually increase in wealth and property. (1961 ed.: 48)

Mercantilism broke with medieval precedent. It was an amoral system, in terms of ends and means, in which the political welfare of the state replaced the spiritual welfare of the individual. However, Sir William Petty, a leading economic thinker of the time, thought that governments should take responsibility for maintaining employment and relieving poverty by fiscal and monetary policies and through public works. In general, mercantalist economists thought that states should foster development (defined as increased national production) through internal improvements (e.g., transportation), by the promotion of national industries (especially manufacturing), and through regulations (internal and external). On the whole, people were taken as they were, by now, presumed to be—pursuing their own self-interest—but were guided by state policy in directions that would enhance the well-being of the state. Mercantilism was, as far as possible, rationalist rather than mystical, believing in the application of science to the solution of practical problems (Newman 1952; Hecksher 1935).

During the seventeenth century, particularly in Britain, there began to emerge, particularly in Protestant mercantile and manufacturing circles, much more definite ideas about a free market economy within, yet partly opposed to, the mercantilist system. The idea of free markets was based on a number of principles: potential harmony between individual self-interest and the public interest *without* state intervention; the equilibrating tendencies of the forces of supply and demand in free markets; the achievement of higher productivity through specialization and the division of labor; and, most importantly, the ability of the market to yield natural or even just prices. A number of writers at the end of the seventeenth century proclaimed the benefits of economic freedom. For example, Pierre Nicole (1625–1695) thought that human ruthlessness could be directed by free markets into beneficent channels (Hutchison 1953: 7). The political philosophers of seventeenth- and eighteenth-century Britain, especially Thomas Hobbes, John Locke, and David Hume, three leading thinkers, were especially important in forming the philosophical basis of classical economic theory: in many ways the three form steps along the path from mercantilism to modern capitalism.

Thomas Hobbes (1588–1679) hypothesized that a "state of nature" would necessarily entail a struggle for power that would frustrate every reasonable person's desire for "commodious living" (i.e., comfort and happiness). Eternal struggle could be overcome by transferring the individual's natural rights to an absolute sovereign, who would impose social order. Hobbes believed that every person's power was opposed by the power of another. Transfers of power were so usual that there was, in effect, a market in which power was traded as a commodity, with the value of the human individual being measured by the deference accorded him or her by others. Even so, Hobbes maintained, people were still bound together through moral obligation. Rather than invoking imagined deities as the basis of morality, as with the medieval theorists, Hobbes thought that rational self-interestedness was as moral an obligation as could realistically be found. Any person could kill any other person, so all people should consider themselves essentially equal in terms of human rights. C. B. Macpherson, formerly professor of political science at the University of Toronto, and author of an outstanding book on the topic, argues that Hobbes seems to have found a rational basis for an emerging possessive market society, albeit one still presided over by the mercantilist state: "If the only alternative is anarchy, every man . . . who sees his true position has no rational alternative but to support a political authority which can maintain that society as a regular orderly system. . . . Every individual . . . must in his own interest acknowledge obligation to a political authority with enough power to enforce the rules of a competitive society" (Macpherson 1962: 87).

The English philosopher John Locke (1632–1704) began by accepting the medieval Christian view that God originally gave the earth and its products to all people in common. Yet, Locke contended, human individuals had a right to preserve their own lives, and therefore had rights to the subsistence (food, drink) derived from the earth. But before the natural produce of the earth could be used, he argued, it had to be appropriated by individuals with rights over their own persons, labor, and work. By mixing labor with earth the individual made nature into property—providing, Locke added, enough was left for others, and products did not perish uselessly in their appropriators' hands. Thus property rights extended from the products of nature and labor to the land people cultivated and improved. Later Locke added that while the natural right to property held in primitive society, the invention of money, together with a tacit agreement to place value on it, removed previous limitations on the extent of property ownership: first, because money did not spoil and people began to desire more than they immediately needed (so that land and money were accumulated as capital); second, because the greater productivity of appropriated land made up for a lack of land available to others (hence appropriation beyond the limits of individual labor took on positive value); and third, because labor was unquestionably the individual's property, it could be sold for a wage, with the buyer (employer) entitled to appropriate the product. For Macpherson (1962: 221), this latter set of arguments justified not only unequal property relations, but also legitimated unlimited individual appropriation and, we might add, legitimated employer–employee wage relations in capitalist societies. Two further points might be added. First, ideas very similar to Locke's were important in the United States which, in Puritan New England especially, was originally settled under the principle of one (white, male) person, one piece of property of appropriate size for family labor. Second, Locke was a shareholder in the Royal African Company whose most profitable "commodity" was slaves. The Lockean notion of human rights presupposed ideas about who was human, which excluded all aboriginal and black people, and usually women as well. The liberating notion of human rights, a founding moment of modern, democratic freedom, was replete with exclusions and rife with contradictions. We live with their effects today.

Finally, the Scottish philosopher David Hume (1711–1776) tried to introduce experimental methods, derived from Newton's physics, into the study of morality. Through observation (presumably of those he found around him), Hume concluded that all humans were compelled by a consuming passion, which he described as an avidity (greed) for goods and possessions, a drive that he found directly destructive of society. Yet people also reasoned that socialization was to their advantage, that is:

"Passion is much better satisfied by its restraint, than by its liberty, and by preserving society, we make much greater advances in the acquiring of possessions, than by running into the solitary and forlorn condition which must follow upon violence and universal licence" (Hume 1987 ed.: 492). In terms of economics, Hume favored the middle class as the best and firmest basis of public liberty, supported free trade against mercantilist restrictions, yet found a need still for government intervention to preserve national economic advantage (Skinner 1992: 223).

In general, the philosophers and political economists of seventeenth- and eighteenth-century Britain theorized on behalf of a new class of merchants and manufacturing entrepreneurs then coming to the fore, and increasingly argued against the entrenched power of the landowning nobility and the state. Their moral desire was to reconcile individual striving with the common good. Increasingly this moral reconciliation was reached in a new way, centered not on religiously enforced morality, nor even through armed force exerted by the mercantalist state, but relying on a modern belief in the freedom of the self-seeking yet responsible, enlightened individual, disciplined by equally modern institutions, principally the market. From this view, progress would occur through possessive individualism while the society retained some semblance of medieval moral concern with the collective good. The seventeenth and eighteenth centuries formed a transitional period when the precursors of modern capitalism, the new individual and novel institutions of social regulation, were being worked out, debated, accepted, and practiced at least by some of the leading forces of the day.

Classical Economics

Classical economics covers a period of thought stretching from Adam Smith's *The Wealth of Nations* (published in the rebellious year 1776) to John Stuart Mill's *Principles of Political Economy* (published in an equally rebellious 1848). During this time economics was part of a broader system of political economy embedded in an even more general moral philosophy. Classical economics asked questions not only about the causes of the growth of wealth, but about the social results of development, particularly its effects on the "lowest orders of society." Classical economics derived, in an immediate, technical sense, from notions developed by the Physiocrats, members of a school of eighteenth-century French Enlightenment thought lying midway between the medieval and the modern.

In the Physiocratic system, laws of human behavior deriving from the will of God could be discovered by theorists and followed by everyone. The Physiocrats thought that God had endowed nature with the capacity to produce wealth, and that God's will was realized through the medium of agricultural labor. Agriculturally derived surplus circulated through the entire society, but was drained off by people engaged in "nonproductive" economic activities, such as commerce and manufacturing. This French theory of the natural (but God-given) origin of value might be compared with British theories developed at the same time, which evidence a greater separation of labor and value from both nature and God. The difference might be explained by the greater development of manufacturing in seventeenth- and eighteenth-century England. It remained for the Scottish moral philosopher Adam Smith (1723–1790) to remove the medieval confusions inherent in the Physiocratic view and synthesize a modern economic science from what was, by then, a considerable legacy of ideas.

It is not generally known that Smith's economics was based in a philosophy of human nature. In his *Theory of Moral Sentiments,* published in 1759, Smith tried to reconcile the conflict between the pursuit of material gain and the maintenance of public morality by discovering the scientific laws covering both. With his friend Hume, Smith opposed the traditional Greco-Christian doctrine that a commitment to spiritual life excluded the pursuit of material advantage. The more skeptical Hume thought that all value judgments were merely "a species of sensation," that morality was relative to the sentiments of each person and, indeed, could be accounted for by the principle of self-love. While deeply influenced by Hume's commercial humanism, Smith believed that there were laws both of external nature and of inner human morality that were divine. God was in the world, although not in the form represented by Christian superstition. Smith subscribed instead to the (Greek and Roman) Stoic doctrine that the individual's highest quest was for virtue, by which he meant exceptional powers of character and mind, the love of that which is dignified, honorable, and noble. How far should the virtuous individual take the duties owed to others? Smith thought that self-impartiality should be the deciding factor. He found people sympathetic, even empathetic toward each other, but in a nonpassionate, scientific way, based on putting the self in the other's position. The individual perceived his or her self through the eyes of the other, through the evaluations of others, a perspective which, once internalized, humbled the individual's arrogance, bringing self-love down to a level others could live with. So the just and wise person would try to model inward sentiments according to the external judgment of an impartial spectator, an abstract good citizen. However, this assent to the representative of humankind, this submission to the substitute for the Deity, was never complete, so that even good people were frequently corrupted by selfish passions. Thus it was that Smith came to believe in a Stoic harmony between the higher and lower motives, between virtue and self-love. In his lectures on jurisprudence (the principles of what laws ought to be) Smith argued that a new, impartial science of morals could be developed that would restrain self-love within socially beneficial limits derived from the impartial spectator's judgment—for example, property rights were justified in the eyes of the impartial spectator when based on the individual's labor (Smith 1976 ed.).

Smith's famous *Wealth of Nations*, published in 1776, elaborated these notions of moral philosophy into a theory of economic behavior. Smith argued that all humans shared certain characteristics, whether innate or resulting from the faculties of reason and speech, which he described as a certain propensity to "truck, barter and exchange one thing for another" (Smith 1937 ed.: 13). It was futile to expect the cooperation and assistance of others from their benevolence alone. Instead, the individual should prevail on the other's self-love, appealing to the other's own advantage to get the other to do what he or she required: "Give me that which I want, and you shall have this which you want" (Smith 1937 ed.: 14)—for, as he added, it is not from the benevolence of the butcher, brewer, or baker that we expect our dinner, but from regard for their self-love. In direct contrast to the Christian disavowal of egotism, Smith wanted to use human selfishness as an economic drive. But he thought that self-love should be both self-regulated and externally limited by laws. Indeed, Smith himself preferred self-interest—self-love mitigated by virtue—as guide to economic behavior. Rather than pure selfishness, he said, justice should be the basis of society (Fitzgibbons 1995). Smithian economics emerges from this tangle of conflicting beliefs.

Economic growth, for Smith, depended on capital accumulation, which in turn depended on saving and the virtues of frugality and self-command. Economic growth also supposed a culture rooted in morality, a system of natural liberty with respect for the higher virtues (Fitzgibbons 1995: 145–148). The system of natural liberty meant, for Smith, that there should be no artificial impediments to trade. From such beginnings, Smith's economics tried to explain why some nations prospered, became wealthy or, in contemporary parlance, experienced economic growth. He found the immediate answer in the division of labor. According to Smith, by specializing the various tasks involved in production, dexterity could be increased, time saved, and labor-saving machinery invented by persons familiar with minute tasks. The products so made were exchanged through trade. And the division of labor was limited only by the extent of the market. With improvements in transport, the market increased in size, labor became more specialized, money replaced barter, and productivity increased.

Smith regarded the market as a driving force for invention, innovation, and risk taking. Against the tendency for trade and commerce to cause moral decline, Smith counterposed the reform of education and religion, in particular the inculcation of a new class of people with a secular morality that would eventually replace Christianity. Opposed to mercantilism, Smith thought that relatively free trade would lead to an efficient allocation of resources, but thought too that a just political economy would also encourage high wages. A society activated by self-interest (even in the sense in which Smith used the term) needed a regulating medium, which turned out to be competition in the marketplace. Any producer motivated only by greed who charged too much for a product, or paid too little for labor, would find himself without buyers or workers. Over the long run, markets and free competition would force prices toward their natural, or socially just, level ("just" in the medieval sense). Self-regulating markets were the "invisible hand" that transformed private interests into public virtue. For Smith, markets were virtuous institutions of social efficiency.

Smith retained the medieval argument that the natural prices of commodities derived from their real costs. Natural prices were not merely levels around which market prices would revolve, they were values that could be translated into moral terms. For Smith, the utility of a thing did not determine its price. Rather, the value of a commodity owned by someone intending to exchange it for other commodities was equal to the quantity of labor the commodity could purchase or command: "Labour . . . is the real measure of the exchangeable value of all commodities" (Smith 1937 ed.: 30). In early societies, Smith thought, the amount of (direct, physical) labor used to produce exchanged commodities determined their value, while the whole product belonged to the laborer. Capital originated in saving from current revenue and was used to hire workers who produced value, putting in motion an additional quantity of industry, which added to the annual product of a country. Yet, when capital accumulates in the hands of particular persons and "they naturally employ it in setting to work industrious people" (Smith 1937 ed.: 42), profits must be given to the risk taker. Similarly, when common land became private property, landlords demanded rent (for "like others they love to reap what they never sowed" and, what is more, were able to get away with it; Smith 1937 ed.: 49). Thus the price, or exchangeable value of a commodity, in more advanced societies, came to be resolved into three parts: wages, profit, and rent. "Natural prices," determined in this way, were brought into equality with market prices by competition. That is, where market prices exceeded natural prices landlords and capitalists would shift land and capital into the more profitable employment, with the reverse happening when market prices dropped below natural prices—hence productive efficiency *and* justice. Also, while the accumulation of capital and its employment in mechanized production might eventually be stalled by scarcity of workers and high wages, Smith thought that population too responded to market incentives, such that more children were born when wages were high, so that growth could continue indefinitely without labor shortages. Hence an automatic mechanism produced productivity and growth without state interference. Self-interested behavior directed resources to where they could best and most profitably be used, while all classes, Smith believed, shared in the benefits of progress. "Natural liberty implied free competition, free movement of workers, free shifts of capital, and freedom from government intervention" (Lekachman 1959: 89). Or, in another interpretation, "Smith's labour theory of value was a defining statement: an impartial system of laws would establish a set of natural prices that in principle would reduce to terms of human liberty, happiness and ease" (Fitzgibbons 1995: 180).

Displaying even more enlightened optimism than Smith, William Godwin, in his *Enquiry Concerning the Principles of Political Justice*, published in 1793, argued that humans were susceptible to perpetual improvement. Human reason, Godwin (1946 ed.) proclaimed, could triumph over human instincts, indefinitely extending life, perhaps even making people immortal. But this kind of optimism about unlimited growth and unbridled human progress could not last forever. As the economist Robert Heilbroner (1986) points out, the optimism of the late Enlightenment was soon countered by the pessimism of the early nineteenth century, with arguments focused on population and progress, social symbols for more basic human instincts and reason. The Reverend Thomas Robert Malthus (1766–1834) responded negatively (and at first anonymously) to Godwin's *Enquiry* and similarly dangerous talk emerging from the French Revolution. Malthus's *Essay on Population*, first published in 1798, argued conversely that human progress would always be limited by uncontrollable "human passion" (he meant sex), causing populations to increase more rapidly than food supplies. Malthus argued that population increased geometrically—2, 4, 8, 16—while food production increased arithmetically—2, 4, 6, 8—with the result that "premature death must in some shape or other visit the earth" (Malthus 1933 ed.: 139). Malthus thought that laws granting aid to the unemployed only made matters worse by encouraging the poor to have children. In Malthus's view, far from ascending perpetually toward a better future, humanity was trapped by passion into an incessant cycle of overpopulation and death. No wonder political economy was termed "the dismal science!"

In the early nineteenth century the political economy outlined by the

Physiocrats, Smith, and Malthus changed again in style, if not in sub-stance. Earlier moral notions about human nature were elaborated in a more quantifiable and predictable way by the British philosopher and economist Jeremy Bentham (1748–1832). As opposed to the earlier Eng-lish philosophers, Bentham thought that the mind did not have active power, but was subordinate to innate principles of mind and body. He defined liberty not as virtue but in terms of the relations between the self and objects of desire (Long 1977: 41). In his *Introduction to the Princi-ples of Morals and Legislation* (1996 ed.), first published in 1780, Bentham simply declared that nature had placed humans under the gov-ernance of two sovereign "masters": pleasure, which made all people happy, and pain, which everyone hated. According to Bentham, the amounts of each could be measured. Bentham's "principle of utility" judged every human action by its effect on augmenting or diminishing the happiness of the individual in question. When the laws of utility were countered by reason, the reasons themselves were based in the same principle of utility. For Bentham, the community, furthermore, was a fic-titious body, and the public interest merely the sum of private interests. Bentham's system, called "utilitarianism," entered economics mainly through the ideas of the "philosophical radicals," active in London in the 1820s and 1830s. (Bear in mind that "radicalism" at this time meant taking the side of the new class of industrialists against the entrenched power of the landed nobility).

One member of this group, David Ricardo (1772–1823), a British millionaire trader in securities, outlined a rigorous system of economics in which real people were replaced by prototypical models, while gener-alizations drawn from national experience were replaced by universal, abstract principles. In *Principles of Political Economy and Taxation* (1817) Ricardo accepted Smith's labor theory of commodity value, with some modifications (commodity value was also determined by scarcity) and Benthamite elaborations (labor was the universal measure of value because it always involved exertion and was a pain, whereas consuming labor's products was always pleasurable), but placed greater emphasis on the distribution of value, especially the part going to rents (the por-tion of value paid to landlords for use of the original powers of the soil). However, Ricardo expressed a greater suspicion that markets might not yield just prices given the entirely different kinds of labor invested in products and the different combinations of labor with capital invested in different kinds of production. Like Smith, Ricardo saw the economic world tending to expand, with capitalists accumulating, building facto-ries, employing more workers, and increasing wages. From the French economist Jean-Baptiste Say (1767–1832) he derived the notion that supply created its own demand, as production generated consumption.

But he followed his friend Malthus in saying that overpopulation reduced the worker's advantages from economic growth. However, Ricardo then added a further pessimistic dimension to the theory of economic growth. He argued that with an expansion of population and an increased demand for food, the margins of agricultural production would expand, bringing into cultivation land of lesser fertility, thereby increasing the cost of grain (the food staple in Britain), yet increasing the returns to landlords owning the better lands, earning them differential rents. In turn, the capitalist would be faced by higher wage costs necessary to sustain workers, while the main class benefiting from economic growth was the landlords even though, the radical Ricardo concluded, they contributed little to the wealth-creating process.

Like Smith before him, Ricardo was against the landowning class. In the early nineteenth century British landlords were protected from foreign competition by a system of Corn Laws (last remnants of the mercantilist system). These imposed a sliding scale of import duties on grains depending on the foreign price, ensuring that landowners benefited from the Industrial revolution more or less in the way Ricardo theorized, except that location near markets assumed greater significance than fertility as the source of differential rents (cf. von Thünen 1966). The British philosophical radicals opposed the Corn Laws by arguing for free trade. Ricardo's contribution to their argument, which eventually led to repeal of the Corn Laws in 1846, was a trade theory based on comparative advantage. Human happiness, Ricardo said, would be increased by each country producing (and then trading) those commodities that it was best fitted to produce by virtue of natural or historical circumstances. Even when one country was consistently more productive than another, trade would benefit both. This was true because total production would be greater through each country specializing in the product for which it had the greatest comparative advantage, or least comparative disadvantage—with production being prevented from concentrating exclusively in one country by the difficulties of moving capital across national boundaries. The theory assumed that all partners in trade benefited from an increase in total production in accordance with their comparative advantages. In this way Ricardo was even more of an advocate for the benefits of free trade than Smith. We must emphasize that Ricardo's principle of trade is reproduced in contemporary economics textbooks and is a basic geographic component of growth theory: Paul Samuelson, Nobel Prize winner in economics and writer of the most popular economics textbook, argues that the principle of comparative advantage makes real incomes higher in all places, while ill-designed tariffs or quotas reduce efficiency and incomes—this, Samuelson (1980: 630) maintains, is the "unshakable basis for international trade."

Ricardo was encouraged to write a formal treatise on economics by the philosophical radical James Mill. In turn, Mill's famous son, the philosopher and economist John Stuart Mill (1806–1873), wrote *Principles of Political Economy*. In this major work Mill argued that the principles of competition were the bases of economic laws that could be outlined with precision and given universal validity by an abstract science. Yet also, by the middle nineteenth century, political economy was resuming that optimistic bent typified earlier by Adam Smith. For Mill, the economic law of diminishing returns, in which additions to the labor working agricultural land were not met by equal additions to product, restricting productivity and growth, could in part be transcended in manufacturing, where productivity could be increased almost without limit. Mill argued that Malthus's pessimistic principle of population could be avoided by workers voluntarily restricting their numbers. With Say and Ricardo, Mill believed that there was no chance of general overproduction (and thus long-term depressions), although specific commodities might temporarily come into oversupply (so there could be short-term economic fluctuations). Here again we see the liberal ideal of unlimited progress.

However, Mill's most significant contribution to classical political economy lay in differentiating science from values. That is, while the scientific laws of economics applied to production with the character of physical truths, the distribution of wealth was a different matter entirely, being a question more of human institutions, as with laws and customs. Once things had been made, people could do with them as they pleased. Society could redistribute wealth through state intervention. Moreover, Mill found the notion of the struggle for existence as an ideal of economic life to be merely a disagreeable symptom of one (early) phase of industrial progress. When more refined minds took over, such coarse stimuli to economic action would be replaced by superior principles spread through education. Mill viewed the relations between workers and capitalists as an association of mutual suspicion, but thought that this antagonism could be relieved by profit sharing, and eventually avoided altogether through partnerships and worker ownership of factories. Mill thought that laissez-faire (the practice of nongovernmental intervention in the economy) should be the general rule, but allowed many exceptions, as with poor relief and factory legislation. Mill was a radical liberal who believed that capitalism would eventually give way to cooperativism. More extreme versions of these ideas were worked out by Marx and Engels, in many ways the final (critical) members of the classical school of political economy. (These more radical ideas are discussed in Chapter 4.)

Most accounts of classical economics end with Mill. There was, however, an alternative economic perspective in the classical tradition presented by Friedrich List (1789–1846), a journalist who lived in the United States and France for a decade after being repeatedly imprisoned for writing about his ideas in his native Germany. List agreed with the principle of free trade proposed by the classical economists. But he thought that free trade presupposed a condition of eternal peace and a single set of laws for a world that had yet to come into existence. He argued that under the actually existing conditions, in which Britain dominated the world's manufacturing industry, free trade would bring not a "universal republic" of equal countries, but "universal subjection of the less advanced nations to the supremacy of the predominant manufacturing, commercial and naval power" (List 1909 ed.: 103). He further argued that a universal republic of national powers recognizing each other's rights, and a situation in which free trade could confer the same advantages to all participants, could only come about when a large number of nationalities had reached the same level of development. In the meantime, List was for the protection of national economies until they could compete on equal terms (Roussakis 1968; Tribe 1988).

The Neoclassical Interlude

In the last third of the nineteenth century economics changed from political economy, part of a moral philosophy critically involved with social issues, to a specialized scientific discipline fascinated by calculus, algebra, and plane geometry, and increasingly removed from social concerns. The central theme of economics changed from growth of the national wealth to the role of the margin in the efficient allocation of resources. Marginal utility, neoclassical economic's leading concept, was anticipated by a little-known Prussian lawyer, Hermann Heinrich Gossen, in a book first published in 1854. Gossen advocated an economics that was utilitarian, mathematical, and centered on consumption rather than production. For Gossen (as for Bentham), the aim of human conduct was to maximize enjoyment. There were laws of pleasure: satisfaction decreased as any activity proceeded (e.g., successive bites of food were less enjoyable) until satiety was reached. To obtain the maximum total enjoyment, the individual with limited resources chose among a mixture of activities, discontinuing each when the amount of pleasure it gave equaled that of all other activities. This last ounce of Benthamite pleasure became the famous economic principle of marginal utility.

The marginalist movement in economics began in earnest, however, when three theorists (Jevons, Menger and Walras) independently, and almost simultaneously, developed the idea of marginal utility, inherent in

Gossen's statement. The British economist W. S. Jevons (1835–1882) proclaimed himself a Benthamite and a mathematician—economics, he said, was a calculus of pleasure and pain, and mathematics was its method, for economic science dealt in quantities rather than qualities. Ricardo and Mill had been able, but wrongheaded. And the notion that value was created by labor was but a minor variation on a major theme that value depended instead on utility. That is, utility was the quality of an object that induced pleasure or prevented pain, depending on the inclination of the person. Jevons emphasized not the total utility given by consuming all of a commodity, but the final degree of utility induced by a very small increment in consumption. Like Gossen, he saw commodities distributed over several alternative uses so that the final (marginal) degree of utility was equal in each case. Exchange took place between individuals owning commodities until equilibrium set in, with marginal utility being equivalent to price. In other words, the final degree of utility given by an object determined its price (Jevons 1911 ed.).

The Austrian Carl Menger (1840–1921) argued that economic phenomena did not express general social forces but instead resulted from the behavior of individuals regarded as "atoms"; hence economics had no ethical or philosophical implications. For Menger, goods had utility because they satisfied wants, either immediately (e.g., bread), or indirectly (e.g., flour). For some goods wants exceeded the quantity available and so possessed "scarcity." Realizing this relationship between wants and quantity produced a judgment of value in the individual's mind, with the subjective value varying with the urgency of the want, and goods used in descending order until the last portion satisfied the least intense want. For Menger, exchange was not due to the individual's inherent propensity to truck and barter, as with Smith, but came as a means of satisfying maximal wants with the available scarce means. Individuals exchanged goods until their marginal utilities were equal (although neither Jevons nor Menger actually used the later term "marginal utility"). Money functioned to quantify subjective values.

The French economist Leon Walras (1837–1910), working in Lausanne, Switzerland, used similar notions of scarcity (which he called *rareté*), with individuals possessing stocks of goods that they exchanged in competitive markets until equilibrium was reached and price was such that demand and supply were equal. Walras's special contribution involved generalizing from the exchange of one commodity to the exchange of all, including factors of production (land, labor, and capital), in what he called "general exchange equilibrium." Competitive markets, he thought, maximized total utility. However, Walras personally favored state intervention, compulsory education, restrictions in working hours, and controls on monopolies (Roll 1942; Lekachman 1959).

As originally formulated, marginalism basically tried to explain consumer choice using a theory of marginal utility. With the partial exception of Walras, it did not extend the marginal principle to the resources used in the manufacture of the exchanged commodities. A second generation of marginalist neoclassical economists created the concept of marginal productivity to cover the productive use of resources. This extended the marginal principle to cover all aspects of production and consumption or, for some, all aspects of life in general. Three main schools of thought emerged in England, Austria, and Switzerland (to which we add an important American contribution).

Alfred Marshall (1842–1924), professor of political economy at Cambridge University, wrote *Principles of Economics* (1920 ed.) in an attempt to improve life for both businesspeople and the poor. Marshall thought that the forces behind supply (stressed by the classical economists) and those behind demand (stressed by the early marginalists) determined value much like the workings of the twin blades of a pair of scissors. On the supply side, work might at first be pleasant, but eventually became painful, so there was a marginal *dis*utility of labor just compensated for by the pleasure of wages. Modifying a notion derived from an earlier British economist, Nassau Senior (1790–1864), that abstinence (from spending) was the justification for earning interest on savings, Marshall argued that "waiting" was a discomfort to the saver overcome by the money returns to invested capital. Like the rational consumer constantly balancing additional purchases of alternative commodities with an aim to maximizing utility, the producer allocated funds among the factors of production, substituting so that the marginal product of each was proportional to its price. Marshall then worked out the conditions of supply and demand using a simple, static model based on the "representative firm" (with all other factors being equal, or hypothetically held constant) and three typical time periods, the market (where supplies were fixed and demand determined price), the short run (where the forces of supply had a larger role), and the long run (where again supply was the more important factor). In long-run partial equilibrium the earnings of each factor of production would equal its marginal real cost. Marshall thought that there were increasing returns to the scale of production, that firms reaped internal and external economies, and that capitalism could raise the standard of living for ordinary people. As with Mill's system, the Marshallian system was full of ethics.

By comparison, the Austrian school of economics, led principally by Menger's students Friedrich von Wieser (1851–1926) and Eugen von Bohm-Bawerk (1851–1914), was abstract and antihistorical in method.

Wieser's notion of opportunity costs abandoned the classical search for the original values of factors of production and saw value as a circular process in which factors were employed so that their alternative uses produced the same earnings. Bohm-Bawerk concentrated on the round-about nature of modern production, that is, the large number of stages intermediate between original factors of production and final consumption that created a demand for capital and justified interest in any kind of economy, socialist or capitalist. At Lausanne, Vilfredo Pareto (1848–1923) set out the mathematical conditions of Walras's general equilibrium in the achievement of an optimal economy ("Pareto optimality"). Altogether this second generation of marginalists formed the crux of the neoclassical school of economics: a science shorn of sociological and historical material, abstract in conception, universal in application, technical and mathematical in methodology. Dynamics and questions of economic growth and development took a back seat to statics and partial and general equilibrium.

Finally, the American economist J. B. Clark (1847–1938) justified the distribution of income under static conditions as according with the rights of property (Clark 1888). In accordance with the laws of marginal productivity, everyone got what he or she deserved, wages were the whole product of labor, interest was the product of capital, profits were the product of the coordinating actor (the entrepreneur). We find with Clark a picture of the enlightened maximizing individual acting within generally competitive conditions in an overall state of static harmony (Hutchison 1953: 260–261). Altogether, neoclassical economic theory asserted that, under conditions of perfect competition, price-making markets yielded a long-run set of prices that balanced, or equilibrated, the supplies and demands for each commodity in production and consumption. Given certain conditions, such as the preferences of consumers, productive techniques, and the mobility of productive factors, market forces of supply and demand allocated resources efficiently, in the sense of minimizing costs, and maximized consumer utilities, in the long run. And finally, all the participants in production received incomes commensurate with their efforts. Capitalism was therefore the best of all possible economic worlds.

Neoclassical economic harmony was disturbed by the critical institutional economist Thorstein Veblen (1857–1929), a Norwegian American from Wisconsin who taught at various universities usually as an assistant professor (his message was unpopular!). Author of *Theory of the Leisure Class* (1912), Veblen differentiated between the rational, technical aspects of modern, mechanized production and the business and entrepreneurial aspects. The first, technical serviceability, produced useful products that satisfied needs; the second, business enterprise, favored chintzy products that would break or displease quickly, leading to replacement and greater profits for business. Veblen argued that pursuit of gain often caused unemployment, higher prices, higher costs, and delayed innovation. He thought that borrowing on the basis of anticipated earnings created business cycles of expansion and contraction that enabled big firms to swallow smaller ones. Rather than class conflict creating the dynamic of capitalist history (as with Marx), Veblen emphasized conflicts between three cultural tendencies: the machine process, business enterprise, and warlike or predatory beliefs. Business enterprise, he thought, would eventually fail and the future system would either involve domination by engineers or reversion to archaic absolutism under military domination (Germany and Japan were his examples). Veblen reversed the arguments of neoclassicism.

Dynamic Analysis

There were other traditions in economics opposing the neoclassical consensus. In Germany a historical school of economics had long been critical of the abstract nature of both Ricardian and marginalist economics. The historical school was influenced by the German philosophical traditions of idealism and romanticism. Originally formulated by Wilhelm Roscher (1817–1894), Bruno Hildebrand (1812–1878), and Karl Knies (1821–1898), and developed further by a second generation led by Gustav Schmoller (1838–1917), the historical school's main themes were the unity of social and economic life, the plurality of human motives, and the relativity of history—all regarded from an organicist or holistic viewpoint (i.e., a view that stressed the natural webs of interconnections between things). The historical school also had an abiding interest in crisis and development. Roscher and other German economic historians thought that it was difficult to keep supply and demand "balanced" in advanced economies and argued that crises were inevitable, particularly when caused by lack of demand, or underconsumption. Other German economists influenced by the historical school stressed the instabilities resulting from psychological factors in economic processes and the booms caused by uneven growth in the various sectors of an economy (e.g., steel, shipbuilding, railroads growing unevenly). The German historical school was empirical, looked at the very long term, and tended to be more critical of capitalism than neoclassical economics. A bitter debate between Schmoller and Menger in the 1880s split German-speaking economics into antagonistic camps for decades. Schmoller thought that classical and neoclassical economics erred in positing universal laws, mistakenly preferred induction to deduction, and was naive in holding the notion that people were motivated entirely by self-interest.

Influenced by the German historical school and by Marxism, but trained at Vienna in marginalist (Austrian) economics, and an admirer of Walras's general equilibrium theory, Joseph Schumpeter (1883–1950) combined methods and theories from all approaches within an overall perspective derived from advanced natural science. For Schumpeter, neoclassical economics, which took basic social variables as given and thought that the play of self-interests in competitive markets would bring resource allocation into equilibrium, was static analysis. His own model saw innumerable exchanges constituting, in their totality, a circular flow of economic life (Schumpeter 1934 ed.: 41). Schumpeter was not interested in small changes, those within the flow that did not disrupt the existing system. Instead, he was fascinated by the truly dynamic developments of economic systems, when the impetus for change came from within the economy (endogenously), with effects that displaced the existing equilibrium. These spontaneous and discontinuous changes, he thought, arose not from consumption, but from production, specifically from new combinations of productive materials and forces. Productive innovations could occur in five different ways: the introduction of a new or substantially different good, a new method of production not before tested, the opening of a new market, the conquest of a new system of supply of raw materials or semifinished goods, and a new organization of production, like the creation of a monopoly position. Because such innovations destroyed old channels of production and formed new ones, Schumpeter called the resulting development process "creative destruction."

The economic subjects responsible for innovations were entrepreneurs. Schumpeter thought that relatively few people in any society tried to change customary practices and introduce new things. Entrepreneurs were dynamic, energetic leaders, distinguished by will rather than intelligence. And rather than viewing hedonism as the basis of economic rationality (the pursuit of pleasure, the avoidance of pain), Schumpeter thought that dynamic analysis required a fundamentally different kind of entrepreneurial rationalism based in the will to found a new domain, the will to conquer and fight, or the joy of creating new things (there are similarities here with the German philosopher Friedrich Nietzsche's rejection of utilitarianism and advocacy of power and will). Schumpeter thought further that creativity could not be predicted from previous facts: creativity shaped the course of future events, yet itself was an enigma. Even so, economics had to deal with psychology and human motivation at a different level than everyday utilitarianism.

Innovative investment was financed not by savings but by credit, with interest paid from the profits generated by innovation. Rather than causing deviations in a kind of dynamic equilibrium, Schumpeter saw the development initiated by innovation as uneven, discontinuous, and taking the form of business cycles. These cycles could be short term (40 months), medium term (9–10 years), and long term, the Kondratieff long waves of 50–55 years (Kuznets 1953), which Schumpeter conceptualized as epochs with different values and civilizational characteristics. For all his praise of the entrepreneur, Schumpeter also thought that an economy satiated with capital and rationalized by entrepreneurial minds would eventually become socialist (Schumpeter 1934 ed.; Shionoya 1997).

Keynesian Growth Theory

With theories like this, temporal variations, or waves in economic growth, began to be theorized in systematic ways. Previously even sophisticated marginalist economists tended toward the bizarre when they left equilibrium to contemplate dynamism—so Jevons, seeing that business and sunspot cycles both had average durations of 10.45 years, postulated that sunspots caused weather variations, which influenced crops, which in turn caused business cycles! In British neoclassical economics most theorists followed J. B. Say in reasoning that general overproduction or unemployment were impossible: production meant hiring labor and purchasing machines and materials, which generated incomes, and increased demand, so that "supply creates its own demand." The main weak spot in "Say's law," noticed by Marshall, was that part of incomes were saved, and thus potentially withdrawn from the upward cycle of growth. However, this was easily explained away, for savings were reinvested (by individuals and banks) and contributed to growth. In the marginalist tradition neither growth nor depressions were relevant economic issues.

This intellectual harmony held until John Maynard Keynes (1883–1946), a Cambridge economist and member of the Bloomsbury circle of artists and intellectuals, began to systematically demolish the postulates of the old approach—for example, the notion that wage earners were maximizers, or that unemployment was voluntary. Keynes's criticism was lent urgency by the onset of the Great Depression in the 1930s. Keynes's *General Theory of Employment, Interest and Money* (1936) argued that the creation of demand by supply (as with Say's law) could occur at *any* level of employment or income, so that full employment was but one of many economic possibilities. The particular level of employment, Keynes thought, was determined by aggregate demand for goods and services in the entire economy. Assuming that the government had a neutral effect, two groups influenced aggregate demand: consumers buying consumption goods and investors buying production equipment. Consumers increased their spending as their incomes rose, although by a smaller proportion: however, this was not the key variable in explaining the overall level of employment, for consumption depended on income, which depended on something else.

In the Keynesian system, real investment (in new factories, tools, machines, and greater inventories of goods) was the crucial variable: changes in real investment fed into other areas of an economy. Investment resulted from decisions made by entrepreneurs under conditions of risk. Investment could be postponed. The decision to invest, Keynes said, depended on comparisons between expected profits and the prevailing interest rate. Here the key variable was "expectation" or, more generally, the degree of investor confidence. Keynes explained the interest rate not in terms of savers postponing consumption, but in terms of speculation about future stock prices, which in turn determined interest rates, as savings moved from one fund to another. This again depended essentially on expectations about the future. Investors bought machines, thereby providing income to machine builders (companies and employees). In turn these spent money, further increasing national income, with the "multiplier effect" (the degree of economic expansion induced by investment) varying with the proportion of additional income that was spent rather than saved (the marginal propensity to consume), and so on; a decrease in real investment had the reverse effects. The government could influence this process through interest rate and other monetary policies, shifting the economy from one equilibrium level to another, generally to higher employment levels.

Keynes himself doubted that merely changing interest rates would be sufficient to significantly alter business confidence and thus investment. Subsequently conservative Keynesian economists have viewed the manipulation of interest rates as a relatively nonbureaucratic, nonintrusive method by which the central bank of a country tries to influence national income and employment; an alternative is tax reduction. Liberal Keynesian economists see government deficit spending as a more effective measure: the "liberal" aspect is that deficit spending improves social services. While favoring the latter course, Keynes thought that government spending, rather than the social part, was crucial: burying banknotes in old mines, filling these with refuse, and having private enterprise dig them up was better than nothing if the goal was higher employment rates and greater national wealth. When capital was scarce, saving was beneficial to an economy. When unemployment rose, however, thrift impeded economic growth. Keynes thus assaulted a basic tenet of Puritan (and Smithian) economics, the identification of thrift with virtue (Lekachman 1966: 111). Keynes also proved theoretically what depression had long shown in practice, that free markets did not spontaneously maximize human well-being.

These ideas became the basis of economic growth theory ("dynamizing Keynes") in an attempt by economists to design policies that would maintain full employment in the social democracies of the West. Keynes's biographer, the Cambridge economist Roy Harrod, asked whether an economy could grow at a steady rate forever. Subsequently the U.S. economist Evsey Domar, a professor at Brandeis University, independently investigated the circumstances under which a growing economy could sustain full employment. The resulting Harrod–Domar model focused "dynamic theory" on the relations between savings, investment, and output. Essentially the model argued that the national saving rate (the fraction of income saved) had to be equal to the product of the capital–output ratio and the rate of growth of the (effective) labor force if the economy was to keep its stock of plant and equipment in balance with its supply of labor so that steady growth could occur. What Harrod (1939) called the "warranted rate of growth" depended on the planned national rate of savings (the proportion of income that individuals and firms planned, or intended, to withhold from immediate consumption and that was potentially available for investment) and the capital–output ratio (the capital needed to produce a given output). The relation between savings and investment was complicated, particularly by uncertainty. The basic problem faced by producers as investors in plant and equipment was that aggregate demand might not behave as expected, so that plant might be worked overtime, or stocks of goods accumulated. The actual capital–output ratio would diverge from what had been planned and output would differ from the warranted rate, producing a series of reactions that moved an economy away from steady-state growth. The limits to divergence were as follows: on the side of higher growth, there was a barrier formed by the growth of the labor force and full employment—the "natural rate of growth"; on the side of lower growth, there was a floor formed by households (or the welfare state) spending to maintain minimum standards of living. For Harrod, the chances of an economy growing at a steady state with full employment were low. Instead, an economy would fluctuate between periods of unemployment and periods of labor shortage. Interest rate policies and public works could decrease fluctuations and increase the possibility of steady growth. In the Domar (1947) version of growth theory emphasis was placed more on the savings rate, which financed investment and achieved a desired rate of growth. In the Harrod–Domar model, increasing economic growth basically involved increasing the savings rate, in some cases through the state budget. Development policies based on the Harrod–Domar model were used in left-leaning countries in the 1950s—for example, in India's First Five Year Plan between 1951 and 1956. In general, Keynesian economic theory established the legitimacy of state intervention into market economies with the aim of achieving growth rates decided on the basis of social policy. Since Keynes, economists have divided into camps favoring the invisible hand of the market or the visible hand of state planning in guiding economic growth.

We might add that the Harrod–Domar model's conclusions about capitalist instability were criticized by the Massachusetts Institute of Technology economist Robert Solow in the 1950s. Solow concentrated on the capital–output ratio, assumed to be constant in the Harrod–Domar model, wishing to replace it with a more realistic representation of technology. Technological flexibility made a range of steady growth situations more feasible. Technological progress, broadly defined to include improvements in peoples' working capacities, allowed long-term growth in real wages and the standard of living (Solow 1970).

Development Economics

During and immediately after World War II most Western governments committed themselves to full employment as a policy objective. The New Deal in the United States had mobilized governmental resources to create employment during the Great Depression of the 1930s. President Roosevelt proclaimed freedom from want everywhere in the world as one of four basic human freedoms. In wartime Britain, two Beveridge reports advocated full employment and welfare services. A full employment pledge was incorporated into the United Nations Charter. And between 1945 and 1950 the United States under the Marshall Plan gave Western Europe $19 billion to finance its economic recovery. An international conference held at Bretton Woods, New Hampshire, in 1944, established the International Monetary Fund (IMF) to regulate the global economy and, as an afterthought, the World Bank, subsequently instrumental in Third World development. There was a widespread feeling that Keynesian principles of macroeconomic management of the economy by governments should be extended to developing countries (Singer 1992). However, this was very much a top-down effort, full of elitism and even racism—Lord Keynes's dismissive description of Bretton Woods, which included 21 small (mainly non-European) countries, as a "monstrous monkey house" (Moggridge 1980, vol. 2: 42) suggests global economic regulation was intended to be directed by the rich, the powerful, and the European.

Economic development outside Europe and the United States was lent urgency by the political context of decolonization, the cold war, and competition for the adherence of Third World countries to either capitalism or communism. In his Inaugural Address on January 20, 1949, President Truman proclaimed the United States's commitment to a "democratic fair deal" for the entire world—greater production, he said, was the key to prosperity and peace. Greater prosperity was understood in terms of rising national per capita income, with benefits "trickling down" to the mass of the population. In terms of foreign commitments, Britain had long been involved in the development of its colonies, especially Australia, Canada, and Kenya (Cowen and Shenton 1996). With its avowed policy of assimilation of the colonies, France invented many development practices in the areas of health care and education (Rist 1997). But the late 1940s and 1950s saw the emergence of a body of economic theory expressly aimed at Third World development, originally in Latin America, but elaborated increasingly in the United States and Britain, as a liberal component of the cold war effort. Growth theory was the theoretical foundation for intervention in the development of poor countries in a kind of global Keynesianism (full employment for everyone throughout the world).

The new specialized field of "development economics" was critical of certain aspects of classical doctrine, found conventional economics too abstract, and often believed, with Keynes, in state intervention in the growth process. Neoclassical economics had assumed that smoothly working market systems and effective price mechanisms organized all economies efficiently. This notion of a universal science ("monoeconomics") was contested by a "structuralist approach" to development economics that insisted instead on the specificity of Third World economies. Two main areas of economic practice came into contention between these positions: trade theory and the causes of inflation.

First, we will discuss trade theory. In Latin America, early development strategies favored an outward-oriented model in which countries provided primary goods, such as coffee or copper, to the Euro-American market. The Great Depression revealed weaknesses inherent in this position; for example, in Brazil, where coffee was a major export, demand fell to the point that coffee was burnt as fuel by the Brazilian railroads. After World War II a coherent Latin American perspective on the development process was formulated in the United Nations Economic Commission for Latin America (ECLA). The ECLA found that conventional (classical and neoclassical) economic theory, especially comparative advantage and trade theories, favored the industrial countries at the center of a divided global system over the agricultural countries at the periphery of the world, and concluded that conventional theory was inadequate for the underdeveloped world. The ECLA argued that appreciation of the different historical contexts and natural situations of these countries, their different social structures, types of behavior, and economies, required a new structuralist perspective. The main tenets of this theory were outlined by Raul Prebisch, formerly head of the Central Bank of Argentina.

Prebisch (1972) saw the world not in monoeconomic terms, as one homogenous system, but as two distinct areas, a center of economic power in Europe and the United States, and a periphery of weak countries in Latin America, Africa, and Asia. Conventional economic theory (comparative advantage) argued that the exchange of the central area's industrial goods for the peripheral area's primary goods was to the periphery's advantage. Technical progress in the center would lead to lower prices for industrial exports, so that a unit of primary exports would buy more units of industrial imports; in other words, over the long term progress would accrue to the periphery, without it becoming industrialized. Instead Prebisch argued that Latin America's peripheral position and primary exports were the causes of its lack of progress, specifically because of a long-term decline in the periphery's terms of trade (the ratio between the value of exports and the value of imports). Using Britain as a case study, Prebisch showed that the terms of trade for center countries had improved with industrialization, from which he concluded that those of the periphery must have deteriorated. Technical advance benefited the center countries rather than the entire world. This was not a temporary phenomenon, but a structural characteristic of the global system. Conventional economic theory failed to work because (1) markets in the center were characterized by imperfect competition and price reductions could be avoided, while competition among primary producers reduced the prices for their goods; and (2) the income elasticity of demand (i.e., the degree to which demand changes with a given change in income) is higher for industrial than for primary goods, so that the periphery's terms of trade tended to decline from the demand side. Prebisch concluded that Latin America's underdevelopment was due to its emphasis on primary exports. The solution lay in structural change: industrialization using an import substitution strategy (i.e., replacing industrial imports with domestic production, under the cover of tariff protection), using income from primary exports to pay for imports of capital goods, state supervision of industrialization, and, paradoxically, the enlistment of foreign companies to help start local businesses. This approach was widely adopted in Latin America, and eventually elsewhere in the Third World, at first with impressive results as industry grew rapidly. Over time, however, import substitution was associated with high-cost, low-quality industrial output, the economically damaging neglect of agriculture, and entrenched positions for foreign capital. In time the remedy came to be seen as the cause of the illness (Blomstrom and Hettne 1984; Chilcote 1984; Harris 1986).

Now we will address the causes of inflation. In the 1940s, 1950s, and 1960s several Latin American countries experienced inflation rates of 80–100% a year against which standard deflationary policies had little effect. Monetarist economists argued that inflation was caused by excessive increases in the supply of money and that price stability could be achieved by decreasing the money supply. Structuralist economists argued conversely that supply and demand operated differently in Latin American countries, with supply being inelastic (i.e., requiring a large price change to bring about small changes in quantities of goods) because of structural characteristics like the domination of agriculture by latifundia (large estates) that did not operate on market principles. The inflation problem could be resolved only by structural changes such as land reform, import substitution (to make countries less dependent on foreign manufactures), increased educational opportunities, and improved fiscal systems (Seers 1962).

In general, structuralist development economics "attempts to identify specific rigidities, lags, and other characteristics of the structure of developing economies that affect economic adjustments and the choice of development policy" (Meier 1984: 118). The main structuralist points were that neoclassical economics was not a universal science, that the price system varied in effectiveness over space, and that a new type of economics had to be developed for the Third World. At least one important development theorist, Dudley Seers, director of the Institute of Development Studies at Sussex University in England, criticized Keynesian economics from the point of view of structuralism. Seers (1983) argued that growth models like Harrod–Domar, which used national accounting statistics as their numerical basis, concealed the real structures of economic change, especially the distributional characteristics (differences between rich and poor, regional and ethnic variations, etc.). Development planning based in Keynesianism was internationalist in orientation, said Seers. It provided a rationale for large-scale foreign aid, imposed technical conformity, and distracted attention from structural policies that would more genuinely serve the interests of the countries concerned. Instead of international Keynesianism, Seers favored greater self-reliance and national development strategies undertaken by regional blocs of nations. In general, structuralist economics argued that developing countries had features that set them apart from the economies theorized by orthodox economics. These features included high levels of rural underemployment, low levels of industrialization, more obstacles to industrialization, and disadvantages in international trade. Structuralist economics in the 1950s and 1960s tried to remedy these problems by removing the obstacles to growth in poor countries.

The development economics that emerged in the 1950s was different from neoclassical and Keynesian economics because of their specific focus on developing countries and their greater practicality in terms of a more immediate policy orientation. At first development economics assumed that economic processes in developing countries were distinct from those in developed countries, as the structuralists argued, but gradually monoeconomics (the position that all economies work in similar ways and that neoclassical economics was universally applicable) was reestablished, although "getting the prices right" was acknowledged to be more difficult in the developing world. Also while population, technology, institutions, and entrepreneurship were exogenous (assumed to be outside the system) in neoclassical economics, they were endogenous (within the system) for development economics; indeed, these were often the main factors requiring economic explanation. The position of development economics eventually became not that neoclassical economics was inapplicable, but that it needed extending, for example, to problems of income distribution, poverty, and basic needs, or that growth economics needed modifying because the unemployment problem was not of the Keynesian variety (Meier 1984: 145–147). The result was a hybrid development economics, a melange of ideas, part structuralist, part neoclassical, part Keynesian, part pragmatic. Some of the leading positions of development economics were as follows:

1. *Dualistic development:* This is the idea that in poor countries a modern, commercial sector developed alongside a traditional sector, resulting in a dual economy. Low labor productivity in the traditional sector (labor with a marginal productivity of zero), together with large numbers of workers eager to transfer to the modern sector, made for a supply curve of industrial labor that was infinitely elastic at the prevailing wage, usually 30% higher than incomes on subsistence farms. Investment capital came from high profits in the modern sector, which expanded until the excess labor was absorbed, whereupon wages rose to a point that might halt capital accumulation. Moreover, the terms of trade for products exchanged between the two sectors might eventually turn against the modern sector unless traditional agriculture was transformed along with the industrialization of the modern sector (Lewis 1955). Other aspects of this model included technological dualism (Higgins 1968), rural–urban migration even when urban unemployment rates rose (Todaro 1971), and the existence of a substantial informal sector providing basic goods and services to low-income people. The main

policy conclusion of the dual model was that attention had to be given to the utilization of labor outside the modern sector.

2. *Mobilizing domestic resources:* Typically, poor countries saved and invested 5% of national income. Development depended on increasing this ratio to 12–15%. The goal was to find ways to increase the savings rate and mobilize domestic savings (through banks and other financial institutions) to make domestic funds available for productive investment.

3. *Mobilizing foreign resources:* However, both a "savings gap" and a "foreign exchange gap" could still remain. These could be filled from external sources in the forms of public financial aid, loans, private foreign investment, and nonmonetary transfers of managerial and technological knowledge.

4. *Industrialization strategy:* Industrialization should produce, often in labor-intensive, capital-saving ways, the simple producer and consumer goods required particularly by rural people. In terms of strategy, some theorists, like P. N. Rosenstein-Rodan (1943) advocated a "big push" in the form of initially large industrial investments to enable external economies to be earned (i.e., lower costs through the growth of several industries at the same time). Harvey Liebenstein (1957), an economist at Harvard University, explained "economic backwardness" in terms of a "low-level equilibrium trap" whereby increased incomes tended to be pushed back down by population growth and consumption in the style of developed countries. Small efforts aimed at gradual change would be counteracted by population growth. For Liebenstein, the solution lay in a critical minimum effort mainly using the existing savings potential, especially funds used unproductively for luxury consumption or land purchases. With such an effort, the scale of investment would enable a growth rate greater than population increases, typically as high as 4% a year. Likewise, other theorists, like Albert Hirschman (1958), advocated deliberately promoting "unbalanced" growth to stimulate investment decisions and economize on scarce entrepreneurial resources. Still others emphasized industrial exporting. Increasingly this school paid attention to the mutually supportive interactions between industry and agriculture.

5. *Agricultural strategy:* Progress in agriculture was thought to be essential for providing food and raw materials, yielding savings and tax revenue for development elsewhere in an economy, earning foreign exchange, and forming a market for industrial goods. Intersectoral relations between industry and agriculture would determine the course of structural transformation in a developing economy. Special help should be given to the rural poor to enable them to take advantage of new tech-

nologies (e.g., the "Green Revolution" in new crop types and fertilizers). Some, more radical, theorists advocated changes in the distribution of land ownership (land reform) and better access for poor farmers to productive resources.

6. *Trade strategy:* Development economists were originally divided on whether free trade increased international inequalities or whether it could contribute to the development of primary exporting countries. They disagreed also on whether development strategies should be inward- or outward-oriented. Increasingly they favored export promotion of semimanufactured and manufactured goods and the liberalization of trade regimes.

7. *Human resource development:* The accumulation of material capital was to be paralleled by investment in "human capital"—that is, improving the quality of people as productive agents—by changing their abilities and skills, even by modifying motivations and values (hence an interaction with modernization theory; see Chapter 3). Population growth strained public services, producing adverse effects, particularly on child nutrition. The idea was to relate health policies to the ecological, cultural, and nutritional situations that permitted disease to thrive in poverty areas. As with technology transfers, there was a need too for an appropriate transfer of medical knowledge and technology. Education had to be seen in relation to employment as an investment good—as "human capital" or "embodied savings."

8. *Project appraisal:* Because investment resources were scarce in developing countries, there was a particular need for the rational allocation of capital and thus for development project appraisals by governments and international agencies like the World Bank. National or social profitability might differ from commercial profitability. So, appraisal involved using applied welfare economics in a world of the second best. A "first best" economy would "fulfill the marginal conditions of perfectly competitive equilibrium in all product and factor markets, with no uncertainty, no externalities, and a given income distribution," but conditions in a developing economy diverged particularly because of price distortions, hence the need to calculate efficient "shadow prices" for project evaluation (Meier 1984: 639).

9. *Development planning and policymaking:* Some development economists voiced criticisms of the market mechanism as ineffective, unreliable, or irrelevant to the problems faced by developing countries and found a need to supersede markets by using state planning. Others found the deficiencies of market systems in developing countries relatively unimportant compared with the benefits deriving from the essential functions of markets. They argued that the best way to strengthen an economy was to strengthen the market system (Meier 1984).

As this last point illustrates, development economics increasingly divided on crucial issues like the efficacy of the market or state planning. At the same time, development economics was subject to a number of critical studies, from the perspective of conventional, established, economic principles, which undercut its scientific validity.

Counterrevolution in Development Economics

The "counterrevolution" in development theory, part of a more general neoliberal or even conservative reaction, opposed Keynesianism, structuralism, and radical theories like dependency in the name of renewed faith in classical, Smithian economics (Dorn et al., 1998). The story of this counterrevolution has been ably told by John Toye (1987), at one time professor at the University College of Swansea, and later director of the Institute of Development Studies at Sussex University. For Toye, the countermovement in development economics began when the University of Chicago economist Harry Johnson (1923–1977) criticized Keynesian economics in the early 1970s. Johnson thought that intellectual movements in economics responded to perceived social needs rather than arising from an autonomous scientific dynamic. Hence the secret of the success of Keynesianism resided in its promise to end mass unemployment. For Johnson (1971), the Great Depression of the 1930s had resulted from the coincidence of several different national problems. Keynes's conclusion that capitalism tended systematically to produce massive economic problems (stagnation, unemployment) was unjustifiably critical of an entire system. Economic policy founded on Keynesian ideas displayed a similar lack of confidence in capitalism. For Johnson, further, development economists erred in adopting industrialization and national self-sufficiency as prime policy objectives, with economic planning as their instrument. This led to unproductive industrial investments in developing countries, especially those of postindependence Africa; encouraged corruption; favored import substitution, which in turn led to balance of payments problems; and in general made for misguided interventions into economic life in futile attempts at achieving social justice. According to Johnson, problems in the developing countries came not from the legacy of colonial history, nor from global inequalities, but from misguided Keynesian development policies. Later Johnson extended this critique to the Harrod–Domar model's "concentration on fixed capital investment as the prime economic mover" (Johnson and Johnson 1978: 232). Johnson argued that a neglect by Keynesian policymakers of the possibilities of technical progress, and their mesmerization by problems of disguised underemployment, especially in rural areas, led to development policies that merely transferred productive resources into industrial production, with no economic gain; by comparison, the Chicago school of economic's view of the rural sector, propounded by T. W. Schultz (1964), was that even poor farmers were efficient profit maximizers.

A more extended critique came from the British economist P. T. Bauer (1972, 1981; see also Little 1982). Mainstream development economics, Bauer argued, was not merely wrong, it was intellectually corrupt. Many of the views taken by orthodox development economics conflicted with obvious, empirical evidence:

> Examples include the thesis of the vicious circle of poverty; the allegation that rich countries have caused the poverty of the underdeveloped world; the idea that substantial economic development of poor countries must be accompanied by a shortage of foreign exchange; the allegation of a secular decline in the terms of trade of poor countries; the insistence on the supposedly inescapable necessity of central planning and of foreign aid for the material advance of poor countries; the opinion that all men are equally gifted by nature, and have equal economic aptitudes; and the practice of economic discussion without price and cost, that is the disregard of the effects of price on supply and demand and of the relevance of the alternative use of resources. (1972: 17)

A small number of theorists opposed to the market system, Bauer said, exercised unwarranted influence on Western people infused with a sense of guilt about the developing countries. Bauer thought that governments (India was his prime example) should stop restricting the energies of their subjects. Reducing poverty in the Third World did not require large-scale capital formation, nor even investment in "human capital." Foreign capital aid and technical assistance might also do great harm. Bauer particularly insisted that nontotalitarian societies should refrain from governmental participation in the economy.

Criticisms like these began to be heard in academic and policy circles during the 1970s. But they were given far greater salience by the coming to power of conservative governments in the United States, Britain, and West Germany in the early 1980s. The news media suddenly discovered the new criticism in 1983 and 1984. By the mid-1980s development economics was finished.

Neoliberalism

Beginning in the late 1960s, a new economics, opposed to Keynesianism, structuralism, and development economics alike, began to receive greater attention and adherence, particularly in Britain and the United

States. Neoliberal economics came from three linked sources: (1) the monetarist economics of Milton Friedman, the Chicago school in the United States, and the Institute of Economic Affairs in Britain, which argued that macroeconomic problems like inflation and indebtedness derived from excessive government spending driving up the quantity of money circulating in a society; (2) the new classical liberalism of economists like Friedrich von Hayek, who argued in *The Road to Serfdom* (1956) that even dalliance with "socialist ideas" (like Keynesian planning) would lead to disaster and that classical Smithian and Ricardian economic principles should be relied on instead; and (3) conservative political and economic ideas glorifying laissez-faire and rugged individualism, long propagated by authors like Ayn Rand (in *Atlas Shrugged* [1957]) and disseminated widely by the American Heritage Foundation and similar right-wing organizations. These ideas began to be taken seriously again in a context of economic crisis. The Bretton Woods agreement broke down in 1971. Oil prices increased rapidly in 1973–1974 and again in 1979. Several waves of inflation occurred. Many economists began saying that Keynesian economics was finished, that planning had been found lacking. Neoliberal economic policies were put into effect by the conservative Reagan and Thatcher governments in the early 1980s. Many had already been tested in Chile, where General Pinochet (who overthrew an elected leftist government led by Salvador Allende in 1973) was heavily advised by Chicago school economists (Overbeek 1990, 1993).

In Toye's (1987) view, the counterrevolution specifically in development economics was extended by Deepak Lal, an economist at the University of California, Los Angeles, and Bela Balassa, professor of political economy at Johns Hopkins University. Lal (1980, 1983) argued that the demise of development economics would promote the economic health of the economies (and economics) of developing countries. Development economics, Lal said, had perverted standard economic principles, such as the efficiency of price mechanisms or free trade, in the belief that developing countries were special cases rather than examples of universal rational behavior. He argued that the fundamentals of growth in the developed countries applied equally to the developing countries (the position of monoeconomics). Development economics had misinterpreted welfare economics, in particular the "second-best theorem," to produce situations worse than laissez-faire would yield. In a necessarily imperfect world, imperfect market mechanisms would do better in practice than imperfect planning mechanisms. On the grounds of individual liberty, Lal argued against income redistribution from rich to poor people. On standard, classical economic grounds, Lal was against all economic controls or government interventions and for "liberalizing" financial and trade controls in a return to nearly free trade regimes. Lal's ideas were complemented by the work of Bela Balassa on commercial policy in developing countries.

For Balassa, free trade did not mean the total absence of government intervention, nor complete acceptance of the pattern of production dictated by freely operating world market forces. There were, for Balassa, permissible government interventions, such as state protection of infant industries, and indeed choice of policy was key to understanding developmental success. Balassa (1981) argued for a stage theory emphasizing the choice of economic policy in setting a course and pushing a country through historical phases of industrialization. Industrial development was said to begin in Third World countries as a response to the needs of the primary sector (processing raw materials, providing simple inputs, etc.). Subsequently, a first or "easy" stage of import substitution entailed the local manufacture of previously imported nondurable goods. These industries were conducted at a small scale and required unskilled labor, but provided rapid growth as tariffs on imports enabled local production to gain increasing shares of the market. With the completion of import substitution further growth was confined to (small) increases in local consumption. Maintaining high rates of growth entailed either second-stage import substitution or exporting. Second-stage import substitution—the replacement of imports of intermediate goods (petrochemicals, steel), producer durables (machinery), and consumer durables (automobiles) by domestic production—was undertaken in the post-World War II period by the Latin American countries, some South Asian countries, and the East European countries. Problems such as the small size of the market (when industries are characterized by considerable economies of scale) led to the need for considerable state protection; in fact, in several underdeveloped countries the cost of protection amounted to 6 or 7% of the GDP. Balassa found that economic growth was distorted in environments protected from outside competition, that agriculture suffered, and that countries following this strategy lagged behind. This led to policy reforms like reductions in import protection and subsidization of exports—a main advantage of exporting being that it enabled economies of scale. Export-oriented policies, which departed least from a neutral state of nonintervention, were adopted by Japan in the mid-1950s; Korea, Singapore, and Taiwan in the early 1960s; and the Latin American countries in the mid- to late 1960s. Korea, Singapore, and Taiwan, all of which implemented "free trade regimes" (exporters could choose to use local or imported inputs in their manufacturing), increased industrial exports rapidly in the early 1960s. In the late 1960s and early 1970s various incentives for exporting in these countries led to further growth in manufacturing employment and higher incomes. Countries in Latin America (e.g., Brazil) that reformed their system of incentives also experienced (somewhat lower) rates of increase in exports and employment. But countries that retained inward-looking strategies (e.g., India, Chile, Uruguay) remained at the bottom of the industrial growth chart. For Balassa (1981: 16–17) the evidence was conclusive: "Countries applying outward-oriented development strategies had a superior performance in terms of exports, economic growth, and employment whereas countries which continued inward orientation encountered increasing economic difficulties." Choice of economic policy was the differentiating factor, and export-led industrialization was the promise of the future for the underdeveloped world. Balassa (1981: 22–23) argued that East Asian countries with high educational levels would replace Japan in exporting skill-intensive products, that Latin American countries would expand their capital-intensive production, and that countries at lower stages of industrial development would export products requiring unskilled labor. This would widen the circle of industrial development to eventually include all. The basic idea that now emerged was that the new industrial countries (NICs) were models for the rest of the developing world to follow.

This view was given credence by the apparent success of the NICs in the 1970s and 1980s. The developed countries had economic growth rates averaging 4.8% a year in the period 1964–1973 and 2.1% a year in the period 1973–1983; the NICs (Brazil, Mexico, Hong Kong, Singapore, Taiwan) collectively had growth rates of 8.4% and 5.3%, respectively, in the same periods, with the East Asian countries sustaining growth rates on the order of 10% a year often for a decade or more (OECD 1988). In the mid-1980s a new wave of industrialization in Indonesia, Malaysia, Thailand, and (later) China seemed to confirm the Balassa theory of an ever-widening circle of industry-led growth. In the view of many, this brought to an end the North–South division of labor involving exchanges between primary commodities and industrial goods. Neoliberal development theorists argued that the success of the NICs confirmed their view that sound development policies could be based on conventional neoclassical economic principles: "Growth and development in the NICs are viewed as natural, inherent properties of open capitalist economies in which market forces are allowed to operate with little state interference" (Brohman 1996a: 107). Putting this a little differently, whereas comparative advantage theory relegated developing countries to providing cheap labor products to the global system, the notion of a ladder leading to increasingly sophisticated products made by better-paid workers suggested a more acceptable development theory.

By the end of the 1980s a system of recommendations based on neoliberal ideas became standard in conventional international economic policy circles. In a book on the debt crisis in Latin America, John

Williamson, a senior fellow at the Institute of International Economics in Washington, DC, outlined the policy consensus reached by the IMF, the World Bank, and the U.S. executive branch (Williamson 1990). The "Washington Consensus" dismissed the conclusions reached in the development literature and relied instead on classical economic theories to reach the following policy recommendations:

1. *Fiscal discipline:* government budget deficits should be no more than 2% of GDP.
2. *Public expenditure priorities:* expenditures should be redirected from politically sensitive areas toward neglected areas like primary health care, education, and infrastructure.
3. *Tax reform:* incentives should be sharpened and sequity improved.
4. *Financial liberalization:* interest rates should be market-determined as far as possible.
5. *Exchange rates:* rates should be sufficiently competitive to induce rapid growth in nontraditional exports;
6. *Trade liberalization:* quantitative restrictions on imports should be replaced with tariffs in the range of 10% over a period of 3–10 years.
7. *Foreign direct investment:* barriers to the entry of foreign firms competing on equal terms with domestic companies should be abolished.
8. *Privatization:* state enterprises should be returned to private ownership.
9. *Deregulation:* governments should abolish regulations restricting competition.
10. *Property rights:* the legal system should secure property rights without excessive costs.

As Williamson (1990: 18) put it: "The economic policies that Washington urges on the rest of the world may be summarized as prudent macro-economic policies, outward orientation, and free market capitalism." The consensus was subsequently widely interpreted by critics as the essence of a neoliberal development policy package (Williamson 1997). Development policy came to consist in withdrawing government intervention in favor of the rationalization of an economy through disciplining by the market and by self-interested individuals efficiently choosing between alternatives in the allocation of resources. In the external sector, neoliberalism entailed the devaluation of currencies, convertible monetary systems, and the removal of restrictions on trade and capital movements. In the internal sector, markets were to be deregulated (including deunionizing) while price subsidies on food were to be reduced and then eliminated. Government spending was reduced, and private consumption restricted (by higher prices) so that incomes flowed into private investment, stimulating growth (Brohman 1996b).

This alternate theory of development was applied to some Latin American countries in the early 1970s, from which it spread to Africa, Asia, and virtually all countries, even a newly liberated South Africa, by the mid-1990s. Likewise, neoliberalism became the West's model for reshaping Eastern Europe in the postcommunist 1990s. A good example was Poland's "return to Europe." Jeffrey Sachs (1991), a Harvard University economist, and an adviser to Solidarity, the Polish workers movement, and subsequently to the postcommunist Polish government, saw structural change occurring through the generalized reintroduction of market forces. Three types of policies were involved in the economic reform program: economic liberalization, the broad rubric for legal and administrative changes needed to create institutions of private property and market competition; macroeconomic stabilization, including measures to limit budget deficits, reduce growth of the money supply, and create a convertible currency with stable prices; and privatization, transferring ownership of state property to the private sector. However, Sachs also advocated a social safety net, to prevent reforms from injuring the most vulnerable sectors of society, and a public investment program, mainly for infrastructure as a complement to economic restructuring. He thought that measures like these could be introduced virtually overnight (like switching the driving side in Britain from left to right) in a process that became known as "shock therapy." The key to economic reform, Sachs said, was that several years had to pass in a vale of tears before the fruits were borne, the time depending on the boldness and consistency of the reforms—if there was wavering, it was easy to get lost in the valley. In one simple statement Sachs summarized the neoliberal approach to development—"liberal" in the classical sense of lack of state control and reliance on markets and the price mechanism, "liberal" in the contemporary sense of concern for victims, but "neo" in the sense that suffering was accepted as an inevitable consequence of reform and efficiency.

World Bank Policy

At the Bretton Woods conference in 1944 two agencies were founded that would prove to be of pivotal importance to development in the second half of the twentieth century. The International Monetary Fund (IMF) was designed to help countries avoid balance of payments problems by giving short-term loans. The World Bank (or International Bank for Reconstruction and Development) guaranteed private bank loans for more long-term investments in productive activities. In the 1950s, under Eugene Black (president 1949–1962), the bank mainly loaned capital for the construction of infrastructure (roads, railroads, dams, etc.) in the belief that development basically meant economic growth and this, in turn, depended on investment. In the mid-1960s, under George Woods (president 1963–1968), emphasis shifted to education and Third World agriculture. Under Robert McNamara (president 1968–1981), the bank increased rapidly in size and changed quickly in orientation. McNamara had been president of the Ford Motor Company and was U.S. secretary of defense during the Vietnam War. In his address to the bank's board of governors in 1972 McNamara said that 40% of the people in the South, or Third World, lived in absolute poverty, which he defined as conditions so deprived as to prevent realization of the potential of a person's genes. The immediate priority was enabling decent living conditions (food, clothing, housing, services), that is, a basic needs approach to development assistance, in which resources were given directly rather than trickling down to the poor. The ultimate goal, McNamara (1981) said, was to raise the productivity of the poor, enabling them to be brought into the economic system. The 1978 *World Development Report* (World Bank 1978) said that the development effort should be directed toward the twin objectives of rapid growth and reducing the numbers of people living in absolute poverty as quickly as possible. The idea was to use resources made possible by rapid economic growth to expand public services. For a while basic needs became the development approach of choice among international agencies (Payer 1982). In 1968 the World Bank's lending for agriculture and rural development totaled $172.5 million; by 1981 this had risen to $3.8 billion (Ayres 1983: 5).

In the early 1980s, with a change in the bank's presidency to A. W. Clawson, the World Bank shifted emphasis again. The first sign of change came with a report on development in sub-Saharan Africa prepared by the bank's African Strategy Review Group coordinated by Eliot Berg (World Bank 1981). The report found that the basic problems of the region—slow economic growth, sluggish agricultural performance, rapid rates of population increase, balance of payments and fiscal crisis—stemmed from a combination of internal and external factors exacerbated by "domestic policy inadequacies": (1) trade and exchange rate policies overprotected industry, held back agriculture, and absorbed administrative capacity; (2) there were too many administrative constraints and the public sector was overextended; and (3) there was a bias against agriculture in price, tax, and exchange rate policies. These areas had to be changed, the group concluded, if production was to be given a higher priority. While reticent in advising specific measures, the bank found that the existing state controls over trade were ineffective, and indicated that private-sector activity should be enlarged, that agricultural resources should be concentrated on small farmers, and that human resources should be improved under an export-oriented development strategy.

During the 1970s the elites of many Third World countries had borrowed as much as they could, ostensibly to finance development projects, although a significant share of the funds ended up in Swiss bank accounts. Third World and Eastern European debt tripled (to a total of $626 billion) between 1976 and 1982 (Kojm 1984). In 1982 Mexico experienced its first debt crisis: the peso lost half its value in a week and the state was unable to meet payments on $20 billion in loans. Along with Argentina, Brazil, and many other countries, Mexico was forced into debt rescheduling (at lower interest rates, with payments over longer time periods) supervised by the IMF. This came at the expense of "structural adjustment," a series of measures first put into place in the mid-1970s, but formalized in 1979 and 1980. By the mid-1980s three-quarters of Latin American countries and two-thirds of African countries were under some kind of IMF–World Bank supervision.

In this context we find the bank's emphasis changing. The 1983 *World Development Report* (World Bank 1983: 29) argued that foreign trade enabled developing countries to specialize in production, exploit economies of scale, and increase foreign exchange earnings. The 1984 *Report* (World Bank 1984: Ch. 3) used "growth scenarios" to argue that developing countries would improve their positions by changing their economic policies: avoiding overvalued exchange rates, reducing public spending commitments, and having an "open trading and payments regime" that encouraged optimal use of investment resources. The case examples cited in the *Report* were the "outward-oriented" East Asian countries. In the following year (World Bank 1985: 145) the bank was warning that a "retreat from liberalization" would slow economic growth. The 1987 *World Development Report* asked, What are the ultimate objectives of development? Generally, the answer was "faster growth of national income, alleviation of poverty, and reduction of income inequalities" (World Bank 1987: 1). The bank stressed "efficient industrialization" as the key economic policy. The bank devised a lending program that supported policy reforms and structural changes across the whole economy of a Third World country. The bank drew directly on Smith's argument that industrialization would be retarded by a low ability to trade, and on Ricardo and Mill in arguing that trade gave advantages that led to productivity increases. Protection of industry in the past, the *Report* said, had led to inefficient industries and poor quality, expensive goods. So the idea was to reduce trade barriers, switch the economy's focus to exports, and compete vigorously in world markets. The bank suggested policy reform in three main areas: trade reform, specifically the adoption of an outward-oriented trade strategy; macroeconomic policies to reduce governments' budget deficits, lower inflation, and ensure competitive exchange rates; and a domestic competitive environment, that is, removing price controls, rationalizing investment regulations, and reforming labor market regulations. To give some idea of what was meant by these innocuous phrases, "reforming" labor market policies meant decreasing minimum wages and ending other regulations that distorted free labor markets. We might note also that reducing government spending meant reducing antipoverty programs, among other things.

The main instrument by which these ideas were put into practice were the structural adjustment programs and stabilization policies imposed on countries borrowing from the IMF and the World Bank. Structural adjustment programs were medium- to long-term economic devices (over three to five years) involving three kinds of measures: expenditure reduction, aimed at improving a country's balance of trade position by reducing demand, decreasing imports, and increasing exports—accomplished via credit and wage restrictions, contractions in the money supply, and reductions in public spending; expenditure switching, aimed at decreasing consumption and increasing savings and investment especially in tradeable goods—to be accomplished by increasing the price of food to stimulate agriculture, and by devaluing the currency and increasing income taxes to raise government revenue; and institutional reforms centered on market liberalization and privatization, in the belief that markets allocate resources efficiently. Stabilization programs were short-term instruments (over one to two years) involving fiscal and monetary policies designed to correct balance of payments and inflation problems (Logan and Mengisteab 1993). Structural adjustment more basically meant changing the structure of an economy so that it mirrored the competitive ideal derived from the Western experience. Most essentially it meant "getting the prices right"—that is, achieving a pricing system that allocated resources efficiently.

Like most policies based on ideals, structural adjustment was subject to modification. In the late 1980s and early 1990s, some commentators found the World Bank shifting slightly to a revised neoliberal model stressing market-friendly state intervention and good governance (political pluralism, accountability, and the rule of law), conditions again found typical in the East Asian "miracle economies" (Kiely 1998). The *World Development Report* for 1990 dealt with poverty for the first time since the McNamara era. The World Bank outlined a two-pronged approach: policies that promoted the use of labor, the poor's most abundant asset, by harnessing market incentives and other means; and the provision of basic services to the poor, like primary health care, education, and nutrition. Such was the state of conventional development policy at the close of the twentieth century. The World Bank has become far more important in setting development policy than its annual $7.4 billion of lending, a mere 2–3% of the capital flows to the Third World, would suggest. As one commentator puts it: "The bank is to economic development theology what the papacy is to Catholicism, complete with yearly encyclicals" (Holland 1998; "yearly encyclicals" refers to the annual *World Development Reports*).

Critique

More than any other social science discipline, economics is unified by a dominant theoretical structure, highly developed, mathematically stated, scientifically conceived, thought and taught as truth, subject only to slight revisions and changes of emphasis within academic and policy circles that reach into the highest echelons of power. Yet, more than other disciplines, economics rests on simplistic assumptions (about human behavior especially) that are taken as given for all time. Economics develops in an intellectual vacuum of high mathematics and unrealistic models, isolates itself from fundamental critiques, and reaches precarious conclusions which, while they affect everyone, are conspicuously lacking in democratic input. These tendencies in contemporary, neoclassical economics are highly related: it is exactly the policy powerfulness of economics that protects it from having to take criticism seriously; it is exactly the mathematical complexity of economics that precludes popular participation in the construction of economic knowledge. Arguments like these apply with double force to the economics of development, which cries out for participation by those "being developed." Thus we spend much of the remainder of this book criticizing development discourse, especially its conventional versions, from the perspectives formed by a number of alternative visions. Several fundamentally opposed economic and sociological notions of development, such as Marxist and neo-Marxist theories, or feminist theories, appear in the coming chapters. However, the discipline has also been criticized from positions within, or on the fringes of, formal, conventional economics. Here we present some of these criticisms.

Institutional economics is one such alternative, critical of the mainstream, yet preserving connections with it. Many institutional economists share the dominant notion of economics as the study of the efficient allocation of resources, but diverge on whether the market is the economy's guiding mechanism. The real allocating mechanism, they say, is the structure of the society, which organizes markets as well as other institutions (Ayres 1957). Institutional economics has a broader interest than the conventional discipline, being concerned more with topics such as power, institutional complexes, individual and collective psychologies, the formation of knowledge in a world of radical indeterminacy, and the relations between culture, income, and control of societies.

This school of economic thought criticizes neoclassicism on a number of grounds. First, institutionalists argue that neoclassical economics employs methodological individualism, treating individuals as independent, self-subsisting entities with inherent drives (pleasure/pain) and possessed of given, utilitarian preferences, rather than as culturally formed (and culture-forming) subjects, even though analyzing markets is clearly a case of methodological collectivism (i.e., economics is the study of collective institutions). Second, the neoclassical quest for determinate optimal equilibrium solutions forecloses on real-world processes that are indeterminate and far from optimal. Third, neoclassical models are static in nature whereas economies are dynamic and evolutionary. Fourth, neoclassicism's analytical categories (i.e., its mental representations of the world) result from formal, logical, and substantively empty abstraction that results in conservative formulations, positions that see institutional changes (in laws or the state) as undesirable interference in otherwise optimal laissez-faire solutions. And fifth, neoclassical demand and supply theory channels analysis along presumptive, prefigured lines that loose contact with other aspects of real-world processes. Some institutionalists criticize both the organization of market economies and the economics of the pure market, while most are more empirical, pragmatic, and open to multidisciplinary approaches (Samuels 1995). Interactions between institutionalism and Keynesianism have produced a school of post-Keynesian economics dedicated to the solution of real economic problems and the achievement of a more just and equitable society (Arestis 1996).

While most institutional thinking in economics derives in some way from the work of Thorstein Veblen, this area contains at least two main variants that are often antagonistic toward each other: new institutional economics and radical institutionalism. In the words of one main theorist, the Nobel Prize–winning economic historian Douglass C. North (1995: 17), "The new institutional economics builds on, modifies and extends neo-classical economic theory" so it can deal with a wider range of issues. Institutions, North says, are the socially devised constraints that structure human interactions. They are different from organizations, in that they are composed of formal rules, as with laws and regulations; informal conventions, for example, norms of behavior and codes of conduct; and the enforcement characteristics or the circumstances that enable rules to have systematic effects. By comparison, organizations are groups of individuals guided by institutions in their actions, as with political, economic, social, or educational bodies. The new institutional economics criticizes the "instrumental rationality" of neoclassical economics. This accepts values as given and constant, postulates an objective description of the world, and assumes unlimited computational powers on the parts of decision makers. Under these conditions, only efficient markets matter, while institutions are unimportant. For the new institutionalists, by comparison, people have limited capacities to process incomplete information; indeed, this is why, according to this perspective, people construct institutions—to impose constraints on their interactions to structure exchange. In conventional economic understanding, the total costs of producing commodities consist of the land, labor, and capital used in transforming the physical qualities of a good. The new institutional economics adds the transaction costs of institutions, as with the resources used in institutionally defining and enforcing property rights over goods which, it claims, make up 45% of the national income of the United States. For institutionalists, the optimizing results of neoclassical economic theory obtain only in an institution-free environment where there are no transaction costs. An exchange process involving transaction costs implies significant modifications in economic theory and different implications for economic performance (Williamson 1985; North 1990). What difference does this make to the theory of economic change?

For North (1995), an institutional/cognitive model of development begins with the different experiences of social groups in different physical environments; the mental models and languages that define their institutional frameworks as they tackle fundamental economic problems of scarcity, exchange, and production; and the processes of learning and cultural transmission that pass institutions through time and space. The application of modern scientific disciplines to technology and the relief of scarcity in the nineteenth century entailed immense transaction costs for coordinating and integrating economies, including the development of a polity (country, nation, state) that would enact and enforce the "rules of the game" for the economy. For North, this suggests a "radically different" development economics and system of policy prescription. Neoclassical development policies based on "getting the prices right" work only when agents already have in place a set of property rights and institutions to enforce them. Economic development is based on the continuous interaction of institutions and organizations in an economic setting of scarcity and competition, with competition forcing organizations to continually invest in skills and knowledge that shape perceptions about opportunities and choices that in turn incrementally alter institutions. This sets economies on certain paths of development in which key elements involve entrepreneurs learning about profitable opportunities. For new institutionalists, the rate of learning determines the speed of economic change, while the kind of learning determines its direction. From North's perspective, economic policy should therefore focus on the institutional framework of development. This turns out to be complex; for example, transferring the formal political and economic rules of one society (the United States) to others (he mentions Latin America, but postcommunist Russia would be a better example) is not sufficient for improving performance because the informal rules differ and the enforcement characteristics may not be in place. Thus privatization is not the universal panacea neoliberals claim it is. For North, the heart of development policy is the creation of polities that enforce efficient property rights: "Long-run economic growth entails the development of the rule of law and the protection of civil and political freedoms" (North 1995: 25). There is no greater challenge, North concludes, than forming a dynamic theory of social change that enables an understanding of an economy's "adaptive efficiency," by which he means a flexible institutional matrix that adjusts to technical and demographic changes as well as to shocks to the system.

By comparison, radical institutionalism is far more critical of the economic status quo than the new institutionalism. Thorstein Veblen advocated fundamental change in capitalism in the direction of an egalitarian system founded on community control of the economy (Tilman 1992). Veblen saw history as absurd, as blind drift, rather than (as with Marx) as dialectical movement shaped by contradiction. Unlike Smith and Marx, Veblen did not believe that the value of a commodity could be traced to any one factor of production, such as labor. Unlike neoclassical economics, Veblen did not see economies headed toward some kind of balance, equilibrium, or optimal state. For Veblen, output was a communal product that should be distributed communally. Drawing on Veblen's ideas, contemporary radical institutionalism, in the view of William Dugger, a major theorist, stresses themes different from the preoccupations of neoclassical economics:

1. The economy is a process of *cumulative change* (improvement, deterioration, underdevelopment, etc.) rather than an equilibrium. An example would be the ideas of the Swedish institutional economist Gunnar Myrdal (1984: 499), who argued that left to itself "economic development is a process of circular and cumulative causation which tends to

award its favours to those who are already well endowed and even to thwart the efforts of those who happen to live in regions that are lagging behind."

2. *Individual rationality* results from socialization in the context of power relations and can be distorted by myths, stereotypes, and emulation, under which the lower orders of stratified societies may burn with desire to mimic the achievements and lifestyles of the upper strata.

3. *Power and status* legitimate authority by turning predatory, exploitative practices into rightful duties. The market does not result from Smith's natural system of liberty, but is defined, and given its leading characteristics, by the state.

4. *Equality is instrumentally effective* in terms of maintaining demand, increasing productivity, and, with full participation, bringing new drive, spirit, and ideas into the community. Progress occurs from the bottom up, being based not on charity but on equality; the redistribution of income and power is an essential component of progress.

5. *Radical institutionalism* is based on an existential philosophy of the

> underground man, the marginal woman, the dissenter who refuses to give up in the face of impossible odds, the resister who does not believe in the inevitable triumph of her cause, who does not believe that life has meaning outside of the meaning she herself infuses. . . . From meaninglessness and hopelessness, the existentialist draws personal commitment to action. (Dugger 1989: 12)

It is also instrumentalist in a *democratic, policy-oriented* way. Radical institutionalists lack the neoclassical faith in the automatic benevolence of the market, believing instead that nations have to plan for their economic well-being.

6. Radical institutionalists are *antiestablishmentarian and democratic* in the sense of participatory democracy (people affected by decisions make them). Indeed, the idea is that the participatory drive (people practically solving problems) pushes the social system forward.

7. Radical institutionalism is a *radical paradigm* predicated on the economy conceived as a *process*, rather than an equilibrium, with radical breaks possible, such as the movement from the free market status quo to national economic planning.

In general, radical institutionalism explains the capitalist economy as a process dominated by power and status, distorted by irrationality, but capable of being transformed into a democratic, egalitarian system of abundance for all (Dugger 1989). Greatly different from its distant cousin, the radical version of institutionalism proposes reconstructing economics from its initial assumptions to the politics of its policy conclusions.

From the critical perspectives of both branches of institutionalism, the theories of growth and development surveyed in this chapter are fundamentally flawed because economics bears deep in its structure an unrealistic, even isolated, view of the world. Rather than social institutions forming the rationalities of economic agents, neoclassical economics takes human behavior as given, as it was supposed to be by Bentham, who reduced the complexity of motivations to the single, utilitarian impulse of the pursuit of pleasure. With marginalist economics, open-ended, dynamic processes composed from the interactions of many people, organizations, and institutions were reduced to static, partial-equilibrium models admired for their mathematical precision rather than for their realistic accuracy—for example, they exclude the possibility of depressions. Even Keynesian growth theory reduces the complex dynamics of economic systems to the interactions between a few "variables." The new classical economics assumes that privatization, markets, and the right prices can solve all problems. Theories like this can be built only by excluding from consideration most real-world institutions and social processes. Yet theoretical exclusion of most of reality from model building has to be conducted carefully, in full realization that results derived from highly abstract models are precarious. Policy statements derived from partial models must be cast in terms of probabilities rather than certainties.

But here we encounter a basic problem of science and scientists. With economics, social science most nearly approaches social physics in the natural scientific sense of the term. Economists become fixated on their own image as scientists, obsessed with the formal beauty of their creations, to the degree that the protests of millions hardly reach their ears—riots against IMF policies, for instance. So while any statement about the social behavior of human beings must always be cast in self-critical terms, economics is stated instead in terms of scientific, mathematical certainty. Versions of economics that break from the fold are either denigrated as mere opinion, or disciplined to return, not just by outside critics, but by insider doubts about scientificity and legitimacy. Thus, in the case of development economics, the notion of a different reality in developing countries, taken seriously, would have meant formulating a completely different approach with different agents in different, often nonmarket relations, with different social relations—economics, however, calls this anthropology. Within the discipline, merely flirting with the possibility of radical difference was dangerous in terms of scholarly respectability. As a result, development economics remained a mishmash of basically conventional ideas, with a few precariously stated alternatives (like the possibility of trade favoring the rich countries) dropped, with relief, as soon as possible. Economics is handicapped by its socially restricted vision.

As radical institutionalism begins to argue, criticisms of economics as "science" must be complemented by criticisms of economics as political ideology. That is the notion developed at greater depth later in this book, that science is not just delusions of grandeur, but is also a disguise ("neutrality") for viewpoints that are actually politically committed. From the beginning, modern economics championed one way of organizing economic activity: the market, for goods, for workers, for capital. Yet, when economists think of the market, science suddenly gives way to mythology. Here we have an institution that magically transforms myriad selfish intentions into homogeneous socially beneficial tendencies, with "beneficial" defined exclusively as the efficient use of resources in the generation of profit and the production of material abundance. Questions of development, issues concerning the distribution of affluence, effects on the natural environment, influences on the mental and physical health of discarded "human capital," and many other dimensions of a truly beneficial economy are relegated to "externalities," disregarded as relatively insignificant, or (worst of all) dismissed (after a few nice words) as the inevitable price of progress. Perhaps the hand guiding market economies is invisible because it does not exist? Perhaps market economies instead are unstable, spontaneous, and utterly destructive?

The selective revival of classical economics in the last third of the twentieth century throws these contentious issues into sharp relief. The ideas of the classical theorists, who considered economy in the broader context of moral issues, was filtered through the supposedly neutral sieve of scientific analytics, to yield an amoral, conservative orthodoxy that now controls the economic imagination. For development theory the results are disastrous. A single developmental model, export-oriented manufacturing within an open, market economy, achieves a position of such dominance that alternative forms of development are dismissed as irrelevant, even by supposedly leftist governments like the Mandela administration in postapartheid South Africa (Republic of South Africa 1996). The fact that Japan, South Korea, Brazil, and Singapore achieved their present status as case studies in "success" through massive state intervention hardly disturbs neoliberal orthodoxy. IMF-imposed structural adjustment programs, designed to produce the social and economic conditions for export-oriented growth, are continually resisted by masses of starving people. And then, in 1997, 1998, and 1999, one by one, the leading export-orientated countries, the miracle economies of Thailand, Korea, Indonesia, Malaysia, Mexico, Brazil, even Japan, not to speak of those precarious economies subjected to "shock therapy," like starving Russia, entered extended periods of crisis which (according to the business-oriented media) threaten global economic stability. In the conventional view, the East Asian crisis is financial in origin, caused by too much borrowing on global financial markets (World Bank 1998) rather than being structural in nature (Hart-Landesberg and Burkett 1998). What is to be done, according to conventional, neoliberal economic opinion? More privatization, less Keynesian interference, even greater trade liberalization. The cause of the problem becomes its solution. As the twentieth century ends, economics closes to alternatives, precludes real solutions, returns to a laundered version of its classical past. Development is inherently a contentious issue. It is time to renew contention, to return to critique, and to begin to think in terms of economic and social alternatives.

Chapter 3

SOCIOLOGICAL THEORIES OF MODERNIZATION

The theories covered in this chapter derive, broadly speaking, from the discipline of sociology, but certain of their aspects were developed by geographers. Rather than covering the entire discipline of sociology, we stress a number of interrelated themes deriving from this academic tradition, the idea being that each, in turn, and in combination, has influenced attitudes toward development. *Naturalistic theories* in sociology and geography saw environments creating societies with uneven potentials for development, with peoples acting in these contexts with different degrees of effectiveness as economic agents. *Weberian sociology* looked to the emergence of a certain kind of culture, specifically, a form of thinking called "rationalism," to explain the progressive transformation of the modern European realm. *Structural functionalism* combined naturalism with rationalism as the philosophical basis of an evolutionary theory of modernization covering all aspects of social activity. *Modernization theory* spelt out the implications for the geography of a global system divided into centers of modern progress and peripheries of traditional backwardness, with the center showing the periphery its future. All these sociological and geographical theories viewed development as far more than economic growth. While conventional in politics, they began by criticizing the narrow focus of neoclassical economics (Parsons and Smelser 1956). Yet, like neoliberalism, they oriented development toward copying the accomplishments of the West. Development is a form of social imagination, and its theories are as much persuasive ideologies as they are models of understanding.

Naturalism

Sociology originated in the "positive philosophy" of the early-nineteenth-century philosopher Auguste Comte (1798–1857). Comte's *Introduction to Positive Philosophy* (1988 ed.) first published in 1824 based on earlier attacks on metaphysics launched by the British empiricists (Hume, Locke, and others) and the French Enlightenment philosophers, laid out an order for the sciences in the form of a hierarchy of generality and complexity, with sociology (in the sense of social physics) at its apex. Comte thought that scientific understanding progressed through theological and metaphysical stages to eventually reach the pinnacle of positive knowledge. The positivistic science of society shared the same logical form as the natural sciences (it too had hypotheses, models, laws) but had to develop its own methodological procedures, for its subject matter was more complex. Human social development, Comte said, might be governed by laws similar to those in nature. Thus Comte introduced the notion of *organicism* into sociology—that is, the study of social organisms, with the family as the cell and social classes as natural tissues. However, variations in the operation of social laws made human deliberative action possible in the rational facilitation of progress. Hence the main difference between social and natural science resided in human consciousness. With this difference, Comte projected a tension between naturalism and rationalism into the positivistic sociological theory he had founded.

One solution to the problem of connecting nature with society, natural science with social science, was proposed by the nineteenth-century British evolutionary philosopher and sociologist Herbert Spencer (1820–1903). For Spencer, societies had natural, functional characteristics like all living things. He argued, through analogy, that the biological principles of organismic evolution also applied to the development of the "social organism." Just as animals derived competitive advantage from their relationships with nature (as with Darwin's theory, for instance), so societies occupying different natural environments were differently endowed in a struggle for survival. According to Spencer, rich natural environments enabled high population densities, thereby increasing economic specialization and division of labor, thus promoting greater political size and armed might—what he called "superorganic" evolution. Natural fertility and population density allowed intense social interaction, that is, people meeting each other more frequently. In turn, social interaction, according to Spencer, was the source of invention, innovation, and progress. In Spencer's theory, the naturally well-endowed areas of the world were areas of innovation, development, and civilization. Moreover, societies went through life cycles, with the young conquering the old, and the whole process of survival of the societal fittest leading toward an eventual worldwide utopian paradise characterized by the more leisurely pursuit of culture (Spencer 1882).

Spencer's ideas were extremely significant in mid- to late-nineteenth-century social thought, especially in the United States (Hofstadter 1955). The Darwinian notion of survival of the fittest, applied to human societies, legitimated laissez-faire, market systems, private ownership of productive resources, and social inequalities. Social Darwinism combined with the doctrine of Manifest Destiny provided a rationale for the Euro-American conquest of the North American continent and the near-elimination of its indigenous inhabitants. Survival of the fittest helped explain the transition to an intensely competitive industrial capitalism and the rise to power of rich people, who revered Spencer and his many disciples in American sociology. As a result of its social and political utility, environmental determinism became the leading school of developmental or evolutionary thought in a number of social scientific disciplines, including geography, in the second half of the nineteenth century.

According to the geographer Ellen Churchill Semple (1863–1932), for example, the natural environment determined people's racial qualities, especially their levels of consciousness, productivity, and economic development (Semple 1911). As with Spencer, and her mentor, the German geopolitician Friedrich Ratzel, Semple believed that Europe's physically articulated yet protected regions were environments conducive to high population densities and the growth of civilizations. So too the confinement of the Anglo-Americans to the Eastern Seaboard for two centuries, yet their separation from England by the Atlantic Ocean, promoted a strong sense of national cohesion, a sense of being "American." She also argued that the trans-Appalachian frontier had a stimulating effect on the Anglo-Saxon "race" in the eighteenth and nineteenth centuries, fostering both democracy and entrepreneurship. Like most environmental determinists, she fully supported imperial conquest and economic domination by powerful nations in the eventual interest of the civilization of all humanity (Semple 1903; Peet 1985).

At the turn of the nineteenth century, the realization that there were great differences between humans and other natural organisms came to the fore in sociology and geography. Humans, it was realized, were self-conscious, aware of what they were doing, able to choose different courses of action (within limits). Humans could plan their own actions and guide their own reactions to nature. Humans interposed complex forms of consciousness, intricate systems of social relations, powerful forces of production, buildings and infrastructures, and so on, between themselves and nature. As the belief in a complex relation between soci-

ety and nature began to spread, the organismic analogy and socio-
biological conceptions of causation came to be thought highly suspect as
bases for sociological and geographical understanding.

Rationalism

At first sight, the idea of human rationality appears contrary to naturalism as a type of social theory—contrary in the sense that, through rational processes, societies may escape the structuring influences of natural
necessity. Yet we find naturalism and rationalism constantly interacting
in sociological theories of development. As we have seen, naturalism
posits social institutions and human behaviors founded on natural
bases—for example, people act on the basis of instinct, or institutions
are social forms of natural functions. In contrast, rationalism valorizes
the capacity for humans to control the world through thought, logic,
and calculation (scientific–technological rationalism), although it also
implies the systematization of meaning patterns and the taking of a con-
sistent, unified stance toward these patterns (metaphysical–ethical rationalism) and the achievement of a methodical way of life based on logical
examination (practical rationalism). In many ways the two metaphilo-
sophies, naturalism as a nonreligious understanding of life's origins and
rationalism as the celebration of the final victory of human mind over
natural matter, are the greatest intellectual achievements of the modern
world, forms of understanding that combine into the modern, materialist, and scientific culture (within which there are positivist, Marxist, and
other philosophical variants). Combining the two perspectives, naturalism and rationalism, into a powerful theory of societal structure and
development was a defining moment in the history of the West.

The stress on rationalism in sociological theory derived from the
work of the eminent German economist and sociologist Max Weber
(1864–1920). Weber's ideas descended from the German school of historical economics outlined in Chapter 2. Weber posited a historical theory of the stages through which modern rationalism emerged and Western culture achieved a rationalized development path of "world-
historical significance." His theory was based on a comparative sociology of religions. Weber's position was that early human societies subscribed to a magical worldview in which there were powers (souls,
demons, deities) behind natural events that had intrinsic meaning as
wholes (the world as an enchanted garden). People contacted the gods
through magic, ritual, and taboos. Magic rather than conduct determined an individual's fate. The break with enchantment began with the

belief that the gods had established rules for human action, expected compliance, and watched over the observance of these rules. Thus worship, sin, conscience, gradually replaced ritual and salvation taboos. More generally, society was marked by the beginning of a dualism between humans and God, between this world and a (magical) other world, or the growth of a (quasi)rationalist metaphysic and religious ethic (i.e., people could choose whether to follow God's rules). Weber focused particularly on the developmental logic within the Judeo-Christian tradition, especially the path leading from medieval Catholicism, through Lutheranism, to Calvinism. Only with Calvinism (the religious doctrine developed by John Calvin in the sixteenth century that formed the basis of Puritan belief) was the process of disenchantment completed, in terms of transcending magical means of achieving heavenly salvation.

Two central doctrines of Calvinism, Weber thought, affected the ethical position of the faithful. First, Calvinism was distinguished from other variants of Christianity by its emphasis on the transcendence of God. While the world originally owed its existence to God, it was as though subsequently God flung the world away, no longer manifesting an interest in its development. Second, individuals had their eventual fates (salvation or damnation in the afterlife) predetermined from all eternity though not revealed to them until the instance of death. Not even practicing strict adherence to the Commandments allowed the faithful to ascertain, let alone affect, the fate God had already assigned them. For Weber, these two religious principles, transcendence and predestination, had a momentous impact on the believer's existential posture, shaping the ethical principles orienting everyday conduct. Rather than being characterized by passive resignation to fate, Weber argued, Calvinist conduct was shaped by a pressing anxiety to gain assurance that God's unknowable decree favored the individual, that the person was among the Elect, the Saints destined for heaven. Weber called this shaping orientation "inner-worldly asceticism," with the "inner-worldly" part meaning practice in the public world of mundane reality and "asceticism" meaning strenuous, protracted effort as a dutiful instrument of God's will, rather than praying or counting beads.

Calvinism shared with Lutheranism a view of each individual's "calling" (occupation) as a center of moral concern. Yet while Lutherans kept in touch with God to reassure their souls, Calvinists found the notion of intimacy with God blasphemous and reduced the significance of religious cult and ritual to a minimum in daily life. In Calvinism, Weber argued, the world was treated as a reality separate from God, deprived thereby of mystery, deprived of symbolic significance, deprived of magical evidences of God's wisdom and lines of access to God's will. Instead, those acting as members of the Elect (i.e., those who thought they would attain eternal grace) treated the world as a set of resistant objects testing their mastering and ordering capacities. The doctrine of predestination induced an acute sense of separation from others because of an intense anxiety about the individual's spiritual standing. The individual was motivated by intellect rather than habit or feeling, with a long-term, planned direction, and continuous rather than intermittent activity, with responsibility for outcomes taken by the person rather than blamed on fate. Underneath was a simple intuition: the individual proved to be a member of the Elect by acting in a God-like way in the sense of relating to the world (including the individual him- or herself) as God does, that is, through mastery, distance, and long-term perspective. In brief:

> The religious evaluation of relentless, steady, systematic work in one's worldly calling is the highest medium of asceticism, and as offering at the same time the safest and most visible proof of . . . a man's faith, must have constituted the most powerful instrument for the affirmation of the conception of life which I have named the "spirit" of capitalism. (Weber 1958: 172)

Calvinists considered themselves ethically bound to sustain profitability over a series of operations through relentless, steady, and systematic activity in business. They strove for maximal returns on assets while abstaining from immediate enjoyment of the fruits of business activity. Hence capital accumulated through continuous investment and repression of all-too-human feelings of solidarity toward others. In Poggi's words, "the entrepreneur is ethically authorised, indeed commanded, to act individualistically" (1983: 73). Or as Weber (1978: 164) said: "The Puritan conception of life . . . favored the tendency towards a bourgeois, economically rational, way of life. . . . It stood by the cradle of modern 'economic man.'" Furthermore, through a study of religious cultures other than Calvinism, Weber concluded that only in the West does science reach the stage of "authenticity" in the forms of mathematics and the exact natural sciences, with their precise rational foundations. Science and technology intersected with the profit motive to produce economic development that followed a path of rationalization unique to the West (Weber 1978: 338–389). Hence, for Weber, the modern rationalism of world mastery was the product of an ethical, religious, and institutional development characterized by "disenchantment" (Weber 1958; Roth and Schluchter 1979; Schluchter 1981).

Structural Functionalism

Weberian notions of rationalism were integrated with the earlier sociological naturalism in structural functionalism, the dominant paradigm of
post-World War II conventional sociology. Structural functionalism drew
on naturalistic conceptions of society derived from the classical sociological writings of Comte and Spencer, but also the works of Emil
Durkheim (1858–1917) the French sociologist. Like Spencer, Durkheim
argued that societal needs were met by social structures that were
institutionalizations of natural functions. Yet Durkheim also emphasized
morality, collective conscience, and culture. For him, the burning question became, How to integrate biologically based functions with social
morality? Or more generally, How to bring together nature, culture,
society, and rationality?

In structural functionalism each component of a system contributed
positively to the continued operation of the whole. In the more biologically orientated versions of this approach, the functional prerequisites
for the survival of societies created urgent necessities to which culture,
economy, morality, and even rationality necessarily responded. In some
versions social stratification into positions carrying differing degrees of
prestige, occupied by classes and castes, was also functionally necessary
to the survival of the social system. Structural functionalism emphasized
the adequacy of methods of dealing with the environment; the differentiation of roles and ways of assigning people to them; communication systems, shared symbolic systems, and shared values; and mutual cognitive
orientations that enabled people to predict what others were thinking in
stable social situations in which people shared an articulated set of goals.
As this perspective developed, we get the further view that societies had
to regulate the means of achieving goals through normative ("ought")
systems and by placing limits on affective (emotional) expression and
disruptive forms of behavior. Hence, structural functional sociology
emphasized the necessity for societies to rigorously socialize their populations, even to the point of promoting common symbols, values, and
emotions, in the urgent context of (naturally based) survival.

This naturalistic, functionalist, and structuralist stream in sociological thought was integrated with the Weberian theme of rationalization
by the Harvard sociologist Talcott Parsons (1902–1979) who published
between the late 1920s and the 1970s. Parsons's early work (summarized in *The Structure of Social Action* [1948]) synthesized the writings
of a number of his predecessors: Weber, Durkheim, and Sombart, in sociology; Marshall and Pareto, in economics; Kant and Marx, in philosophy. Together with the sociologist Neil Smelser, Parsons argued that the

economy was but one subsystem of a society and that the study of economics was a special case of the general theory of the social system (Parsons and Smelser 1956). In the next phase of his work, centered on the social system, Parsons (1971a) integrated ideas derived from Freudian psychoanalytic theory (especially internalization of social and cultural norms), psychological notions of purposeful behavior and the choice of alternative possible objects in a cognitively mapped environment, and ideas from structural and functionalist anthropology, including the theories of Bronislaw Malinowski (1884–1942) and A. R. Radcliffe-Brown (1881–1955). Parsons later responded to criticisms that structural functionalism could not deal with social change, nor respond to real problems, by resorting even more to biological theory and cybernetics in a neoevolutionary, functional theory of society.

Parsons argued that sociology was the study of meaningful social action. Action was interpreted as voluntary and subjective, yet patterned into a structure, or social order. Social patterning occurred through the normative orientations of actors, their norms, beliefs, values, and the like. This was intended as a critique of nineteenth-century positivist approaches to social science (e.g., neoclassical economics), which Parsons found incapable of accounting for human consciousness, interpretation, and reflection. From Durkheim came the idea of a collective conscience, or system of common values, that secured social order and solidarity. From Weber come notions of types of rational action together with an emphasis on ideas and values as driving forces in social change. For Parsons, the social actor was a selective, perceiving, evaluating agent, or a personality system, acting in a social system characterized by institutionalization—that is, stable patterns of social interaction were controlled by norms mirroring cultural patterns in areas like religion and beliefs. The "unit act" was composed of the actor; an end, or objective; a situation, including conditions and means; and a mode of relationship between the elements such that normative orientation drove social action. Acts were processes occurring in time (rather than in space, which Parsons found to be a condition irrelevant to the theory of action) that had a probabilistic character within an action frame of reference. Humans were goal-seeking beings, active in creating their own lives. Actors made choices between variable properties of the action system, which Parsons termed "pattern variables." Action guided by values was necessarily a matter of choice, with each choice conceptualized as a dilemma between two polar opposites. Parsons believed it was possible to categorize the pattern variables in terms of the following polarities: (1) a social actor might judge a physical or social object according to criteria applicable to a range of objects (universalism) or by criteria peculiar to the object (particularism); (2) an actor could judge an object by what it did (performance) or in itself (quality)—this he also described as the difference between achievement and ascription when referring to people; (3) an actor could set feelings aside in making judgments (affective neutrality) or could directly express feelings in relation to objects (affectivity); (4) actors might be in contact with each other in specific ways (specificity) or be related through multiple ties (diffuseness); and (5) actors could aim at achieving their own interest (self-orientation) or the aims of the community (collectivity orientation). These variables connected norms in the social system with individual decisions in the personality system. Here we find sophisticated synthetic notions of socialization, such as Freud's theory of the introjection of normative standards into developing personalities, combined with Durkheim's powerful ideas of the influence of the social context, and equally intricate versions of the idea of social control in which the actor is an autonomous agent, yet reacts to contexts of social constraint.

For Parsons, the study of societies was guided by an evolutionary perspective, with humans conceived as integral parts of the organic world, and human culture open to analysis in the general framework of the life process. Parsons saw human action systems responding to four social–functional imperatives (Table 3.1): *adaptation* (A), a society's generalized adaptation to the conditions of the external environment—that is, deriving resources and distributing these through the system; *goal attainment* (G), establishing goals and mobilizing the required effort; *integration* (I), maintaining coherence or solidarity, coordinating subsystems, and preventing disruption; and *latency* (L), or pattern maintenance, storing motivational energy and distributing it through the system, this involving pattern and tension maintenance. These four imperatives made up the functional basis of the social structure (*AGIL*). Basically, Parsons correlated the AGIL with the functional requirements of all social and natural systems. In human action systems, *cultural systems* provided individuals with the norms and values that motivated them. *Social systems* integrated the acting units (human personalities engaged in roles). *Personality systems* defined system goals and mobilized resources around goal attainment. *Behavioral systems* adapted functions to transforming the external world. The lower levels (nonsymbolic) provided energy for the higher (symbolic) levels, which, in turn, controlled the lower levels. This produced a cybernetic hierarchy in which social subsystems high in information, but low in energy (culture), regulated other systems higher in energy but lower in information (biological organism).

Moreover, Parsons thought that basic concepts of organic evolution, like variation, selection, adaptation, differentiation, and integration, could be adjusted to Weberian social action theory and used as central

TABLE 3.1. The Societal Community and Its Environments

Functions in general action systems	Extrasocial environments of societal community	Intrasocial environments of societal community	Environments of action	Cybernetic relations
			"Ultimate reality"	High information (controls)
(L) Latency: Pattern maintenance	Culture system	Maintenance of institutionalized cultural patterns		
(I) Integration	Social system	Societal community		
(G) Goal attainment	Personality system	Polity		
(A) Adaptation	Behavioral system	Economy	Physical–organic environment	High energy (conditions)

Hierarchy of controlling factors

Hierarchy of conditioning factors

Source: Parsons (1966, pp. 28–29).

components of a synthetic analysis. Thus social development, like organic evolution, would proceed by variation and differentiation from simple social forms, like gatherer-hunter bands, to progressively more complex forms, like industrial societies. Advances in the biological sciences, Parsons thought, had generated new conceptions of the fundamental continuity between organic and sociocultural evolution. Evolutionary theory enabled the construction of a more sophisticated social developmental scheme than had been possible in Spencer's time, one with considerable variability and branching among developmental lines (Parsons 1966; Hamilton 1983).

For our purposes, we need to focus more on Parsons's notions of development or, rather, the evolution of social systems. The most important change process in neoevolutionary perspectives like Parsons's was the enhancement of a society's adaptive capacity, either internally (originating a new type of structure) or externally through cultural diffusion (importation of new factors). Adaptive upgrading basically involved differentiation, as subsystems specialized and divided. That is, each subsystem became better able to perform its primary function, while societies became better able to cope with their problems. But problems of integration or coordination arose among the proliferating subsystems derived from differentiation. Thus, for Parsons, the other vital component of the change process was the value system, the cultural pattern that, when institutionalized, established and reinforced the continuing desirability of a given social order. Adaptation, differentiation, integration—these were the themes of evolutionary development.

The state of any society or system of ordered societies was the complex result of progressive cycles involving these (and other) processes of change, while at any stage there was a fan-like spectrum of societal types. Some variants favored additional evolution more than others; some variants were so beset with internal conflicts that they could hardly maintain themselves, and might deteriorate. Somewhere in the variegated system of societies, a developmental breakthrough occurred, a disturbance that endowed a society with a new level of adaptive capacity, increasing the resources available to the system, changing its competitive relations with other societies, and in other ways giving it advantages. Parsons saw the enhancement of adaptive capacity as an "advance" or, more generally, as "social evolution." Societies could destroy this innovation, adopt this innovation (the drive to modernization among underdeveloped societies is a case in point), confine it to an insulated niche, or lose their social identity through disintegration or absorption by a larger societal system (Parsons 1966: 24). History took the form of an increasing differentiation between systems of action (e.g., between the social and cultural systems) and progressive control over nonhuman factors by purely human (cultural) factors in an evolutionary series of stages in which societies moved from primitive to modern (Parsons 1960, 1961, 1971a; Parsons and Shils 1951; Parsons and Smelser 1956; Roches 1975; Savage 1981; Ritzer 1992).

Sociological Modernization Theory

According to S. N. Eisenstadt (1973: 12–15), a leading sociological exponent, modernization theory elaborated differences between societies in terms of their positions on various indices of modernity or development that measured their similarity to the model of modern industrial society. Modernization theory asked What is impeding advance (toward this industrial model) and What are the conditions and mechanisms of social transition from traditional to modern? As in Parsons's theory, traditional societies were viewed as limited by the environments they could master. Similar to Parsons too, modern societies were regarded as expansive, able to cope with a wider range of environments and problems. The more the characteristics of structural specialization could be found in a society, the higher its position on an index of modernization. And the more thorough the disintegration of traditional elements, the more a society could absorb change and develop the qualitative characteristics of modern societies such as rationality, efficiency, and a predilection for liberty. Hence, the main structural characteristics of modernization were identified by Eisenstadt as

> the development of a high extent of differentiation: the development of free resources which are not committed to any fixed, ascriptive groups; the development of wide non-traditional, "national," or even supernational group identifications; and the concomitant development, in all major institutional spheres, of specialized roles and of special wider regulative or allocative mechanisms and organization, such as market mechanisms in economic life, voting and party activities in politics, and diverse bureaucratic organizations and mechanisms in most institutional spheres. (1973: 23)

More specifically, in the economic sphere, modernization meant specialization of economic activities and occupational roles, and the growth of markets; in terms of sociospatial organization, modernization meant urbanization, mobility, flexibility, and the spread of education; in terms of the political sphere, modernization meant the spread of democracy and the weakening of traditional elites; in terms of the cultural sphere, modernization meant growing differentiation between the various cultural and value systems (e.g., a separation between religion and philosophy), secularization, and the emergence of new intelligentsia. These developments were closely related to the expansion of modern communications media and the consumption of culture created by centrally placed elites, manifested as changes in attitudes, especially the emergence of an outlook that stressed individual self-advancement. In general, modern societies were able to absorb change and assure their own continuous growth.

In the 1960s, the Committee on Comparative Politics of the United States Social Science Research Council produced an influential series of studies using a modernization approach within an overall structural functional framework. Development, these studies concluded, was an evolutionary process in which the human capacity increased in terms of initiating new structures, coping with problems, adapting to continuous change, and striving purposefully and creatively to attain new goals. The "development syndrome," they found, increased equality, capacity, and differentiation, which produced strains and tensions that might abort or arrest change in traditional societies (Coleman 1971).

Economic Modernization Theory

Parsons's theory of social action was also used to reformulate theories of growth, stemming from the works of Keynes, Harrod, Lewis, and others, that stressed purely economic variables. Emphasis was placed on broad social and cultural differences between modern and traditional societies, with these differences becoming the bases of development policies. The economist Bert Hoselitz, a faculty member at the University of Chicago, and for years editor of the influential journal *Economic Development and Cultural Change*, played a leading role in criticizing economics and proposing a sociological alternative. Hoselitz was unusual for an economist in that he questioned the economics of growth and was more interested in the impact of growth on living standards. Hoselitz emphasized cultural change as a precondition for economic development.

Hoselitz (1960) used Parsons's "pattern variables" to look at differences in behavior between peoples in modern and traditional societies. He argued that in traditional societies (i.e., undeveloped economies) particularism prevailed in the distribution of economic roles, whereas in more complex societies (i.e., developed economies) universalism underlay a more efficient allocation of labor and resources. Traditional societies, he said, usually exhibited a lack of reliance on individual achievement, emphasizing ascription (e.g., kinship relations) as the basis for distributing economic goods. In traditional societies the performance of

economic tasks was typically diffuse, whereas in advanced societies economic tasks were characterized by specificity of roles. And finally, in
undeveloped societies the elite was self-oriented, whereas in the
advanced countries elites exhibited collectivity-oriented attitudes. These
positions are summarized in Table 3.2.

Hoselitz then applied these differences to an analysis of the development process under the assumption, drawn from Adam Smith, that
increasing productivity was associated with more detailed social divisions of labor:

> A society on a low level of economic development is, therefore, one in
> which productivity is low because division of labor is little developed,
> in which the objectives of economic activity are more commonly the
> maintenance or strengthening of status relations, in which social and
> geographical mobility is low, and in which the hard cake of custom
> determines the manner, and often the effects, of economic performance.
> An economically highly developed society, in contrast, is characterized
> by a complex division of social labor, a relatively open social structure
> in which caste barriers are absent and class barriers are surmountable,

TABLE 3.2. Hoselitz's Ideal-Type Societies Using Parsons's Pattern Variables

	Hoselitz's ideal-type societies	
Parsons's pattern variables (dilemmas)	Underdeveloped or "backward" societies	Developed or "modern" societies
I Choice between types of value orientation: universalism versus particularism	Particularistic norms	Universalistic norms
II Choice between modalities of the social object: performance versus quality	Quality (ascription)	Performance (achievement)
III Gratification–discipline dilemma: affectivity versus affective neutrality	Not relevant	Not relevant
IV Definition of scope of interest in the object: specificity versus diffuseness	Functional diffuseness	Functional specificity
V Private versus collective interest: self-orientation versus collectivity orientation	Self-orientation	Collectivity orientation

Sources: Parsons (1971a); Hoselitz (1960, pp. 41–42).

in which social roles and gains from economic activity are distributed essentially on the basis of achievement, and in which, therefore, innovation, the search for and exploitation of profitable market situations, and the ruthless pursuit of self-interest without regard to the welfare of others is fully sanctioned. (Hoselitz 1960: 60)

As a consequence, a sociological theory of economic growth had to determine the mechanisms by which the social structure of an underdeveloped economy was modernized—that is, altered to take on the features of an economically advanced country. Hoselitz's answer was based in the "theory of social deviance": the capitalist entrepreneur of late medieval and early modern Europe was the prototype of a socially or culturally marginal individual who originated important new forms of economic activity. By extension, entrepreneurs or bureaucrats imbued with modern ideas could do the same for underdeveloped countries today. In terms of the geographical place of deviant behavior, Hoselitz argued that the city was the focal point for the introduction of innovative ideas and new social and economic practices. In underdeveloped countries, cities modeled after the urban centers of the West exhibited a spirit of difference from the traditionalism of the countryside. In terms of policy, therefore, Hoselitz favored a shift in political power to promote the economic leadership of the urban modernizers in undeveloped countries (see also Barnett 1989).

Psychocultural Theories of Modernization

Another group of modernization theorists turned their attention more specifically to the psychological, cultural, and behavioral dimensions of modernization. Everett Hagen (1962) linked differences in human personality to technological progress and more generally to social change in an attempt at reformulating purely economic theories of growth. People's images of the world in traditional societies, he said, included the perception that uncontrollable forces restricted and dominated their lives. Fearing the world and its problems, traditional people were uncreative and authoritarian. But the authoritarian personality could change if groups of people experienced a reduction in respect, for example, through domestic or external conquest, or through migration, and then searched for a satisfactory new identity through withdrawal and social deviancy. As retreat deepened through successive generations, the circumstances of home life and social environment eventually became conducive to the development of an innovative personality, for example, through a high need to achieve. Under certain cultural circumstances, creative individuals saw technological prowess as a path to the satisfaction of their needs. The values of a new generation might turn in the direction of innovations in production, institutional reform, and economic growth. The deviant group then led the society toward modernization.

A similar, if more extreme, position was taken by the American psychologist David McClelland (1961). Part of the push for economic development, he thought, came from a psychological characteristic, which he called "n-Achievement," or the need for achievement, which suited particular individuals for entrepreneurial roles. Societies with high levels of need for achievement produced energetic entrepreneurs who, in turn, led rapid economic development. The amount of n-Achievement could be enhanced through "achievement motivation training," which McClelland recommended as a low-cost way of stimulating economic development in "low achievement countries" (McClelland and Winter 1971).

The sociologist Daniel Lerner (1958) contrasted traditional and modern society in terms of village versus town, illiteracy versus enlightenment, resignation versus ambition, and piety versus excitement. Modern societies, he thought, encouraged mobility, rationality, and empathy. Similarly Alex Inkeles and David H. Smith (1974) argued that enlightened, modern "man" was characterized by traits like rationality, abstractness of knowledge, scientific thinking, and urbanity. In a case study of East Pakistan they compared "Ahmadullah," the traditional man, with "Nuril" a modern urbanite, using a dichotomy of characteristics (Table 3.3). In brief, economic development originated in the modern personality, the person with a high need to achieve that is satisfied through innovative behavior.

Historical Stages of Modernization

Ideas concerning stages of growth have a long history in various Enlightenment theories of human progress, in Marx's modes of production, and in the German school of historical economics; in this latter case examples include the theories of Friedrich List, Bruno Hildebrand, Karl Bucher, Gustav Schmoiler, and Werner Sombart. The most recent successor to this theoretical tradition is W. W. Rostow, who in his *Stages of Economic Growth* (1960) proposed an alternative to Marx's theory of history. A historian at the University of Texas, Rostow argued that, in their economic dimensions, all societies lay within one of five historical categories:

TABLE 3.3. Traditional and Modern Man

Traditional	Modern
Not receptive to new ideas	Open to new experience
Rooted in tradition	Change orientation
Only interested in immediate things	Interested in outside world
Denies different opinions	Acknowledges different opinions
Uninterested in new information	Eager to seek out new information
Oriented toward the past	Punctual; oriented toward the present
Concerned with the short term	Values planning
Distrustful of people beyond the family	Calculability; trusts people to meet obligations
Suspicious of technology	Values technical skills
Places high value on religion and the sacred	Places high value on education and science
Traditional patron–client relationships	Respects the dignity of others
Particularistic	Universalistic
Fatalistic	Optimistic

Sources: Inkeles and Smith (1974, pp. 19–34); Scott (1995, p. 29).

1. *Traditional societies* had limited "production functions" (i.e., combinations of factors of production) based in pre-Newtonian science, primitive technologies, and spiritual attitudes toward the physical world. These placed a ceiling on productivity and limited economies to the agricultural level. A hierarchical social structure, in which political power was held by landowners, provided little scope for social mobility. The value system was derived from long-run fatalism. Rostow admitted that placing infinitely various, changing societies in a single category said little about them, but he justified such historical conflation as necessary for clearing the way to get at his main subject, the posttraditional societies where each of the major characteristics of the traditional society was altered to permit regular growth (Rostow 1960: 6).

2. The second universal stage was the development of a set of *preconditions for takeoff*. These cohered in Western Europe in the late seventeenth and early eighteenth centuries as the insights of modern science were translated into new production functions in agriculture and industry in a setting given dynamism by international expansion. Favored by geography, trading possibilities, and political structure, Britain was first to develop these preconditions. Elsewhere they arose not endogenously, but exogenously from intrusions originating in more advanced societies. These external influences shook traditional society and either began, or

hastened, its undoing. Essentially this undoing involved the spread of the idea of progress, not just as a possibility but also as a necessary condition for some other purpose judged to be good—for example, national dignity or private profit. Education expanded, new people came forward, banks appeared, investment increased, the scope of commerce broadened, manufacturing plants sprang up—all, however, within societies still characterized predominantly by traditional methods, structures, and values.

3. *Takeoff* was the "great watershed in the life of modern societies," when blockages and resistance to steady growth were finally overcome. In Britain and the "well-endowed parts of the world populated substantially from Britain" the proximate stimulus for takeoff was mainly technological, but elsewhere a political context favorable to modernization was also necessary. During takeoff the rate of effective investment rose from 5% of national income to 10% or more, new industries expanded, profits were ploughed back, urban industrial employment increased, and the class of entrepreneurs expanded. New techniques spread to agriculture and, in just a decade or two, the social and political structures of society were transformed so that steady economic growth could be sustained. A question immediately arose: If the breakup of traditional societies came exogenously, from demonstration effects from other societies, how could the first takeoff in Britain be accounted for? Rostow's answer (1960: 31) was that a combination of necessary and sufficient conditions for takeoff in Britain was "the result of the convergence of a number of quite independent circumstances, a kind of statistical accident of history which, once having occurred, was irreversible, like the loss of innocence." The more exact answer to the question unfolded as a synthesis of two features of postmedieval Europe: external (geographic) discoveries and the internal development of modern science. Rostow also found crucially significant Britain's toleration of religious nonconformists (i.e., Hoselitz's "social deviants"), the country's relatively open social structure, and the early achievement of a national consciousness in response to threats from abroad—this last, he said, placed the first instance back into the general case of societies modernizing in response to intrusions from abroad.

4. Following takeoff, a society *drives toward maturity* over a long interval of time as modern technology spreads over the whole front of its economic activity, 10–20% of the national income is invested, and growth outstrips any increase in population. Some 60 years after takeoff a society attains maturity, that is, a state in which there is sufficient entrepreneurial and technical skills to produce anything it chooses— machine tools, chemicals and, electrical equipment industries were examples.

5. This led eventually to the final stage of *high mass consumption*, where the leading industrial sectors become durable consumer goods and services. Real income rises to a level permitting a large number of people to consume at levels far in excess of their needs, and the structure of the work force changes toward the urban skilled and office types of employment. Western societies at this level might choose to allocate increased resources to social welfare and social security. Stage 5 was reached by the United States in the 1920s and, more fully, in the immediate postwar decade; Western Europe and Japan entered this stage in the 1950s; the Soviet Union had the technical capacity to enter Stage 5 should its communist leaders allow (Rostow 1960: 12).

Such were the universal stages of growth lying between traditional and modern, undevelopment and development. Rostow's stage theory occupied a leading position in conventional development thinking in the 1960s, when liberal attitudes toward the Third World were being established: for example, these ideas formed the basis of the historical understanding in much of development economics (Meier 1984), while versions of Rostow can be found in the foreign policy sections of speeches by John F. Kennedy (his Inaugural Address, for instance; see Chapter 6). The policy implications of this stage theory were clear: traditional societies wishing to develop need only copy the already-proven example of the West, while generous Western governments should send armies of modernizers, like Peace Corps volunteers or retired corporate executives, to the benighted people of the Third World awaiting the rational spark of business-oriented thinking. In economic and geographical terms, given the initial development of modernity in the restricted space of Euro-America (and Japan), "backward" countries should encourage the diffusion of innovation from the advanced center, should adopt markets as the mode of economic integration, and should welcome U.S. aid, investment, corporations, and direction.

Modernization Geography

As this term implies, the historical schema could be spatialized by placing the highest stages of growth in one core area (Europe and the United States) and seeing the rest of the world as a series of peripheral zones, each representing a stage of the past, persisting into the present, and awaiting change through the diffusion, or spread, of innovative changes. Many of these economic and sociological theories implicitly recognized the uneven development of modernization processes in space. But the spatial implications of modernization theory were more explicitly drawn out by geographers. The Swedish geographer Torsten Hagerstrand (1952), a professor at Lund University in Sweden, pioneered work on the diffusion of innovations, seeing these as waves of change moving across space that gradually lose power due to the friction of distance. Thus areas close to an origin of innovation received change early, while those more distant got it later. Peter Gould (1964), a geographer at Pennsylvania State University, argued that innovations diffused over space in patterns because people were persuaded to adopt new things through communication with each other, and communicative possibilities were constrained by distance.

These geographical versions of diffusion theory were then synthesized with ideas from the main body of modernization theory to yield a "geography of modernization." In this view, Third World countries were isolated, parochial, technically primitive subsistence economies in which disease, hunger, and malnutrition were daily problems. Change showed as islands of progress in a sea of stagnation, while transformation was viewed as a progressive spatial process of the diffusion of innovations:

> Unlike former days . . . people . . . act today in response to the new foci of change, the towns and the cities. Modern transport systems extend the length and breadth of the country [Sierra Leone], bringing new ideas, new methods, new people even to the most remote corners. . . . These changes which affect all spheres of life—political, social, economic, and psychological—constitute the modernization process. (Riddell 1970: 43–44)

Modernization was seen as a spatial diffusion process, originating at contact situations, such as port cities or colonial administration centers, with patterns of change moving across the map, cascading down urban hierarchies, and funneling along transport systems. This process could be measured by the spread of modern institutions, like schools or medical facilities, and mapped as a *modernization surface*. In keeping with the strongly quantitative temper of the social sciences in the 1960s and early 1970s, the research objective was to devise statistical indices to measure real variations in modernization, such as (1) the development of transport networks; (2) the expansion of communication and information media; (3) the growth of integrated urban systems; (4) the breakdown of traditional ethnic compartmentalization; (5) the emergence of a money economy; (6) the development of education; (7) participation in nonparochial forms of organization and activity; (8) proximity to, and interaction with, urban cores that act as concentrators, adapters, and distributors of modernization; and (9) physical or geographic mobility. Modernization, however, "is not simply an increase in a set of indices. It involves profound changes in individual and group behavior" (Soja 1968: 4). In many ways this simple statement summarized the whole modernization approach.

Critique

This set of theories, moving from naturalism through rationalism to structural functionalism and modernization, is symptomatic of the entire modern cultural paradigm. Modernization theories express, but also reinforce, an entire system of European attitudes toward the world. Naturalism in its strong geographical form of environmental determinism says that Europe was dominant because the environment endowed Europeans with superior natural characteristics, especially greater natural intelligence. Naturalism in its weaker sociological versions, such as Spencer's fertility–density theory, stresses the superior social systems developed in rich natural environments. With Parsons, we find naturalistic theory updated by appeal to Darwin, with the social mediations between nature and culture articulated through appeal to the finest intellects of the nineteenth and early twentieth centuries—Weber, Durkheim and Freud, Malinowski and Radcliffe Brown, Marshall and Pareto—together with the integration of post-World War II developments in systems theory and cybernetics. In the structural functionalist version of modernization theory the rise of Europe is endowed with natural inevitability so that, with Rostow's stages, global history is reduced to a series of copies made from distilling the experience of the West. And with modernization theory Europe shows the world its common future. These are more than academic theories; they are cultural attitudes displaying the West's idea of itself and its relation to the "rest of the world."

The sociological theory of modernization, especially the idea that progress means replicating the rationalizing processes of the West, underlies most conventional development theories, including contemporary neoliberal economic policy. This notion of societies structured by similar, functionally based processes is a political as well as a theoretical statement. Structural functionalism, together with its offshoot modernization theory, came into prominence in the post-World War II period, in the era of cold war competition between the West and the East, of McCarthyism in the United States, and the political disciplining of social science. "Development" came from a society assuming its allotted place within a global order already determined by the heroic rise of the West. Development meant assuming the mental models of the West (rationalization), the institutions of the West (the market), the goals of the West (high mass consumption), and the culture of the West (worship of the commodity). For most critics, the basic problem with Weberian sociology, and its structural functionalist offshoots, is that it inverts the historical process. Weber himself was interested in a comparative sociology of world religions as the basis of a series of different developmental trajectories. Yet Weberian sociology, as it emerged in the postwar period, emphasized purely internal processes in explaining Western supremacy. Global processes of imperialism, colonialism, exploitation, and domination were either relegated to secondary status or reinterpreted as necessary elements in the diffusion of progress.

Beginning in the late 1950s, but gaining momentum in the mid-1960s, modernization theory was subjected to intense political and intellectual criticism—indeed, criticism was ferocious when coming from dependency theorists (e.g., Frank 1969a) or political leftists (e.g., Szentes 1976). Attacks were launched on all aspects of the theory, from its original base in structural functionalism, to the politics of its policy prescriptions. Beginning with the base in structural functionalism, the sociologist Alvin Gouldner (1970: 168) said that Parsons "more than any other contemporary social theorist has influenced . . . academic sociologists . . . throughout the world." Gouldner argued that functional theories, like those of Parsons, were devoted to maintaining the existing social order. While stressing the importance of the goals humans pursued, or the values they followed, Parsons never asked whose goals and values these were. He stressed value transmission, rather than value creation. Gouldner found theoretical emphasis placed on the individual's plastic potential for conforming with the requirements of his or her social position—that is, people were seen as hollow containers dependent on training in social systems for their characters. For Gouldner (1970: 218–219), the reason for stressing value transmission and social malleability was to eliminate conflicts between the individual and the group. This neglected resistance, power imbalances and exploitation (Gouldner 1970: 240). With this went a focus on equilibrium, that is, stable systems of interaction which, once established, tended to remain unchanged over long periods of time. When it did come, change was cyclical or rhythmical, rather than transformative. Differentiation was a way for systems to change in an "orderly" manner, that is, in a manner not threatening to existing power centers. All of this contributed to a crisis in functional theory, and in academic sociology more generally (Gouldner 1970: 351–361). For our purposes, we stress that Gouldner finds structural functionalism unsuited to a theory of social dynamics because of its bias toward equilibrium, unidirectional and nonthreatening types of evolutionary change. We might also note that many of these criticisms of structural functionalism apply with equal force to neoclassical economics.

Anthony Giddens (1977), long a sociologist at Cambridge University, but later director of the London School of Economics, traced modern functionalism (via Comte, Spencer, and Durkheim) to advances in biology in the nineteenth century. Functionalism borrowed biological principles (by analogy) to explicate the anatomy and psychology of social life. Its intellectual appeal derived from a desire to demonstrate the logical unity between the natural and social sciences. Giddens found functionalism to be teleological, allowing for only a limited and deficient explication of purposive human action because the end of history was already implicit in the historical process. Homeostatic processes (in which change in one element causes change in another which then causes readjustment in the first) had to be seen as fulfilling some systemic need. In functionalist social theory this turned out to be a social system's "needs." Yet Giddens thought that social systems were unlike organisms in that they did not have "needs"; rather, social actors had wants (different from a society's "needs"). Giddens also found that structural functionalism mistakenly assimilated the notions of structure and system—structure was like anatomy, while system included how the anatomy functions. For Giddens, structures (patterns) only existed in social life to the degree that they were constantly produced and reproduced in human action. Furthermore, purposiveness in human affairs could not be grasped as a homeostatic process involving merely cybernetic control through feedbacks of information. Rather, human action involved not just self-regulation, but self-consciousness or reflexivity: "purpose" in relation to human affairs was related in an integral way to the possessing of reasons for action, or to the rationalization of action in processes of self-reflection. In this respect, purpose was quite different from whatever teleology was involved in self-regulating processes in nature (Giddens 1977: 116). For Giddens, structural functionalism saw change stimulated by exogenous rather than by internally generated factors (e.g., social struggles); evolution in the animal world operated blindly, whereas there was an attempt to consciously control human development; and the relation of human society to its material environment was ill-conceived as mere adaptation—as Marx said, humans actively transform nature (Giddens 1977: 118–121).

This led Giddens (1977: 118) to an alternative sociological notion which he termed "structuration": the modes whereby systems were produced and reproduced through social interaction. According to Giddens, rather than being natural, repeated social practices involved, reflexive forms of human knowledgeability, "reflexivity" being understood not merely as self-consciousness but as the mental monitoring of the flow of social life (i.e., watching and learning from actions). And rather than responding automatically to natural urgencies, intentionality characterized acts that agents believed would have particular outcomes. For

Giddens, actors made things happen, although they could behave in cognizance of what they took to be social needs. Action involved power in the sense of transformative capacity—in this sense "power is logically prior to subjectivity" (Giddens 1984: 15). The "duality of structure" in power relations referred to the drawing on, and reproduction of, resources as structured properties of social systems by knowledgeable agents (see also Cohen 1989; Spybey 1992).

Structural functionalist modernization theory has also been criticized for its concept of history or, more exactly, for its ahistoricism, with critical attention focused on Rostow's concept of the universality of the process of modernization (i.e., change does not change but is the same everywhere at all times), his notion of a single, fixed end-stage for development, and his ethnocentrism. The radical dependency theorist Andre Gunder Frank (1969a) was particularly effective in exposing the politics of Rostow's "theory of history" (dependency theory is covered in Chapter 4). First, Rostow described all "backward" societies in terms of a uniform traditionalism that equated Imperial China, Aboriginal Australia, Mayan Central America, and the tribal civilizations of southern Africa, with feudal Europe. This denied the specific precapitalist histories of Third World societies, reducing them to a common "backwardness," whereas in fact many were more developed than feudal Europe, the more to disguise the (underdeveloping) effects contact with European capitalism had on the world's civilizations. Second, the developmental history of Euro-America was generalized into a sequence of stages of economic growth that all societies had to follow. Frank asked how could history repeat itself when Europe's development had already altered the context in which historical events occurred? Specifically, the development of capitalism had already created a center of power and a dependent periphery, so that progress in the underdeveloped world must contend with a global structure inimical to progress. Third, high mass consumption of the North American type was propagated as the end point for all development, yet many would wish to live well without the social and environmental problems associated with overconsuming societies. Rostow subverted peoples' dreams of a better future and converted them to the worship of the almighty dollar. In brief, Frank (1969a: 40) found this entire approach to economic and cultural change attributing a history to the developed countries but denying histories to the underdeveloped countries. An economic policy for the underdeveloped societies had to be based on their specific historical experiences—for Frank, their active underdevelopment through contact with developed societies.

Weberian sociology and structural functionalism in general can also be criticized as Eurocentric. In his historical-empirical work Parsons (1971b), like most European and North American theorists, traced the origins of European modernization only as far as the "seedbed" societies of ancient Israel and Greece. Elements derived from these sources, after undergoing development and combination, comprised the main cultural components of modern society. In doing so Parsons failed to see that classical Greece was not the cradle of a distinctively Western civilization, but was itself derived from African and Asian sources. As the Marxist historian Martin Bernal (1987) argues, the "ancient model" of the Afro-Asian origins of Western civilization, which had admitted this extra-European influence, was downplayed in the nineteenth century in favor of an "Aryan model" that conformed better with the racialism and imperialism of the time. The earlier model cast an entirely different light on the more diverse African and Asian origins of modernization. We should note that Bernal's critique initiated intense debate on the origins of Western progress.

In a parallel argument, the geographer James Blaut (1976), of the University of Illinois, compared Eurocentric ideas about self-directed growth with Third World ethnoscientific models of the world as multi-centric. In a Third Worldist understanding, Blaut said, the multicentered pattern of relatively equal levels of development was disrupted not by the autonomous rise of rational Europe, but by the European plunder of the New World (European "discovery" being due solely to the fact that the Iberian centers of expansion were closest to America), the flood of bullion into Europe, and the resulting commercial, industrial, and scientific–technological development. "Thereafter the dialectic of development and underdevelopment intensified, and the world economy fixed itself in place" (Blaut 1976: 1). Blaut argued against the notion of the "European miracle": (1) Europe was not superior to other regions prior to 1492; (2) colonialism and the wealth plundered from Third World societies (rather than rationalization) were the basic processes leading to the rise of Europe; and (3) Europe's advantage lay solely in the "mundane realities of location," that is, its nearness to the Americas (Blaut 1994).

Structural functionalism and modernization were components of a modern, scientific project, which included most of classically based economics, to explain the world from an advanced European perspective. We need to stress the liberal nature of this project. Rather than naturally based racial characteristics directly determining human behavior, as with environmental determinism, structural functionalism conceived people as the products more immediately of socialization and enculturation and only indirectly as the products of nature. Structural functionalism, as outlined by Parsons, argued that societies had structures similar to those of all organisms, that there were imperatives that the functional order had to pursue, and that culture and socialization responded quite automatically to these needs: people were what their society needed them to be. In the structural functionalist conception, too, development was one more instance of the natural (eternal) process of differentiation—in this case, with the component parts of society, or of the various aspects of an economy, specializing and separating in complex divisions of labor. This formed the naturalistic basis of modernization, the notion that there was a single (universal) process of the evolution of civilization, with Euro-America occupying the eventual position toward which all societies tend. Development for the periphery was reduced to a process of spatial diffusion of innovation from the global center of civilization. The policy conclusion was that societies wishing to develop should open their borders and let change in; should become part of the existing global system; should welcome and indeed encourage multinational corporations, advanced technology, and export-oriented economic activities; should withdraw state aid and privatize their economies; and should allow the market to discipline their economies. In other words, modernization and neoliberal policies coincided. Modernization was a cold war attempt at legitimating U.S. domination of the global system. Neoliberalism was its continuation in an era of market triumphalism. The notion that there is a proven path to development that can be read from the experience of the West is embedded in modern culture to the point that mere academic critique is relatively powerless. Modernization can be countered only through alternatives that are more convincing and persuasive, alternatives written from the positions of excluded groups, or alternatives based in criticisms of the very concept of development. These alternatives form the themes of the following chapters.

Chapter 4

MARXIST AND NEO-MARXIST THEORIES OF DEVELOPMENT

arxism is far more than radical politics: it is a materialist philosophy of social existence and a dialectical theory of human development. Writing in the mid-nineteenth century, the founders of this school of thought, Karl Marx and Friedrich Engels, were enlightenment modernists who believed in social progress and the perfectability of humankind, in the transformative potential of science, and in the material plentitude made possible by technological advance in Western societies. Yet they thought differently than most modernists. They saw modern processes of production as emancipation but also as alienation from nature; as a process of human self-creation, but one directed by a few powerful people; and as progress in material life, but driven by a mainspring motivated by socially and environmentally irrational drives. Marxian analytics thus became not the scholastic pursuit of truth for its own sake, and certainly not legitimation theory for the rich and famous, but a guide to radical political practice aimed at changing society so that it met the needs of the working class. Marx and Engels came to liberate modernism, not to praise it.

Idealism and Materialism

We should first counterpose historical materialism, the philosophy of Marxism, with its opposite, Hegelian idealism. In idealism, reason is the source of material progress. This "reason" can be human reason, in the form of logical thought; transcendental Reason, in the form of Spirit; or some combination of the two. In the late Enlightenment, the German philosopher G. W. F. Hegel (1770–1831) connected the individual's rational consciousness with a collective and transcendent World Spirit, or Absolute Idea, a kind of Rationality inherent in the world (Hegel capitalized the first letter of transcendent terms and we will follow him in this usage). Rather than believing that people think and then act on their thoughts in a rational way, Hegel believed that movements of Spirit precede both human thought and material events, in some way causing both. In idealism, development of the World Spirit is the Transcendent Force behind all things (Hegel 1967 ed.).

In their youths, Marx (1818–1883) and Engels (1820–1895) adhered to a radical, material version of German (Hegelian) idealism. As their thinking matured, they developed an alternative, indeed contrary, conception of social existence. In opposition to idealism, they called this conception "historical materialism." As they put it at the time:

> In direct contrast to German philosophy which descends from heaven to earth, here we ascend from earth to heaven. That is to say, we do not set out from what men say, imagine, conceive, nor from men as narrated, thought of, imagined, conceived, in order to arrive at men in the flesh. We set out from real, active men, and on the basis of their real life-process we demonstrate the development of the ideological reflexes and echoes of this life-process. . . . Life is not determined by consciousness but consciousness by life. (Marx and Engels 1981 ed.: 47)

In materialism, human rationality is the mental result of the working of the brain, and the brain is conceived as originating purely through evolution as a natural organ. Human consciousness is the ability to understand in a self-reflexive way, that is, to know that we exist, to be able to think about existence, and to represent existence through symbols (words, ideas, paintings, etc.). Consciousness in a materialist understanding comes from real experience in a material world that precedes thought. Consciousness is the deposit of experience in the memory, interpreted and reinterpreted by the human brain. Thus, consciousness is a social product.

Dialectics

Marx and Engels turned spiritual belief back on its material base: for them, consciousness was the product of matter rather than its origin. Yet they retained from Hegel's idealism key dialectical ideas, for example, development through contradiction and the notion of individuals and societies transcending their former identities. In dialectical understanding, the natural and social worlds are not viewed as systems eternally the same, but are seen instead as developmental processes capable of rapid change. What brought change about, from a dialectical perspective? Dialectics was a theory of development that saw all things as complex wholes composed from parts. The "inner" relations that bound the parts of a thing together had to be complementary and cooperative so that an object had coherence—for example, the mind was in touch with the body (within the whole person), or communities had cooperative social relations (within the total social group). Yet inner relations were also contradictory, giving an object immanent potential for change—for example, body and mind could move in different directions (the body contradicts the mind's intent), or communities are riven with conflict (as when one class or gender exploits another). But there was also an "outer," external–relational dimension to dialectical thinking that has been especially appealing to geographers and others fascinated by earth space. In the spatial dialectic, objects also developed through "inter" relations with the external environment of other things, and these relations were likewise simultaneously both cooperative and competitive. Fundamental, transformative change occurred when contradictions built to the breaking point—for example, when two people could no longer stand the sight of each other, or when environments were destroyed by overproduction and too much consumption. Changes transmitted from external sources could not have transformative effects unless a given thing (held precariously together by contradictory internal relations) was already made highly unstable by inner conflict. The developmental process was thus a synthesis between inner and outer dialectics; the two aspects of change might alternate in significance; the types of their interaction were multiple and complex (cf. Ollman 1976).

Production as the Transformation of Nature

In historical materialism, therefore, the origins of human life were sought in the natural evolution of a distinctive kind of eventually conscious social animal. For Marx and Engels, the writing of history began with the natural bases of life, and the modification of nature (internal human nature and external natural environment) through human action. As with other animals, the assimilation of natural materials ("metabolism") was "the everlasting nature-imposed condition of human existence . . . common to all forms of society in which human beings live" (Marx 1976: 290; Timpanero 1975). However, humans distinguished themselves from other animals when they began to *produce* their means of subsistence, that is, when they consciously and exactly transformed natural resources into materials that satisfied their needs:

> Labor is, first of all, a process between man and nature, a process which man, through his own actions, mediates, regulates, and controls the metabolism between himself and nature. He confronts the materials of nature as a force of nature. He sets in motion natural forces which belong to his own body, his arms, legs, head, and hands, in order to appropriate the materials of nature in a form adapted to his own needs. Through this movement he acts upon external nature and changes it, and in this way he simultaneously changes his own nature. He develops the potentialities slumbering within nature, and subjects the play of its forces to his own sovereign power. (Marx 1976: 283)

For Marx, there was no such thing as eternal or essential human nature. Rather, the human character was actively created and re-created under definite natural and social conditions. "Human nature" emerged and changed during the struggle, along with and against others, to gain a livelihood from the rest of the natural world. Human nature derived from experience, particularly in production, in the labor process, but more generally in the reproductive process, in the making of a whole existence.

Originally, according to Marx, human labor was similar to the animal's hunting or gathering: it was the exertion of the forces of the body in necessary activities that made further life possible. For Marx (1976: 228), the transformative (developmental) moment differentiating social from natural history came when human beings put consciousness and deliberation into effect, most significantly in the making of "instruments of labor"—tools, implements, machines—that added greatly to the available means of the production of livelihood. Instruments allowed nature to be transformed in an intentional way; they also confirmed human effectiveness and reinforced intentionality. As a result, the forces available for development became labor, physical means like tools, and mental conceptions. By applying these productive forces, necessary labor time ("necessary" in terms of providing the essentials of life) could be shortened and more time devoted to conceptualization, technology, and the production of tools, the economic sources of development. Development of the human ability to transform nature enabled the possibility of higher material standards of living and thus the potential for a more liberated existence—liberated, that is, from the ravages of nature, or from eternal, back-breaking work.

How did the productive forces advance? Marx had a dialectical understanding of the relations tying productive elements together, in the sense that while these formed a unity, they were also ridden with conflicts. In particular, for Marx, the social relations that combined labor with means of production determined the quantity and quality of productive development. Social relations were therefore Marxism's most essential analytical category.

Production as Social Relations

The analytically distinguishing feature of Marxism resides in the emphasis placed on social relations. Clearly, social relations take many forms: relations between individuals within families, relations between people who are friends, relations within communities, and so on. Marx emphasized relations of reproduction broadly, and relations between people in the material production of their existence specifically—"material" in the direct sense of transforming natural materials into products that make life possible. In examining the social relations of production, it should be remembered that even relations fundamental to existence, functional relations in structural terms, were characterized in Marxism by a dialectical interplay between cooperation and competition, collaboration and struggle. In Marxism, the productive base of society was inherently conflictive and therefore subject to developmental change.

Human existence was secured by applying productive forces to the extraction and processing of resources from nature in the making of products that satisfied human needs and demands. For Marx, the most essential aspect of social relations was control over the productive forces and resources available to a society. Thus social relations were concerned with power in its fundamental guise as control over the possibility of continued existence. In Marxist theory, a second transformative historical moment took place when the means of production came to be controlled by a ruling elite. This created a fundamental social cleavage, a class relation, between the owners of the productive forces and the laborers who performed work. The aspect of this class relation crucial for economic development was the extension of the working day beyond necessary labor time: "Wherever a part of society possesses the monopoly of the means of production, the worker, free or unfree, must add to the labor necessary for his own maintenance an extra quantity of labor in order to produce the means of subsistence for the owner of the means of production" (Marx 1976: 344). Marx's term for the extraction of unrewarded surplus labor time was "exploitation." This concept formed the social relational basis of Marxian economics, lending this version of the classical labor theory of value an entirely different orientation with a revolutionary political conclusion. Now to help the reader to understand this revolutionary idea, we must present an outline of the main contents of Marx's economics.

Marx opened his main work, *Capital*, which first appeared in German in 1867, with an analysis of the commodity form of products, his intention being to uncover the social relations hidden in objects. The commodity, for Marx, had three valuable aspects—use value, exchange value, and value—which could be looked at both individually and in combinations. First, *use value* was the material aspect of the commodity, the qualities of the physical body of the object that satisfied human wants and needs, and therefore created demand for it. Rather than emphasizing demand in Benthamite terms of the maximization of individual pleasure, Marx's use value concept placed wants and demand in the context of needs, with needs being part of social reproduction; that is, people consumed primarily so they could work and raise families. More generally, *social reproduction* was that system of consumptive activities by which the productive resources of a society (labor, instruments, infrastructures) were reproduced from one time period to the next so that they could continue to function. In Marxism, use value thus referred to needs that are far more socialized than in classical, and especially neoclassical, economics.

Second, *exchange value* was the expression of use value in terms of a commodity chosen to represent value (i.e., money); exchange value was the basis of market price. Marx agreed that demand and supply led to market equilibrium and set prices in an immediate sense, but he found that this market equilibrium was tangential to the real inner laws of capitalist production. For one thing, the money commodity itself had an exchange value, a use value, and a value, and money served various functions—measure of value, medium of the circulation or exchange of commodities, store of value, and so on—that might conflict one with another. Indeed, by analyzing these functions, Marx was able to show how money as means of payment became capital as social relation and process. The commodity form of circulation entailed one use value exchanging for another with money as intermediary—that is, C–M–C, or Commodity (e.g., wheat)–Money (e.g., gold)–Commodity (e.g., coat)—with the result that farmers satisfied their needs for clothing. But there was also the possibility of starting with money, buying another commodity, and exchanging this commodity for money again, or M–C–M. The only possible motive for performing the latter exchange, which was not driven by need, was to have more money at the end of the circulation than at the beginning, or M–C–M′, to use Marx's simple notation. Money circulating in such a way was *capital,* money put into circulation to make a profit. Economic analysis entailed finding the source of profit in a commodity that could expand money. From this perspective, Marx critically reexamined the classical theory of value.

Third, Marx began by following Ricardo in arguing that the exchange of qualitatively different use values implied some content they had in common, some identical social substance; for both Ricardo and Marx, this common content was human labor. Commodities were congealed quantities of labor, or "crystals of a social substance," and as such were *values* (Marx 1976 ed.: 128). Marx differed from Ricardo in distinguishing between concrete useful labor, or labor exercised to produce a specific use value (e.g., coat making), and human labor in the abstract, labor whose differences have been obliterated by market exchange—the average labor needed to make a piece of clothing, for instance—which Marx termed "socially necessary labor time." For Marx, it was the socially necessary labor time invested in a product—the labor expended under normal conditions at any particular time, with average skill and average intensity of effort—that formed its value (hence economic analysis was historical rather than timeless). Money was the measure of this social substance. By facilitating exchange, money was also the condition for distilling abstract labor out of the many types of concrete labors. Money brought thousands of producers into relation (via markets) with each other; hence the *fetishism of commodities*, the relation of individual to individual not via direct social relations, but via commodities or, more revealingly, via money. From this came Marx's theory of alienation (Ollman 1976) and also the entire social analysis of value, its types, relations, and meanings.

The exchange of commodities and the value they contained presupposed, for Marx, the ability of individuals to freely dispose of their labors and the freedom of equals to meet in the market, or the conditions advocated by Hobbes, Locke, Hume, and Smith as the essence of human freedom and equality. But Marx saw these conditions of equality as merely an exchange surface that disguised entirely different production relations, conditions in which apparent individuality, equality, and liberty disappeared. For Marx, the circulation of money as capital shifted the focus of analysis from the sphere of circulation and exchange to the sphere of production. In capitalism, money was expended to buy commodities that functioned as means of production; specifically, money was expended to buy labor in the marketplace. As a commodity, labor had an exchange value, which was the socially necessary labor time necessary for its production at a certain standard of living and with the requisite skills—this was the price of labor, or its wage. As a commodity, labor also had a use value, its power to produce not only further commodities (coats, flour, etc.) but, importantly, more value than it originally contained, a *surplus of value* over and above the socially necessary labor already invested in the production of the laborer (hence there was a difference, missed by Ricardo, between labor and labor power). For Marx, labor power was the source of surplus value, surplus value the source of profit, and profit was the expansion of money expended as capital (M–C–M'). When owners of money controlled the conditions under which labor made commodities, surplus value could be expropriated (or taken) from its producers, thereby expanding the original stock of money. Used in such a way, money was capital (hence capital was a social process) and the social relation between capitalist and laborer was exploitative (hence contradictory in the sense of dialectics).

For Marx, nature had not produced on the one side owners of money and on the other side owners of labor power, nor was the relation between capital and labor common to all historical periods. Rather, this exploitative relation resulted from the destruction of older systems of social relations and the gradual formation, during historical processes full of social struggles, of the capitalist system. In particular, these struggles involved denying peasants ownership of land, or rights to their own means of production, and their projection onto the labor market as owners merely of their own persons, with labor powers they were forced to sell to capital. This lends the sociology of development (as the study of the production of the social conditions for capitalist development) an entirely different, critical quality than either structural functionalism or modernization!

As for capital, capitalists, and the relations between owners, these too were historically produced. Capital came from the surplus made in earlier periods of history, from merchant's capital (in which profits were made by buying cheap and selling dear), from savings and hoarding, and from raiding other societies for their labor and accumulated wealth:

> The discovery of gold and silver in America, the extirpation, enslavement and entombment in mines of the indigenous population of that continent, the beginnings of the conquest and plunder of India, and the conversion of Africa into a preserve for the commercial hunting of blackskins, are all things which characterize the dawn of the era of capitalist production. These idyllic proceedings are the chief moments of primitive accumulation. (Marx 1976: 915)

Capitalists were originally commercial farmers or small manufacturers who put accumulated capital into use to produce profit. Under market conditions, they had to produce commodities at prices regulated by the average conditions of production. Competition was the exact mechanism of this compulsion: competition was the external, coercive law that directed the capitalist effort. Competition forced capitalists to extract surplus value from workers in two ways: absolutely, by extending the working day, and relatively, when the productivity of all kinds of labor increased, and the costs of reproducing labor power diminished (hence a smaller portion of the working day could be devoted to necessary labor). Competition propelled capitalism toward perpetual revolution in the productive forces. Most especially, it compelled the substitution of capital invested in machines ("constant capital" in Marx's parlance) for capital invested in labor power ("variable capital," because this was the source of the expansion of money) in an effort to make production more efficient than the social average. Competition forced the adoption of new technologies and innovative types of organization (e.g., corporations as compared with family firms, multinationals as compared with national corporations). Each technological or organizational change would then have multiplier effects throughout an economy. Rather than seeing this historical process as a series of equilibriums, Marx conceptualized development as uneven and contradictory, with crises periodically necessary for restoring the conditions of profitability destroyed by fierce competition. For Marx, development was a process of capital accumulation that occurred unevenly in terms of class (with the owning class becoming richer) and space (with some countries becoming richer than others). Development was a contradictory process (Marx 1976; Harvey 1982; Becker 1977; Weeks 1981).

Mode of Production

For Marx, class control over production and development had profound implications for sociocultural life as a whole. Marx's own summary of the complex social and economic structure, the layers of institutions, social relations, and practices intervening between economic necessity and symbolic consciousness, reads as follows:

> In the social production of their existence, [people] inevitably enter into definite relations, which are independent of their will, namely relations of production appropriate to a given stage in the development of their material forces of production. The totality of these relations of production constitutes the economic structure of society, the real foundation, on which arises a legal and political superstructure and to which correspond definite forms of social consciousness. The mode of production of material life conditions the general process of social, political and

intellectual life. It is not the consciousness of [humans] that determines their existence, but their social existence that determines their consciousness. (Marx 1970: 20–21)

Marx did *not* say, in this passage, that a social "machine" called "economic structure" stamped out parts called "political superstructure" and "consciousness." Dialectical terms for structural relationships like "correspond" and "condition" cannot imply such a mechanical process of determination. Marx *did* argue that the level of development of a society's productive forces—society's ability to transform nature—limited its social and political development and, indeed, directed its entire cultural mode of existence. Putting it simply, the economic structure (forces and relations of production) "determined" the superstructure of society (culture, politics, consciousness). Beyond this very general determination, phrased by Marx in terms of influences and pressures, we have to look at the particular historical and geographical conditions to see exactly how economy conditioned social and cultural development.

For Marx, societies were exploitative when uncompensated surplus labor, or its products, were taken from the direct producers by elites and their organizations, be these states or corporations. Surplus was not easily extracted. Particularly at a low level of development of the productive forces, when the margin of survival was narrow, exploitation might mean the difference between life and death during times of natural scarcity—exploitation meant the death of children and elderly people. So the exploitation process was seen by Marx as an arena of struggle, in which the dominant used a combination of economic, political, and ideological force to ensure their control over socially produced surplus, and in which the dominated resisted through overt means like organization and rebellion and hidden means like reluctant compliance—although the exploited might be induced to "volunteer" their own exploitation with the right persuasion. In such a context, consciousness had to take ideological forms that rationalized and legitimized exploitation. Organized religion was one such form—for example, the notion of heaven as a realm of eventual peace, with a place in paradise gained by good deeds like hard work and devotion to law and order. Yet even religion was a contradictory ideology, so that oppositional groups formed alternative interpretations of spiritual principles—liberation theology, for example, or humanism as a nondeified admiration of the good in people.

If we turn to the political aspects of superstructure, a society characterized by exploitation and conflict had to develop collective institutions for ensuring elite domination and for socially reproducing the conditions and infrastructures of production (Hirsch 1978). Many of these institutions were accumulated in the apparatus of the state, governed by an appropriate kind of politics (e.g., representative democracy in advanced capitalism). Again, however, while the necessity for a complex of institutions called "the state" originated in the contradictory nature of production, its exact character could be found only by examining the particular, empirical circumstances of a given time period (Marx 1983: 927–928). Hence, for Marx, there were structural connections between the economic base of a society and its cultural and political superstructures. These connections limited and directed the forms of social consciousness and the kinds of states and politics that came into existence, but people living in specific times and places created their more exact historical forms. Notice that this entailed two kinds of social analysis: structural and empirical.

In summary, the Marxist concept "mode of production" entailed a system of social relations that organized and directed the forces of production in the transformation of nature (Figure 4.1). The social objectives of economic activity were the production of material goods used to reproduce the conditions of production (necessary labor) and the production of a surplus of values (surplus labor), used partly for investment in new means of production and partly to support and protect the lifestyle of the elite. The social ability to transform nature, measured by the level of development of the forces of production, and guided by exploitative social relations, limited and directed consciousness in multiple ideological forms, while the state monopolized violence, rationalized inequality, and guaranteed the continued reproduction of the social order. For Marx, this whole process was suffused with social, political,

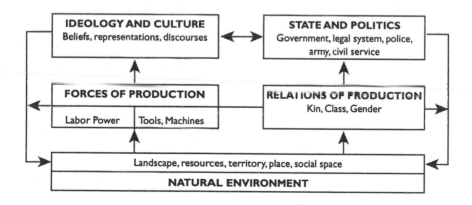

FIGURE 4.1. Mode of production.

and ideological struggles generated by contradictions at the very heart of society—in the relations that bound social actors together as collectivities of producers.

Development and Transformation

Development, for Marx, occurred through the buildup of forces of production, especially the addition of tools, machines, and infrastructures to human labor power. Social transformations involved shifts from modes of production at low levels of the forces of production to modes at higher levels of productive force. Marx envisioned these qualitative changes as violent episodes undertaken by desperate people only when the productive possibilities of the old social order had been exhausted:

> At a certain stage of development, the material productive forces of society come into conflict with the existing relations of production or—this merely expresses the same thing in legal terms—with the property relations within the framework of which they have operated hitherto. From forms of development of the productive forces these relations turn into their fetters. Then begins an era of social revolution. The changes in the economic foundation lead sooner or later to the transformation of the whole immense superstructure. (Marx 1970: 21)

In other words, material development was full of crises. These sharpened and intensified the social struggles endemic to class societies, opening the door to possible structural changes, with the process led by political and ideological transformations. And the new social relations put into place through struggle did not materialize out of thin air, nor from utopian thought alone, but from embryonic relations already present in the dying body of the old society.

The culminating moment in this line of thought is a reconceptualization of history in terms of temporal sequences of modes of production and of geography in terms of articulations of modes of production. Marx thought it possible to theorize "laws of social transformation" between modes of production—"laws" being understood dialectically as tendencies or probabilities—leaving the specifics of historical change to be worked out by empirical research. Marx only began an outline of the main modes of production that have characterized human history, and investigated only one mode (capitalism) in detail. Marx's knowledge of noncapitalist modes of production was biased by the (colonial) nature of the available information. However, in notes, posthumously published as *Grundrisse* (Marx 1973: 471–514), and in subsequent work, Marx seems to have seen societies passing through the following general types: primitive communist mode of production, kin-ordered mode of production, tributary mode of production, capitalism, and socialism.

In early, simple statements Marx tended to see all societies passing through a few simple stages, or modes of production, in a unilinear conception of history. In later statements Marx indicated that each mode of production contained several different societal types, and that any particular society could move through some modes but not others, might skip a mode, or even reverse track, in a multilinear theory of history. What first appears as a simple process of societal evolution turns out to be a complex process of uneven development, such that capitalism could appear in Europe, the previously dominant civilizations (China, India, Egypt, Mayan and Inca America) remained in "Asiatic" tributary systems, while much of the rest of the world was tribal or communal. Spatial relations between societies during any time period took the form of "articulations" (combinations and interpenetrations) between modes of production with unequal powers, for example, between state formations in southwestern North America and tribal systems on the Great Plains, or between the Incas and the hunter–gatherer–agriculturalists of the Amazon Basin, or between European imperialistic capitalism and kin-ordered, tribal systems in Africa. Each of these "articulations" had developmental and underdevelopmental effects as surplus was extracted as value or tribute, techniques spread, and political power expanded. The geographical study of development became an analysis of the articulations between modes of production in space.

Structural Marxism

This notion of articulations as combinations and interactions of modes of production emerged most strongly in structural Marxism. Structuralism originated in the structural linguistics of the early twentieth century and was particularly important in European social theory in the 1950s and 1960s. Structuralism affected Marxism mainly through the work of the French Marxist philosopher Louis Althusser, who developed a rigorous analysis of the concept of mode of production. This involved elucidating the necessary structural relations between the various "levels" or "instances" of a society (economy, consciousness, and politics) by determining precisely how surplus extraction determined the types and relative importance of the superstructures: "Economic relations, centrally those between owners and direct producers, are always determinant (in the last instance) but . . . this determination by the economic structure takes the rather indirect form of assigning to the other, non-economic levels, their place in a hierarchy of dominance with respect to one another, and the kind of articulation between them" (Benton 1984: 72). In structural Marxism, revolutionary change, from one mode of production to another, occurred through a "condensation" or "fusion" of several contradictions occurring at different levels in a social structure—for example, simultaneously material and ideological. Structural change was a complex process in which dominance might be displaced from one instance to another—for example, from the political to the economic instance during the transition from feudalism to capitalism (Taylor 1979), or from the state to the mass media in advanced capitalism. In this conception, each mode of production had a characteristic structure, typical complexes of contradictions, and a dynamic, or system of courses of development. A central tendency in a mode was counterbalanced by other tendencies to produce the complex rhythms of social change that typified any epoch. Each mode of production contained several divergent developmental tendencies in dynamic tension, and several modes of production were present in an actually existing society, or "social formation" (Althusser 1969; Althusser and Balibar 1970).

Structural Marxism had significant implications for development. Modes of production, characterized most basically by their social relations, entailed different capacities for the development of the productive forces. But social formations were formed by the articulation of several modes, so that the economic dynamic of a specific society had several, often conflicting, developing and underdeveloping tendencies, often located in different regions within a society (i.e., geographically uneven development). Surplus was extracted by ruling elites within a given social formation, and was transferred across space between formations, according to principles of hierarchy and domination that were both social and geopolitical. Spatial systems of surplus extraction were protected and expanded by state action—for example, imperialism and colonialism—and spatial inequalities were legitimized by ideologies—for example, the notion of "white man's burden." Structural Marxism offered a powerful, complex way of understanding intersocietal relations.

Imperialism

From the Marxist perspective, capitalism was a social form of development based on the extraction of surplus from workers: extraction might be internal to a social formation, or it might be external, between societies. Marxist theories of imperialism looked at society's external or spatial relations. Lasting from the fifteenth to the nineteenth centuries in Europe, mercantilist forms of imperialism involved the plundering of ancient stockpiles of wealth from precapitalist civilizations, unequal trade relations with dominated societies, and the production of bullion and exotic commodities using coerced (often slave) labor in the Americas. Mercantilism involved massive state control over external relations to the point of declaring war on foreign competitors and heavily regulating trade and commerce to the advantage of the home country. Once the forces of production had achieved economic advantage for Britain, the leading mercantilist country, protectionism was dropped and "free trade" (between unequal partners) promoted for continued global economic dominance. However, by the second half of the nineteenth century, several large industrial countries competed for global domination and, at times of depression (such as in the 1870s and 1880s), struggled for economic survival. This was the context in which a "second imperialism," more violent than the first mercantilist version, suddenly emerged in most of the economically advanced countries.

Between 1870 and 1900 the European states *added* 10 million square miles of territory and 150 million people to their areas of control, one-fifth of the earth's land surface and one-tenth of its people. Britain extended its empire so that it now controlled one-fifth of the globe, and one-quarter of its people by the end of the nineteenth century, gaining an empire on which "the sun never sets." France took possession of much of North and West Africa and Indochina, and Germany seized parts of Africa and the Pacific. Italy and Belgium were active in Africa, the United States in the Pacific and Caribbean, and Japan in East Asia and the Pacific (Cohen 1973). Why did the Euro-American social formations show a suddenly renewed, ferocious appetite for foreign domination? Schumpeter (1952) sought explanation in sociopsychological compulsion; he argued that instinctive inclinations toward war and conquest bubbled to the surface as people and nations struggled to avoid extinction. Other theorists saw imperialism as an act of state power or as a political expression of modern government. By comparison, radicals influenced by Marxist ideas identified a relationship between the maturation of industrial capitalism, with its tremendous material demands and competitive pressures, and the redevelopment of imperialism.

The British journalist John Hobson (1858–1940) linked the internal class relations of industrial capitalism with an external need for territorial control. He reasoned that because of the limited purchasing power of underpaid workers, capitalist societies tended toward economic stagnation unless a place outside such societies could be found to invest unneeded capital; imperialism was therefore a contest between the industrial capitalist powers to monopolize external markets for capital exports (Hobson 1902; Zeitlin 1972). The Austrian socialist economist Rudolph Hilferding took Marx's idea of monopoly capitalism (competition concentrating capital in fewer hands) a stage further to include finance capitalism, capital accumulation by banks. Finance capital seeking domination needed a state strong enough to pursue an expansionist policy and acquire colonies. Such expansionism was given justification by racial ideology, but was essentially a matter of economic necessity since "any faltering of the onward drive reduces the profits of finance capital, weakens its powers of competition and finally turns the smaller economic area into a tributary of the larger" (Hilferding, quoted in Mommsen 1980: 37). The notion of the export of capital was retained by Vladimir Lenin (1870–1924), the Russian Marxist and revolutionary. Lenin (1975 ed.) saw the developing capitalist powers caught in a struggle to repartition the global system of investment domains, with the latecomer Germany attempting to acquire colonies at the expense of the older imperial powers (Britain and France). By comparison, the Polish-German Marxist Rosa Luxembourg (1871–1919) saw the contradictions of capitalism focused on the inadequate purchasing power of workers, such that additional markets for commodities had to be sought in noncapitalist societies. As these would not submit voluntarily to having their manufacturing industries destroyed, there was a need for state violence and political control (i.e., imperialism) to force trade at disadvantageous terms (Luxembourg 1951 ed.). Other theories stressed labor needs or energy and raw material supplies (Caldwell 1977). Despite their differences, all radical theories of imperialism had essentially the same dialectical logic: external imperialism served to relieve contradictions internal to the capitalist system. Imperialist expansion of all kinds (exporting of capital, gaining of external markets, opening of new territories) accelerated the accumulation of capital. Capitalism in an expansionist phase was less vulnerable to crisis.

Colonialism was the system of political control forced on conquered peoples. Beginning with the Spanish conquest of Central and South America in the sixteenth century, colonialism lasted until the late 1940s and 1950s, with some colonized countries not achieving political independence until as late as the 1970s. However, this decline in Euro-American political control occurred only when the economies of Third World societies had already been captured, in structure and orientation, by the capitalist world market—"independence" was therefore termed "neocolonialism" by many radical theorists. From this perspective, the tendency toward "globalization" entailed the increasing homogenization of societies with the incorporation of world space into a single social, economic, and cultural system dominated by the old imperial powers.

Dependency Theory

Marxism forms the philosophical and theoretical basis for a range of neo-Marxist theories that combine historical materialist notions with a number of other critical traditions; examples most obviously include dependency and world systems theories, but also neostructural notions, like regulation theory. The basic message of the dependency school was that European development was predicated on the active *under*development of the non-European world. For dependency theorists, Europe's development was based on external destruction: brutal conquest, colonial control, and the stripping of non-Western societies of their peoples, resources, and surpluses. From historical processes like these came a new global geography of European First World center and non-European Third World periphery. The relationship between center and periphery assumed, for the Brazilian geographer Teontonio Dos Santos (1970), the spatial form of dependence, in which some countries (the dominant) achieved self-sustaining economic growth, while others (the dominated and dependent) grew only as a reflection of changes in the dominant countries. The incorporation of Latin America into the capitalist world economy, directly through (Spanish and Portuguese) colonial administration, but more subtly through foreign trade, geared the region's economies toward demands from the center, even when the export economy was locally owned. Dependence skewed the region's social structure so that local power was held by a small ruling class that used the gains from exporting for luxury consumption rather than investment. Real power was exercised from external centers of command in dominant ("metropolitan") countries. Dependence continues into the present through international ownership of the region's most dynamic sectors, multinational corporate control over technology, and payments of royalties, interest, and profits.

The theory behind the dependency position came from two main sources. In the United States a school of neo-Marxist thought centered on the socialist journal *Monthly Review* developed a theory of "monopoly capitalism" to refer to the dominant form of social organization in the twentieth century. Beginning in the late nineteenth century, large corporations increasingly took over, or outcompeted, small companies. Monopolization controlled competition, corporations accumulated surpluses from excess profits, and capitalist economies tended toward underconsumption and economic stagnation. Economic crises were avoided by stimulating individual demand through advertising and collective consumption through the growth of the military–industrial complex. Paul Baran and Paul Sweezy (1966), leading lights of the *Monthly*

Review school, found this an irrational kind of development. Genuine development could be achieved, they argued, only by withdrawing from the world capitalist system and reconstructing economy and society on a socialist basis.

The second main source for the dependency school was critical, radical economists in Latin America. The ideas of the Economic Commission for Latin America (ECLA) and Raul Prebisch (discussed in Chapter 3) were criticized by the Latin American left for ignoring class relations. State intervention in the economy, such as the protection of infant industries, could end up subsidizing the profits of the local bourgeoisie, with consumers paying higher prices (at one time the tariff on refrigerators imported into Mexico was 800%). A more radical *dependentista* position was pieced together by writers such as Osvaldo Sunkel (1972), Celso Furtado (1963), Fernando Cardoso and Enzo Falleto (1979), and Teontonio Dos Santos (1970), and popularized in the English-speaking world through the writings of Andre Gunder Frank (1969a, 1869b, 1979).

Frank was a leading critic of development economics and modernization theory. He mounted a detailed criticism of the "dual society" thesis, which maintained that underdeveloped societies had a dual structure of traditional and modern sectors, each with its own dynamic (see Chapters 2 and 3). For Frank, attributing underdevelopment to traditionalism (or feudalism) rather than to capitalism was a historical and political mistake. World capitalism destroyed or transformed earlier social systems even as it came into existence, converting them into sources of its own further development (Frank 1969a). For Frank, the economic, political, social, and cultural institutions of the underdeveloped countries resulted from the penetration of capitalism, rather than being original or traditional. Frank focused on the metropole–satellite (or center–periphery) relations he found typical of Latin America. The underdevelopment of peripheral–capitalist regions and people, he said, was characterized by three contradictions: the contradiction of the monopolistic expropriation of economic surplus, the contradiction of metropolis–satellite polarization, and the contradiction of continuity in change. Drawing on Marxist analyses of the class expropriation of surplus value, especially Baran's (1960) version, which emphasized the potential surplus that could be made available for investment under noncapitalist circumstances, Frank argued that external monopoly resulted in the expropriation (and thus local unavailability) of a significant part of the economic surplus produced in Latin America. The region was actively *under*developed (made less developed) by the expropriation of its surplus product (the source of investment capital in Marxist theory). Using a case study of Chile, Frank described the pattern of surplus movement as a massive, geographical expropriation system reaching the most remote corners of the region:

> The monopoly capitalist structure and the surplus expropriation/appropriation contradiction run through the entire Chilean economy, past and present. Indeed, it is this exploitative relation which in chain-like fashion extends the link between the capitalist world and national metropolises to the regional centers (part of whose surplus they appropriate), and from these to local centers, and so on to large landowners or merchants who expropriate surplus from small peasants or tenants, and sometimes even from these latter to landless laborers exploited by them in turn. At each step along the way, the relatively few capitalists above exercise monopoly power over the many below, expropriating some or all of their economic surplus. . . . Thus at each point, the international, national, and local capitalist system generates economic development for the few and underdevelopment for the many. (1969b: 7–8)

This idea of surplus transfer over space was further developed in Frank's second contradiction, whereby center and periphery become increasingly polarized as capitalism developed the one and underdeveloped the other in a single historical process. In this perspective, only a weaker or lesser degree of metropole–satellite relations allowed the possibility of local development. These two contradictions suggested a third to Frank: the continuity and ubiquity of structural underdevelopment throughout the expansion of the capitalist system.

From this perspective on underdevelopment, Frank generated more specific hypotheses that could be used in guiding development theory and policy. In contrast to the development of the world metropolis, which was satellite to no other region, the development of national and regional metropolises was limited by their satellite status. For example, local metropoles such as São Paulo, Brazil, or Buenos Aires, Argentina, could only achieve a dependent form of industrialization. Real development thus entailed separation and autonomy from the global capitalist system. Similarly, in a hypothesis directly opposed to the finding of modernization geography, that development was spread through contract with the metropolis, Frank hypothesized that the satellites experienced their greatest development when ties to the metropolis were weakest— historically during wars, geographically in terms of spatial isolation. By extension, regions that had the closest ties to the metropole in the past were most underdeveloped in the present. Frank found this thesis confirmed by the "ultraunderdevelopment" of the sugar-exporting region of northeastern Brazil and the mining regions of Bolivia. In summary, underdevelopment in Frank's theory was not an original condition, nor the result of archaic institutions surviving in isolated regions, nor even did it come from Third World irrationalism. Underdevelopment was generated by the same processes that developed the center; in particular, underdevelopment in the periphery resulted from the loss of surplus that was expropriated for investment in the center's development (Frank 1969b, 1979).

An immediately noticeable weakness in Frank's theory resided in its failure to specify the economics of surplus extraction. In some cases the mechanisms of surplus extraction were obvious—for example, when European, North American, or Japanese corporations owned land and factories in Latin American countries and withdrew surplus as rent or profit, or when center banks loaned capital to peripheral states and enterprises and withdrew surplus as interest. But what of peasant producers, owning their own land, and producing cash crops for export to center markets, a situation typical of much of the peripheral agriculture in the nineteenth and twentieth centuries? Here the beginning of an answer was provided by Arghiri Emmanuel (1972; see also deJanvry 1981) with the theory of unequal exchange. Like the ECLA economists, Emmanuel argued against neoclassical trade theory, which said that the international division of labor and system of trade had advantages for all participants (see Chapter 2). Emmanuel argued instead that international trade made poor countries poorer and rich countries richer. Emmanuel assumed the perfect international mobility of capital, but the immobility of labor between countries; hence wage rates persistently differed greatly between the two. Peripheral countries exported agricultural products that embodied large quantities of cheap labor and imported industrial products that embodied small amounts of expensive labor. This led to terms of trade favoring the higher cost products of the center, while devaluing the lower cost exports of the periphery. Peripheral countries were prevented from achieving development because they sold their goods at prices below values (the socially necessary labor embodied in the products), while rich countries sold goods at prices above values. For Emmanuel, unequal exchange (through trade) was a hidden mechanism of surplus extraction and a major cause of the economic stagnation in the periphery. Samir Amin (1976: 143–144), director of Forum Tiers Monde in Dakar, Senegal, estimated the amount of surplus transferred from poor to rich countries via unequal exchange to be 1.5% of the product of the rich countries, but 15% of that of the poor countries, an amount, he thought, that was "sufficient to account for the blocking of the growth of the periphery." From the perspective of dependency theory, the peripheral countries borrowed back their own surplus to finance "development schemes." The geopolitical implications of this theory were explosive!

Yet, there were other, more serious, criticisms of Frank. The Brazilian economist Fernando Cardoso (1982) found the notion of the development of underdevelopment a neat play on words, but not helpful in concrete terms. In Latin America, he argued, multinational corporations invested in modern industrialization, while supposedly traditional sectors (agriculture, mining) operated in technically and organizationally sophisticated ways, and both were parts of an advanced but dependent capitalist development. However he added that in countries like Argentina, Brazil, and Mexico spatial and sectoral dualism emerged, composed of advanced economies tied to the international capitalist system, and backward sectors, or internal colonies. Multinational corporations were interested in at least some prosperity for dependent countries because of the markets this prosperity provided. But the Latin American countries remained dependent for technology on the United States. In contrast to Frank's universalism, Cardoso advocated looking closely at specific situations in particular parts of the Third World, where development and dependence could be found existing in tandem. We might note that, on becoming president of Brazil in 1994, Cardoso adopted a neoliberal development posture directly contrary to his previous dependency views.

Dependency theory was holistic in that it attempted to place a country into the larger (global) system. In its simple form, it stressed the external causes of underdevelopment rather than those internal to a peripheral society. A strong emphasis was placed on economic rather than social or cultural interactions. In Frank's version, the accent was on regions, spaces, and flows, rather than on class. For most theorists, dependency and underdevelopment were synonymous, although Cardoso, for example, thought that dependent forms of capitalist development could be achieved. And finally, dependency theory was politically radical, with most of its adherents proclaiming the need for some kind of socialist revolution, although a purely nationalist politics (merely cutting a peripheral country off from the world capitalist system so that it could develop autonomously) could also emerge from purely spatial versions of the dependency perspective.

World Systems Theory

World systems theory has obvious affinities with the dependency school. But it had antecedents, too, in a theory of history named after *Annales: Economies, Societies, Civilisations*, the journal founded in 1929 by French historians Lucian Febvre and Marc Bloch. The *Annales* school aimed at remaking the discipline of history. Dissatisfied with conventional history because it was isolated and unrealistic, the *Annales* historians used a comparative method involving long sweeps of time to examine differences and similarities between societies. The French geographer Vidal de la Blache, who believed that *genre de vie*, or way of life, mediated between people and nature, deciding which of nature's possibilities came to be used (environmental possibilism), was an ally of the school, which always had a strong geographical component in its regional histories, geohistories, and studies of transportation. The main themes of the *Annales* school were social history, especially of the material conditions of the masses; structural factors, or relative constants; the long term as a common language for the social sciences; and, while this was not a Marxist school of thought, a concern with the relations among economy, society, and civilization. Ferdnand Braudel (1972, 1973), the most famous of the school's second-generation scholars, was particularly interested in structural limitations on material and economic life, the great slopes of historical change over centuries, regional histories, and the sudden breakup of ancient ways in the nineteenth century. This view was found to be suited to the study of the long-term history of the peoples of the Third World and the sudden changes thrust upon them through contact with the First World.

A more obvious connection with development theory was forged by a leading English-speaking representative of the *Annales* school, the sociologist Immanuel Wallerstein of the State University of New York at Binghampton. Wallerstein retained the broad spatial scale and long historical time span of *Annales* scholarship by treating world history as the development of a single system. By "system" Wallerstein meant a social entity with a single division of labor so that all sectors or areas were dependent on the others via interchanges of essential goods. The past was characterized by minisystems, small entities with a complete division of labor and a single cultural framework, as in simple agricultural or hunting and gathering societies. But the recent integration of the hill tribes of Papua New Guinea, and the bushmen of the Kalahari into the capitalist world system meant that minisystems no longer existed. World systems, characterized by a single division of labor and multicultural systems, have long been dominant. The outstanding example, for Wallerstein, was the capitalist world economy, in which production was for profit and products were sold on the market. In such a system production was constantly expanded, as long as profits could be made, and producers innovated to expand the profit margin; hence the secret of capitalist success was the pursuit of profit. In the past, world economies, held together by strong states, were unstable and tended to become world empires, as with China, Egypt, and Rome. Surplus was extracted from peasants using various methods of political coercion. With capitalism, by contrast, power passed to the private owners of means of production, with the state guaranteeing conditions for capital accumulation. The capitalist world economy resisted various attempts to create a world empire (e.g., by Britain and the United States), and capitalism has therefore proven to be a lasting way of regulating and coordinating global production (Wallerstein 1979).

According to Wallerstein, within the world system there are three main economic zones: core, semiperiphery, and periphery. The core consists of countries with efficient, complex production systems and high levels of capital accumulation. Core states are administratively well organized and militarily powerful. Peripheral countries have the opposite characteristics, while the semiperiphery combined elements of both. World systems theory saw spatial relations as exploitative, that is, involving the flow of surplus from periphery to core. For world systems theory, most of the surplus accumulated as capital in the core came from local sources (the exploitation of local workers) but the addition of peripheral surplus reduced the level of class and interstate conflict in the core (Chase-Dunn 1989). For the periphery, loss of surplus meant that capital needed for modernization was not available, while the system of intense labor exploitation at low wage levels shaped peripheral class relations and fostered political conflict. Semiperipheral states functioned to prevent political polarization in the world system while collecting surplus for transmission to the core (Shannon 1989: Ch. 2).

For Wallerstein, the capitalist world economy originated in sixteenth-century Europe, an era and place of increased agricultural production for growing urban markets. At the core of the developing world economy, in England, the Netherlands, and northern France, a combination of pastoral and arable production required high skill levels and favored free agricultural labor (yeoman farmers). The periphery of the system, in Eastern Europe and increasingly the Americas, specialized in grains, cotton, and sugar together with bullion from mines, all of which favored the use of coerced labor (either a kind of serfdom that Wallerstein calls "coerced cash crop labor" or pure slavery). In between lay a series of transitional regions (e.g., northern Italy), mainly former cores degenerating toward peripheral status, making high-cost industrial products, giving credit and dealing in specie, and using sharecropping in the agricultural arena. Whereas the interests of capitalist landowners and merchants coincided in the development of the absolute monarchy and strong, central state machineries in the core, ruling class interests diverged sharply in the periphery, leading to weak states. Unequal exchange in commerce was imposed by the strong core on the weak

peripheries and the surplus of the world economy was thereby appropriated (Wallerstein 1974: Ch. 2 and 3). From this geosociological perspective, Wallerstein outlined the main stages in the history of the world capitalist economy:

1. The European world economy emerged in the "long sixteenth
century" (1450–1640). The crisis of feudalism posed a series of dilemmas that could only be resolved through geographic expansion of the
division of labor. By the end of the period Northwest Europe had established itself as core, Spain and the northern Italian cities declined into the
semiperiphery, and Northern Europe and Iberian America were the main
peripheries of the system.
2. A mercantile struggle during the recession of 1650–1730 left
England as the only surviving core state.
3. Industrial production and the demand for raw materials
increased rapidly after 1760, leading to geographic expansion of the system, which now became truly a world system under British hegemony.
Russia, an important external system, was incorporated into the semiperiphery, while the remaining areas of Latin America and Asia and
Africa were absorbed into the periphery. This expansion enabled former
areas of the periphery (the United States and Germany) to become
semiperipheral, and eventually core, states. The core exchanged manufactured goods with the periphery's agricultural products. The mass of
industry created an urban proletariat as an internal threat to the stability
of the core of the capitalist system which the industrial bourgeoisie eventually had to "buy off" with higher wages. This also solved the problem
of what to do with the burgeoning output of manufacturing.
4. World War I marked the beginning of a new stage characterized
by revolutionary turmoil (the Russian Revolution ended that country's
further decline toward peripheral status) and the consolidation of the
capitalist world economy under the hegemony of the United States. After
World War II, the urgent need was expanded markets, which the hegemonic power met by reconstructing Western Europe, reserving Latin
America for U.S. investment, and decolonizing South Asia, the Middle
East, and Africa. Since the late 1960s a decline in U.S. political hegemony has increased the freedom of action of capitalist enterprise, now in
the form of multinational corporations.

The world system thus had structural parts (center, semiperiphery,
periphery) evolving through stages of alternating expansion and contraction. Within such a framework, Wallerstein argued, comparative analyses of the whole system and the development of its regional parts could
be made.

Regulation Theory

It is often said that Marxist and neo-Marxist theories are ridden with tensions between structural imperatives and peoples' struggles to change the conditions of their lives—that is, between the unfolding of a world system and the acts of people in creating history, or between structure and agency. Various solutions to this tension have emerged as different schools of Marxist thought. One response was the Italian Marxist Antonio Gramsci's concept of "ideological hegemony." Writing from prison in the 1920s, Gramsci compared the Marxist notion of *domination*, by which was meant direct physical coercion by police, army, and law in political society, with that of *hegemony*, or ideological control through consent in civil society (unions, schools, churches, families, etc.). Civil institutions, Gramsci thought, inculcated an entire system of values, beliefs, and morality supportive of the established order and its dominating classes: hegemony was a worldview diffused through socialization into every area of daily life which, when internalized, became part of "common sense." Hegemony mystified power relations, camouflaged public issues and events, encouraged fatalism and political passivity, and justified deprivation for the many so that a few could live well. Hegemony worked to induce oppressed people to consent to their own exploitation and misery.

Along with many other theorists, Gramsci was fascinated by the development of capitalism in the United States. In his concept of "American Fordism" Gramsci explored a new kind of hegemony: the achievement of willing consent through mass consumption. We can add to this the consumption oriented mass media as inducers of social passivity and the worship of the spectacular. Revolutionary political transformation, Gramsci argued, was not possible without a crisis of ideological hegemony: changes in civil, as well as political, society. Socialist movements, Gramsci concluded, had to create a "counterhegemony" to break the existing ideological and cultural bonds and penetrate the false world of appearances as prelude to the making of new ideas and values for human liberation (Gramsci 1971; Boggs 1976).

Based on these ideas, the neostructural French regulation school, which developed in Paris in the 1970s, 1980s, and 1990s, thought that the overall societal framework of capitalism contained several historical and geographical variants. This school divided the history of capitalism into *regimes* based essentially on the prevailing labor process: manufacture, dominant in the capitalist countries between 1780 and 1870; machinofacture, dominant between 1870 and 1940; scientific management (called "Taylorism" after its main practitioner) and Fordism, beginning at the turn of the century and dominant from 1940 to the late

1970s; and flexible accumulation, or post-Fordism, beginning with the economic crises of the 1970s and expanding rapidly in the late twentieth century (Dunford and Perrons 1983). The regulation school theorized society in terms of development models, their parts, and their transformations: *regimes of accumulation* described the main production–consumption relationships, *modes of regulation* described cultural habits and institutional rules (Lipietz 1985, 1986, 1987; Aglietta 1979).

What the regulation school called "Fordism" (the term originally used by Gramsci) was pioneered by Henry Ford in the immediate pre-World War I years, and generalized in the United States from the 1920s. Ford linked two innovations: the semiautomatic assembly line, adopted between 1910 and 1914, and the $5.00, eight-hour day, inaugurated on January 5, 1914. As Gramsci (1971 ed.) had said, Ford's goal was to create a new kind of worker, thoroughly Americanized, committed to conventional morality, who would never join a union. Fordism entailed standardization of production and separation of conception, organization, and control from manual work, a system that resulted in a rapid rise in the volume of goods produced per person. This expansion in productivity was counterbalanced by an equally massive growth in consumption, first by unionized wage earners, later by all sectors of the population. In the Fordist mode of regulation, the competitive mechanisms of the nineteenth century declined in favor of compulsory agreements between capital and labor (collective bargaining), the hegemony of large companies, and state control through Keynesian macroeconomic policies. Regulation of the population was also achieved by advertising and the control of imagination by mass-mediated popular culture. The massive growth of consumption exacerbated environmental crisis through mass wasting of resources. Fordism thus consists of a number of interdependent elements generating rapid economic growth over several decades (Figure 4.2).

As an intensive regime of accumulation centered on mass consumption Fordism became generalized in the capitalist social formations of the center countries after World War II. This produced typical economic growth rates of 4% a year. International trade was of secondary significance to the postwar Fordist model; the driving forces of Fordism were the transformation of production processes and the expansion of the internal market by increasing mass purchasing power. However, peripheral social formations supplied labor and raw materials, with U.S. military domination assuring continued control over these resources. In the 1930s in Latin America and the 1950s in Southeast Asia some countries developed an import-substitution industrialization (ISI) policy. Although initially successful, the ISI strategy ran into difficulties in the 1960s because it failed to enter the "virtuous circle" of Fordism (in terms of

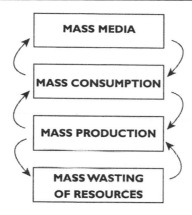

FIGURE 4.2. Fordism.

limited technology, restricted worker and peasant incomes, and confined foreign earnings from raw material exports). For regulation theorists like Alain Lipietz, of the University of Paris, these regimes were therefore caricatures of Fordism, what he referred to as "sub-Fordist." Early experiments with relocating unskilled tasks in a search for lower wages occurred in the 1960s, again in the immediate peripheral countries, including some in Latin America and Southeast Asia. New industrial countries (NICs) opting for a new regime of accumulation via "export substitution" employed a number of strategies, of which two were significant: (1) Primitive Taylorism, which involved the transfer of types of production with high rates of exploitation (in terms of wages, length of the working day, and labor intensity) from the center to peripheral countries like South Korea, Taiwan, Singapore, and Hong Kong in the 1970s, with a second wave to Malaysia, Thailand, the Philippines, and China in the 1980s and 1990s; and (2) peripheral Fordism, in which countries with autonomous local capital, significant markets formed by sizeable middle classes, and elements of a skilled working class (South Korea since 1973, Mexico, Brazil) were able to develop significant aspects of the Fordist developmental logic. Both strategies resulted in extensive industrialization of Third World countries.

What the regulation school terms a "crisis of Fordism" occurred with a decrease in the growth of productivity and a fall in profitability in the late 1960s and a more general economic crisis in the 1970s, characterized by the internationalization of production, state austerity programs, unemployment, and eventually a crisis of demand (i.e., an underconsumption crisis). All these resulted in a new post-Fordist regime of "flexible accumulation" from the mid-1970s to the present (Leborgne and Lipietz 1988;

Piore and Sabel 1984). Allan Scott (1988), a geographer at UCLA, has argued that the typically rigid mass production processes of Fordism gave way to changeable, computer- enhanced processes, situated within systems of malleable external linkages and labor market relations. The turn toward flexibility produced a new geography: older centers of Fordist mass production, characterized by unions, rigid labor relations, and governmental restrictions on producers, were avoided as flexible production began to ascend again in North America and Western Europe—for example, high technology industries were located in the suburbs of large metropolitan areas and in previously unindustrialized communities in the South and West; in the Third World the spatial margin of production expanded while industry converged on major growth centers (Scott and Storper 1986). The neo-Marxist notions of Fordist and post-Fordist developmental systems are leading examples of the continuing validity of radical theory in explaining contemporary global capitalism.

Critique

Dependency and world systems theories enjoyed wide support among critical social theorists and radical development practitioners in the 1960s and 1970s, particularly in Latin America, India, and sub-Saharan Africa, while world systems theory remains a leading source of innovative ideas and historical research today, much of it published in the journal *Review.* But these theories have also come in for more than their share of criticism. For some critics, dependency theory is so dated it can no longer be taken seriously. As one author proclaimed, dependency theory "is all but dead . . . it is now a theoretical–political memory" (James 1997: 205). Changes in the global capitalist system, such as industrialization and economic growth in Latin America and East Asia, supposedly contradict dependency theory's notion of blocked development in the periphery. Characterizing Frank and others as taking the position that capitalist development was impossible in the periphery, so that only underdevelopment was possible there (Bienefeld 1981), a number of writers (e.g., Jackman 1984) have showed that dependent countries can have economic growth rates higher than those of nondependent countries, or more generally that capitalism could develop the productive forces in the periphery. Behind empirical inaccuracy, some critics said, lay basic errors in philosophy and theoretical methodology. Frank's mistake, in the view of sociologist Gabriel Palma (1978), lay in the "mechanico–formalistic" structure of his analysis, which rendered dependency theory static and unhistorical. Palma was particularly referring to dependency theory's tendency to see the internal structures of Third World countries as "mechanically determined" by external relations with the First World. Palma wanted instead more specific studies that included the possibility of capitalist development in Latin America (see also Palma 1981). Many later critiques followed a similar line of criticism.

David Booth (1985), a sociologist at Hull University in England, argued that the Marxist sociology of development (including dependency theory) reached an impasse in the 1980s related to generic difficulties in its underlying social theory. For Booth, the basic problem with Marxist theory was its metatheoretical commitment to demonstrating that events were necessary results of the objective laws of the teleological unfolding of capitalism. This commitment to necessity was expressed in development theory in two main forms:

> The first operates through the way in which it is usual to conceive of the relation between the theoretical concept of the capitalist mode of production and the national or international economies, politics and social formations under analysis. The other—if anything more persistent and fundamental—involves a form of system teleology or functionalism. (Booth 1985: 773)

Booth relied on a critique developed by former structural Marxists Barry Hindess and Paul Hirst (1975, 1977; Cutler et al. 1977–1978) that Marx read the characteristics of social formations from the laws of motion of the capitalist mode of production. Hindess and Hirst objected to the idea that social totalities had necessary effects inscribed in their structures. Booth found this to be a telling criticism of Marxist development theory. Either development problems were explained by their particular insertion into international capitalism, or socioeconomic processes took local forms that contributed to the wider process of capitalist accumulation. For Booth, ideas like these persisted because social scientists were seduced by notions of system teleology—for example, they wanted to discover deeper, more teleological, more functional reasons for development problems. In common with Giddens (1981) and following Hindess and Hirst, Booth found this damaging to Marxism's intellectual standing. Functionalism reified certain social institutions, placing them by metatheoretical fiat further beyond human control than they could empirically be shown to be. Booth argued that this was socially and politically corrupting. It was wrong to pretend that functional claims were explanatory in sociology—for example, Booth doubted the existence of feedback mechanisms of the type claimed by functionalism, whether Parsonian or Marxian. All this, he said, accounted for the repetitive, noncumulative character of the dependency literature, the forcing of Marxist theory along restricted lines, and its failure to systematically explore urgent empirical issues. The rich complexity of reality, Booth concluded, could not be captured by the "theoretical nonsense" of the simple "laws of motion" of a system.

Further criticisms soon followed. Peter Vandergeest and Frederick Buttell (1988) of Cornell University criticized neo-Marxist theories from a Weberian perspective. Weber had criticized Marx for assuming that theoretical constructs, like mode of production, were empirically valid to the point of being "real," whereas they were actually just "ideal types." Neo-Weberian Marxists instead constructed generalizations from grounded historical work and insisted on a continuing dialogue between theory and empirical evidence. For Vandergeest and Buttell, a synthesis of Weber and neo-Marxism would reconceptualize formal models as (Weberian) ideal types which, they explained, might be used for understanding, but not explaining. They wished to discard some of the materialist tenets of historical materialism, like the base–superstructure metaphor, while modifying Weber—for example, by replacing the notion of rational disenchantment of the world with comparative analyses of types of rationalization and derationalization. The Marxist conception of power would be broadened to include more varied kinds, while power itself would be reinterpreted as liberating and productive. Neo-Marxism's impoverished theory of the Third World state would be broadened to include theories of modern bureaucracy (from Weber) or reconceptualized to see the state as enabling and not just repressive (as with the social theorist Karl Polanyi [1944]). The incorporation of culture into a new neo-Weberian approach to development would look at how social groups (e.g., ethnic, class, or gender) viewed their worlds. Neo-Weberianism rendered the notion of "obstacles" to development irrelevant. For Vandergeest and Buttell, development studies should deal with subjects whose behavior could not be fully understood. They preferred an agenda emphasizing empowerment and participation. In brief, they did not reject neo-Marxist development sociology but wished to augment it with neo-Weberian ideas.

However, the outstanding critique of dependency and world systems theories came from a historian who remained in the Marxist camp. For Robert Brenner (1977), an entire line of Marxists and neo-Marxists intending to negate the optimistic model of economic advance derived from Adam Smith (i.e., widening trade and a deeper division of labor bringing economic development) ended up with a theory that was the mirror image of Smith's model. Frank found the dynamic of capitalist expansion to reside in the rise of a world commercial network, with growth or backwardness originating in the surplus appropriation chain. Wallerstein carried this idea to its logical conclusion by defining capitalism as production for profit via exchange and focusing on the expansion of the world market. With this market came a world division of labor, the development of different methods of labor control in the various specialized zones, and the creation of strong and weak states in core and periphery. For Brenner, both kinds of analyses erred by displacing class relations from the main body of development theory. Brenner argued that the incorporation of more productive resources into the world system did not determine the economic development process, nor did the transfer of surplus and buildup of wealth in the core, nor even specialization of labor control systems. Capitalism differed from all previous societies in its systematic tendency to economic development. This was achieved through increasing labor productivity, which made it possible for workers to reproduce themselves in less time than previously, and thus make a larger surplus ("relative surplus labor," in Marx's terms). By comparison, precapitalist societies were confined to extending absolute labor, for example, by lengthening the working day, gaining control over more workers, and the like. Under capitalist social relations, workers were free to be combined with machines at the highest possible level of technology, while competition forced capitalists to innovate. Capitalist development thus derived from the class structure of the economy as a whole, exactly the position ignored by Frank and Wallerstein, according to Brenner. Brenner's political conclusion was that while Frank's "circulationist" argument could be construed as arguing merely for regional autonomy (i.e., development could be achieved through cutting lines of surplus outflow), he himself argued instead for changing the relations of production in favor of a new class system characterized by efficiency but also equity. With this, neo-Marxist development theory was thrown back in the direction of a more classically Marxist position centered on class rather than space.

Soon after Brenner penned these words (in the late 1970s), Marxism in its classical sense as well as in its neo-Marxist versions came in for even more criticism as politics, philosophy, and theory of development. The decline and eventual fall of the Soviet Union left a political field so dominated by neoliberalism that the conservative thinker Francis Fukuyama (1989) could proclaim "the end of history" in the sense of an end to any alternative to capitalism. Broad changes in critical intellectual culture were marked generally by a retreat from radicalism. What was taken for granted in one decade became unmentionable in the next. Development alternatives stemming from critical liberal, dependency, and socialist sources, for example, notions of relative autonomy from the global system, using local productive resources to meet basic needs, the belief that the state should direct the economy toward developmental objectives, were dropped from development discourse as naively irrelevant. The intellectual groundwork for this transformation in economic policy was prepared by a barrage of criticisms aimed at the epistemology and social ontology of Marxism, the leading alternative philosophy to neoliberal theory. Historical materialism was called, among other things, "economistic" (the economy determines everything), "functionalist" (functions automatically produce human actions), "totalistic" (things have significance only in terms of their place within overarching structures), "totalitarian" (the whole taking precedence over the part justifies suppressing the individual), and "teleological" (history has a predetermined end). Marxists replied that the notion of structural inevitability read into Marxism was largely a figment of the critics' imagination—for example, it ignored the many empirical studies using the concept of articulation of modes of production (Long 1975; Post 1978; Rey 1973; Watts 1983). Far from elaborating utter structural necessities while leaving the empirical details of history and geography to be "read off" objective laws of motion, Marx's own work, and the work of Marxist theorists, show a rich complexity of structural necessity and contingent freedoms, so that historical events fit into contradictory structures, yet result also from local, specific actions. Indeed, the dialectic between necessity and freedom lies at the heart of materialist analysis. Non-Marxists, or very simple mechanical Marxists, have a nondialectical conception of structural determination, in which structures mechanically cause things to happen, stamping out events like a machine stamps out spare parts. Dialectical structuralism is nothing like these simple caricatures—as this chapter abundantly demonstrates.

Dependency theory counters the notion that European development derives, exclusively or mainly, from European sources. The theory played an important role in the critique of conventional theories—whether the theory of comparative advantage in mainstream economics or modernization theory in mainstream developmental sociology. It accounted for the historical experiences of the peoples of peripheral societies by proposing, in opposition, that contact with capitalism led to underdevelopment rather than to development. The notion of dependent development more accurately describes the experiences of East Asian and Latin American countries than neoliberal economic theory. Dependency theory opened our eyes and made us see the world from the perspective of oppressed peoples living in its "distant" corners. This was quite a contribution.

Chapter 5

POSTSTRUCTURALISM, POSTCOLONIALISM, AND POSTDEVELOPMENTALISM

B etween the mid-1960s and the early 1980s, critical thinking about development was dominated by Marxist and neo- Marxist theories. Dependency theory and world systems theory were primary areas of debate in the late 1960s and for much of the 1970s. Marxist structuralism and articulations of modes of production were particularly important for radical thinking about development in the Anglo-American intellectual world of the late 1970s and early 1980s. With the easy wisdom of hindsight, we can see structural and systemic theories as culminating triumphs of radical modern social philosophy. These highly generalized theories tried to position every historical event, and place each social characteristic, as a component of some more general, overarching system, be it mode of production, world capitalist system, or global market. The aim was a systematic theory of social totalities and their parts with nothing unexplained or left to chance, although some aspects might have to be examined empirically. For the true structuralist, empirical analysis was an admission of theoretical failure.

However, the notion of structures and totalities came under increasing suspicion—in the sense both of societies as wholes and of theories as holistic explanations—in the 1970s and early 1980s. Critical theorizing began to assume various *post*structural forms, particularly in France during the 1970s, with these philosophies spreading to Britain and the United States in the 1980s, and coming into full intellectual prominence in the 1990s. The appearance of Edward Said's *Orientalism* in 1979 was a significant moment in the application of poststructural ideas to the relations between the First and the Third Worlds. And from the mid-1980s on, poststructural ideas influenced critical developmental and even postdevelopmental thought.

Some poststructural thinkers continued structural themes in new applications. The French poststructural sociologist Jean Baudrillard (1983) argued that structures took novel forms—for example, a structural shift had occurred from mode of production to code of production—and that signs and cultural codes, rather than the forces and relations of material production, were the primary constituents of social life. According to Baudrillard, we live in a "hyperreality" of simulations, in which image, spectacle, and the play of signs have replaced the logic of production. But many other poststructural thinkers saw events erupting spontaneously from a far more anarchic world than structuralism had suggested. Theirs was a world of discontinuities rather than continuities, of complexity rather than structural simplicity. Whereas structuralism saw transcendent systems lending significance to the individual, many poststructualists wanted to return significance to the singular person or event. Whereas structuralism, in its critical forms, usually employed economic languages to criticize capitalism, poststructuralism used cultural language to criticize modernity. Whereas structuralism saw potential for human emancipation in modern development, poststructuralism saw development as a strategy of modern power and social control. These and other markers indicated a divide in critical social thought as wide, some said, as that between premodern and modern thought; hence the notion of a *post*modern era of thought and culture, characterized by disillusionment and loss of faith in modern metanarratives (great stories) like truth, emancipation, democracy, revolution, and development (Lyotard 1984). For the postmodern theorist, it was as though the Enlightenment and its progeny had finally been laid to rest and a new era had begun.

The Enlightenment and Its Critics

The philosophies that characterized the modern Western world, from Descartes, through the Enlightenment thinkers of the eighteenth century, to the scientific positivists of the nineteenth century, and finally to the modernization theorists of the twentieth, saw human reason and rational behavior as the mainsprings of social progress. Thought in careful, empirically based, but also logical and deductive, forms intervened productively between human beings and the rest of the natural world. Reasoned thinking produced science and technology, which led to new sources of material progress and human well-being; science replaced religion as mode of understanding; happiness on earth now replaced heavenly salvation in the afterlife as the reason for living. Modernists believed that by examining the lessons of experience, social norms, values, and morals could be humanly reasoned, rather than magically divined from the whispered hints of God's mysterious intent. Hence morality could be accepted as just, right, and reasonable by all thoughtful, responsible people. By synthesizing science with morality, a normative science could act on behalf of humanity, enabling emancipation from nature and want, and from superstition and ignorance. People could act rationally in all aspects of their lives. In a phrase, for the modernist, reason made possible science, which enabled development on behalf of humanity.

The philosophers of the Enlightenment considered all people to be "indefinitely perfectible." Everyone was capable of self-guidance solely by the light of reason. And "reason is the same for all thinking subjects, all nations, all epochs, and all cultures" (Cassirer 1951: 5, 13–14). In geographical terms, according to the modernists, reason and the freedom from nature that it brought had reached their highest, most developed forms in Europe. In *Sketch for an Historical Picture of the Progress of the Human Mind* the radical Enlightenment philosopher Antoine-Nicolas de Condorcet said:

> Our hopes for the future condition of the human race can be subsumed under three important heads: the abolition of inequality between nations, the progress of equality within each nation, and the true perfection of mankind. Will all nations one day attain that state of civilization which the most enlightened, the freest, and the least burdened by prejudice, such as the French and the Anglo-Americans, have attained already? Will the vast gulf that separates these peoples from the slavery of nations under the rule of monarchs, from the barbarism of African tribes, from the ignorance of savages, little by little disappear? . . . These vast lands . . . need only assistance from us to become civilized [and] wait only to find brothers amongst the European nations to become their friends and pupils. (de Condorcet 1972: 141)

An Enlightenment map of the world saw global space divided between a center of reason, knowledge, and wisdom in Western Europe and a periphery of ignorance, barbarity, and only potential reason elsewhere. The "idea of progress," which social theorist Theodore Shanin (1997: 65) argues is the main legacy of modernity, envisaged all societies advancing "up" a route leading from diverse barbarisms to a singular, European-style rationalized democracy. Europe was destined to lead the world. But its enlightened generosity should be demonstrated by helping others ("our pupils"). And with this, poststructuralists claim, the democratic Enlightenment turned into its opposite, oppressive Rationalism, the conception of a teleologically directed history and a predestined geography, with European reason at the heart of the human endeavor.

Poststructural philosophy revealed the flaws in this modern, confident stream of thought. Poststructural thinking, especially in its more extreme postmodern forms, emphasized the other side of rational modernity, its peasant, female, and colonized victims; its disciplinary institutions (schools, prisons, psychiatric clinics); and the sacrifice of spontaneity, emotion, and pleasure suppressed under rational control—the idea that modern people suffered by continually scrutinizing the emotional upsurge of pleasurable, free behavior through the lenses of logic, thought, and rationalized ethics. In poststructural philosophy, modern reason was reinterpreted critically as a mode of social control that acted openly through disciplinary institutions; that worked in more disguised forms through rationalized socialization; and, most subtly, that operated seditiously through rational self-discipline. In the *poststructural* view, modern philosophy's claim to universal truth was practically impossible. The poststructural philosopher Richard Rorty, of the University of Virginia, criticized modern theories of "representational truth," in which systems of symbols (statements, theories, models) accurately reflected ("mirrored") real and separate structures of events. In poststructural thinking, by comparison, representational theories of truth at best provided perspectives seen from the views of particular thinkers. For poststructural philosophy, especially the French philosopher Jacques Derrida, the relations between reality and mind were not direct, and therefore objectively accurate ("truthful"), but instead were linguistically mediated and historically specific. Poststructuralism attacked the central tenets of modern progress: reason, truth, accuracy (Best and Kellner 1991). The postmodern end of poststructural theory abandoned the notion of the rational, unified subject in favor of a socially and linguistically decentered and fragmented subject, the notion of multiple identities.

In particular, as Robert Young (1990: 9), of Oxford University, pointed out, a special interest of French poststructural philosophy concerned the relation between the universal truth claims of the Enlightenment and the universalization of European power. The new stress on this relation, he said, had stimulated a "relentless anatomization of the collusive forms of European knowledge." Especially important is the geophilosophical notion buried in Western modernity that European thinking was universal reason—for example, that classical economics, born from a particular conjuncture of European history, was a universal economic science capable of guiding development the world over. Added to this notion was the normative expectation that copying European rationality was good for everyone, what all people *should* do. Hence Derrida (1971: 213) said: "The white man takes his own mythology, Indo-European mythology, his own *logos*, that is, the *mythos* of his idiom, for the universal form of that he must still wish to call Reason." In brief, poststructural and postmodern criticism considered "reason" to be a historical and regional form of thought rather than a universal potential.

Marxism has either been seen as an integral component of Enlightenment rationalism or as its most persistent critique. On the one side, there were elements in Marxist thought that conformed to Enlightenment principles—for instance, development as the growth of the forces of production guided by rationality. On the other side, there were aspects of Marxism confounding the Enlightenment, as with the notion of rationalism as an ideology serving the interests of a ruling class. Both of these positions clearly had significant content. So Marxism can be seen as modernist, but in a highly critical form—that is, sharing modernism's optimistic belief in the potential of science and technology to bring a better life for humanity, but pessimistic about the misuse of this potential in societies ridden with class and gender inequalities. As a result, critical thought at the turn of the millennium can be divided into critical modernism on the one side and critical poststructuralism and postmodernism on the other, with debate between the two positions focused particularly on the vexing question of development. Is development yet another European mechanism to control the world, or is it capable of transcending this origin to offer hope for poor and downtrodden peoples? The present chapter debates this question.

Post-Enlightenment Criticisms

Modern, rational thinking, with its secular beliefs and scientific attitudes, has continually encountered resistance. It cannot be automatically assumed that modern rationalism is so clearly the final, superior form of thought that everyone immediately succumbs to its logical charms, like lost sailors hearing the Sirens' call. Nor should the finest product of rationality, the plentitude of modern life, with its high mass consumption, its ability to match even the most trivial (consumptive) whim, be seen as capable of satisfying all with its seductive, sedative, selfish appeal. Even as modernist rationality initially formed, opposition to it was encountered from philosophers like Giovanni Battista Vico (1668–1744), who defended the irrational forces creating human nature and common sense (Vico 1984). Likewise, the poet–philosopher Friedrich Nietzsche (1844–1900) thought that "truths are illusions we have forgotten are illusions" and "truth is the kind of error without which a certain kind of being could not live" (Nietzsche 1968: 493). Modern life, Nietzsche said, was compelled to found itself on the unquestioned principles of spirit, progress, and truth. Yet the modern world brought an impoverishment of experience to the degree that people no longer found meaning or truth (Clark 1990: 1–3). Likewise, the phenomenology of Edmund Husserl (1859–1938) criticized modern rationalism's intellectual product, the realist, empiricist, and scientific positivism of the nineteenth century (Husserl 1970: 5–6). Empirical science's inability to provide answers for normative, evaluative questions created a cultural crisis in modern life. For Husserl, science as knowledge of the objectively real relegated the "life-world" (the world as experienced in everyday, prescientific activities) to the inferior status of subjective appearance. Instead, Husserl wanted to unearth the experiential roots of all thoughts in their original, intentional contact with real phenomena. Husserl wanted phenomenology to rediscover the radical, primary foundations of all knowledge as the basis of a new kind of science.

Similarly, the existential phenomenologist Martin Heidegger (1889–1976) searched for a radical foundation, not only for knowledge (as with Husserl), but also for the qualities of being human. Heidegger's best-known work, *Being and Time* (1962), argued that philosophy had to arise from, and return to, the whole existence, and not come merely from the disengaged attitude of knowing (i.e., humans as disembodied rational consciousnesses). He saw the history of Western philosophy as one long misinterpretation of the nature of reality, inevitable once the detached standpoint of theoretical reflection was adopted (i.e., stepping back to get an impartial, objective view of things), for then the world went dead, that is, things lost their meaningfulness. Following the lead of "life philosophy," an influential school of thought at the turn of the nineteenth century (Nietzsche, Henri Bergson, Wilhelm Dilthey), Heidegger hoped to recover an original sense of things by setting aside the view of reality derived from abstract theorizing and focusing instead on the ways things showed up in the flux of everyday, prereflective activities. For Heidegger, the meaning of being (i.e., the basis of intelligibility) was an "absence of ground," or an "abyss," in that there was no *ultimate* foundation for the holistic web of meaning that made up being-in-the-world. In his "Letter on Humanism" Heidegger (1977) took these arguments against modern certainty a step further by criticizing the Enlightenment project of emancipation as the subjection of nature through the mastery of rational will; for Heidegger, the (ultimately insecure) modern subject manipulated an objective world, dominating nature according to his or her own (subjective) priorities. This fundamental critique of modern humanism passed into poststructural and postmodern thought through the antihumanism of the French philosopher Michel Foucault (1926–1984).

Power–Truth–Knowledge

Foucault shared with Nietzsche a fascination with the power–truth–knowledge complex and with Husserl and Heidegger a critical attitude toward modern rationalism. Foucault saw reason saturating life, intruding the gaze of rationality into every nook and cranny of existence, with science classifying and thereby regulating all forms of experience. Foucault launched two kinds of attack on the philosophy of modern, rational humanism. First, he argued that modern reason metaphysically grounded an image of universal humanity on traits that were culturally specific (to the Europeans). Second, he maintained that the values and emancipatory ideals of the Enlightenment (autonomy, freedom, human rights) were ideological bases for a normalizing discipline that imposed an "appropriate identity" on modern people. Like the Frankfurt school Marxists Max Horkheimer and Theodore Adorno, writing in *Dialectic of Enlightenment* (1991), Foucault believed modern rationality to be a coercive force focused on the minds of individuals. In analyzing this rationality, he employed a method different from that of the Marxists which, after Nietzsche, he called "genealogy."

Genealogy involved diagnosing relations of power, knowledge, discourse, and the body in modern society. Genealogy was opposed to most modern methods of inquiry in that it claimed to recognize no fixed essences or underlying laws, sought discontinuities rather than the great continuities in history, avoided searching for depth, and sought out and recorded forgotten dimensions of the past. The genealogist found hidden meanings, heights of truth, and depths of consciousness to be shams of the modern imagination; instead, genealogy's truth was that things had no essence (Foucault 1972: 142). Whenever genealogy heard of original truths, it looked for the play of power-driven wills; when talk turned to meaning, value, goodness, or virtue, the genealogist heard tales of domination; instead of explicit human intentionality, the genealogist found abstract force relations worked out in specific instances. For the genealogist, there was no conscious rational subject moving history forward. Instead, events came from the play of forces in any situation. History was not the progress of universal reason but, rather, humanity moving from one form of domination to another.

Foucault (1972; 1973) was particularly interested in the careful, rationalized, organized statements made by experts—what he called "discourses." In *The Archaeology of Knowledge* (1972) Foucault saw the human sciences as autonomous, rule-governed systems of discourse. Within these discourses, Foucault claimed to discover a previously unnoticed type of linguistic function, the "serious speech act," or statements with validation procedures made within communities of experts (Dreyfus and Rabinow 1983: 45–47). Foucault was interested in the various types of serious speech acts, the regularities they exhibited in "discursive formations," and the transformations these formations underwent. Discursive formations had internal systems of rules determining what was said about which objects. Foucault called the setting that decides whether statements count as real knowledge the epistemological field, or *episteme*. So by *episteme* he meant the set of relations between discursive practices in a given period that created formalized systems of knowledge (Foucault 1973: 191). Discourses had systematic structures that could be analyzed archaeologically (identifying their main elements and the relations that form these into wholes) and genealogically (how discourses were formed by nondiscursive, social practices, especially by institutions of power).

Modern discourses were founded on appeals to truth. Yet, for Foucault, modern Western knowledge was integrally involved in the clash of dominations. For Foucault, knowledge did not detach itself from its practical, empirical roots to become pure speculation, subject only to the demands of reason. Rather truth, power, and knowledge operated in mutually generative ways:

> Truth is not outside of power. . . . Each society has its own regime of truth, its general politics of truth. . . . There is a combat for the truth, or at least around the truth, as long as we understand by the truth not those true things which are waiting to be discovered but rather the ensemble of rules according to which we distinguish the true from the false, and attach special effects of power to "the truth." (Foucault 1980a: 131)

Foucault argued that modern "biopower" emerged as a coherent political technology in the seventeenth century, when the fostering of life and the growth and care of populations became central concerns of the early modern state. Systematic empirical investigation of historical, geographical, and demographic conditions engendered the modern human sciences. Their aim, for Foucault, was not human emancipation, but the making of docile yet productive bodies (Dreyfus and Rabinow 1983).

In two lectures given in 1976, Foucault (1980a: 78–108) stressed certain aspects of genealogy particularly interesting for the question of development. For Foucault, thinking in terms of totalities reflected an urge for theoretical unity, but it also curtailed and caricatured local research. Instead he favored autonomous, noncentralized theorization that did not depend for its validity on gaining approval from established regimes of thought. He favored local knowledge, the "return of [forgotten] knowledge," an insurrection of subjugated knowledges, blocs of historical knowledges usually disqualified as inadequate, naive, mythical, beneath the required level of scientificity. By resurrecting histories of local struggles and subjugated knowledges, Foucault thought that critical discourse could discover new essential forces. Genealogy undertook the rediscovery and reconstruction of the forgotten, a task that would not be possible unless the tyranny of globalizing discourses (e.g., monoeconomics, modernization, modes of production) was first eliminated. Genealogies, then, were antisciences, opposed not necessarily to the concepts of science, but opposed to the effects of organized scientific discourses linked to centralized power systems. In Foucault's words, "It is really against the effects of the power of a discourse that is considered to be scientific that genealogy must wage its struggle" (1980a: 84). By genealogy, Foucault (1980a: 83) also meant "the union of erudite knowledge and local memories which allows us to establish a historical knowledge of struggles and to make use of this knowledge tactically today." In genealogy, Foucault examined anew the multiple relations of domination. For him, these were not global kinds of domination, that is, one large group of people over others, center over periphery, but multiple forms of domination, exercised in many different forms: power in its regional and local forms and institutions; power at levels other than conscious intention; power as something that circulated or functioned in the form of chains and networks; power starting from the infinitesimal personal relations, and then colonized by ever more general mechanisms into forms of global domination; power exercised through the formation and accumulation of knowledge. In brief, the interactions between power, knowledge, and discourse were the province of Foucault's genealogy.

According to Foucault, The control of space was an essential constituent of the modern, disciplinary technologies (Philo 1992). In modernity, space took the form of grids (vertical and horizontal lines) with slots or positions on the grid assigned values; individuals were placed in preordered, disciplinary spaces, for example, with military hospitals, factories, classrooms with numbered desks, suburbs ranked by socioeconomic status, or for that matter countries placed in tables according to GNP/capita. Discipline "made" individuals through this kind of distribution in space, by training, through hierarchical observation, through normalizing judgment, examination, documentation, with help from the human (social) sciences (i.e., psychology, anthropology, sociology, geography). The phrase "academic discipline" was no accident: for Foucault, the academy was linked with the spread of disciplinary technologies in the same matrix of power.

Foucault believed all global theories, such as modernization theory, Marxist mode of production theory, or world systems theory, to be reductionist (reducing complexity to a few tendencies), universalistic (making everyone and everything the same), coercive (implying force), and even totalitarian (implying total control). He attempted to "detotalize" history and society as wholes governed by a central essence, whether production in Marxism, World Spirit in Hegelian idealism, or progress in modernization theory. As opposed to existential phenomenology he decentered the subject as a consciousness constituting the world, and instead saw people as socially constructed identities. Society was understood in terms of unevenly developing discourses. Whereas modern theories of human emancipation drew on broad, essential themes to reach macropolitical solutions—for example, solving world poverty through Western intervention—Foucault respected difference and favored micropolitics, allowing people the freedom to define and solve their own problems (Best and Kellner 1991; Peet 1998).

Postcolonialism

This extreme skepticism about the Western project of reason, truth, and progress, formulated mainly in Paris, paradoxically at the center of the Enlightenment world, intersected with an increasingly sophisticated critique coming from intellectuals from the previously colonial countries, ironically often from scholars who had lived, or who had been partly educated, in the West. These thinkers spoke from hybrid, in-between positions, drawing on several traditions of thought, including Western reason and poststructural criticism, revealing a number of conflicting experiences in a critical discourse that came to be known as "postcolonialism."

Postcolonial criticism now occupies a prominent position in a number of disciplines, such as modern languages, literature, history, sociology, anthropology, and geography. In the words of the Princeton historian Gyan Prakash (1994: 1475), the idea of postcolonial criticism was to compel "a radical rethinking of knowledge and social identities authored and authorized by colonialism and Western domination." According to Prakash, previous criticisms of colonialism had failed to break free from Eurocentric discourses. For example, Third World nationalism attributed agency to the subjected nation, yet staked its own claim to colonialism's order of Reason and Progress. Or, in another example, Marxist criticism was framed theoretically by a historical schema (modes of production) that universalized Europe's experience. The postcolonial critique, by comparison, sought to undo Europe's appropriation of the Other (the non-European) within the realization that its own critical apparatus existed in the aftermath of colonialism. Following Derrida, it could be said that postcolonial criticism "inhabited" the structures of Western domination it sought to undo. More complexly, postcolonial literatures resulted from an interchange between imperial culture and the complex of indigenous cultural practices, the idea being that imperialism was, in part, resisted, eroded, and even supplanted in hybrid processes of cultural interaction (Ashcroft et al. 1995).

Postcolonial criticism began with the writings of the West Indian/ Algerian psychoanalyst of culture Frantz Fanon in his well-known book *The Wretched of the Earth* (1968), but also in the lesser known *Black Skin, White Masks* (1986). Fanon's bitter, violent words forced European readers to rethink their experiences in relation to the history of the colonies then awakening from "the cruel stupor and abused immobility of imperial domination" (Said 1989: 223). Fanon's challenges to fixed ideas of settled identity and culturally authored definition were part of a broader convergence between the critical study of colonialism and a renewed interest in the recurring topic of subject formation—that is, how peoples' identities were formed (Gates 1991). Here Fanon drew from the French structural psychoanalyst Jacques Lacan the idea that the ego (conscious self) was permanently schismatic. The infant's "mirror stage" (when the child saw its behavior reflected in the imitative gestures of an other, discovered "that is me") was thought, by Lacan, to be deceptive, for the mirror was a decoy, producing mirages rather than images. Hence ego construction, for Lacan, was an alienated process and the resulting individual was permanently discordant with himself or herself (Bowie 1991). Third World intellectuals turned Lacan's ego theory into a critique of the certainty of the Western, rational identity. Thus Fanon thought that the black person, the Other (not-self) for the white European, was unidentifiable and unassimilable, a confusing mirage, a hallucination rather than a confirming mirror image. Conversely, he maintained, the historical and economic realities of colonialism formed the more accurate basis of the (white) Other for a more securely defined black identity (Fanon 1986: 161). In the postcolonial literature the argument was subsequently made by Homi Bhabha (1986) that Fanon too quickly named a singular Third World Other to the First World Same; but others countered that Fanon's conqueror–native relation was an accurate representation of a profound global conflict. From such differences derived a number of postcolonial positions, all stressing contacts between Europe and the civilizations of the rest of the world, but differing over similarity or variability in this set of experiences (among many other things).

Postcolonialism has usually been said to begin in a more organized way with the work of the "subaltern studies group" in the early 1980s—"subaltern" meaning subordinate in terms of class, caste, gender, race, and culture (Guha and Spivak 1988). One of the founders of this group, the Indian theorist Ranajit Guha (1983: 2–3), thought that elitist bias in colonial historiography denied peasants recognition as subjects of history. Acknowledging peasants as makers of rebellions, by comparison, meant attributing to them a consciousness (cf. Gramsci 1971). Guha tried to identify the (recurring) elementary aspects of such a rebel consciousness as part of a "recovery of the peasant subject," his argument being that subaltern peoples acted on their own, with autonomous politics, in forms of sociality and community different from nation or class, which therefore defied the conventional models of rationality used by Western historians. However, the postcolonial critic Gayatri Spivak (1987: 206–207) later saw subaltern studies' attempts at retrieving a subaltern, or peasant, consciousness as a strategic adherence to essentialist and humanistic notions, like consciousness, derived originally from the European Enlightenment. As long as such Western, modernist notions of subjectivity and consciousness were left unexamined, she said, the subaltern would be narrativized in what only appeared to be theoretically alternative ways (MacCabe 1987: xv). Spivak's own alternative involved the structural notion of "subject positions," in which the "subject," of a statement, for example, was not the immediate author, but instead the "author" was "a particular, vacant place that may in fact be filled by different individuals" (Foucault 1972: 95; see also Foucault 1980b: 196–197). With this idea Spivak sought to reinscribe the many, often contradictory, subject positions assigned by multiple colonial relations of control and insurgency, so that a subaltern woman, for example, was subjected to three main domination systems: class, ethnicity, and gender. From this she reached the extreme position that subaltern woman had no coherent subject position from which to speak: "The subaltern cannot speak" (Spivak 1988: 308). Her argument was that in straining for a voice of indigenous resistance, critics of colonialism succumbed to the romantic quest for a transparent "real" voice of the native, one that might give trustworthy evidence in the Western sense of "presence"—the sureness of knowledge gained by being on the spot. Like Bhabha (1986), she was critical of simple "binary" (twofold) oppositions, like colonizer/colonized, and wanted to explore the heterogeneity of colonial powers. Yet notice that Spivak herself drew on a central notion (subject positions) from the (Western) poststructural theorist Michel Foucault!

Another main source of postcolonial ideas was the Palestinian literary critic Edward Said's (1979: 2; 1993) notion of orientalism, a "mode of discourse with supporting institutions, vocabulary, scholarship, imagery, doctrines, even colonial bureaucracies and colonial styles" through which European culture "produced" the Orient (politically, imaginatively) in the post-Enlightenment period. Said used Foucault's notion of discourse to look at the political and cultural dimensions of interregional power relations, arguing that binary oppositions, such as East/West, determined all interactions between Europeans and other peoples. Said argued that constructed notions of "the Orient" helped define a contrasting image of Europe as its spatial and cultural Other. Also, because orientalist discourse limited thought, the Orient was not, and is not, a free subject of thought or action. In this sense Said found localities, regions, and geographical sectors, like "Orient" (East) and "Occident" (West), to be humanly "made." So we could ask, "Whose East was that?" (East of what?). Similar was the British theorist Benedict Anderson's (1983: 13–15) view that nationalisms were cultural artifacts or, more generally, that all human groupings larger than primordial villages of face-to-face contact were "imagined communities." Subsequent work extended these "discourses on the Other" to histories of the different European conceptions ("science fictions") of "alien cultures" (McGrane 1989; Hulme 1986; Todorov 1984). Such conceptions, or imaginaries, became perhaps the most significant bases of the new approach to culture and postcolonialism (Ashcroft et al. 1989; Bhabha 1994; Spivak 1988). In this vein we find a number of sophisticated analyses of the psychology of imperialism and colonialism, for example, critical admissions of the appeal of the idea of modernity for progressive Third World intellectuals (Nandy 1983).

For the Lacanian theorist Homi Bhabha (1983: 19; 1986), who teaches at the University of Chicago, representations of the Orient in Western discourse evidenced profound ambivalence toward "that otherness which is at once an object of dislike and derision." Colonial discourse, for Bhabha, was founded more on anxiety than on arrogance, and colonial power had a conflictual structure. Hence colonial stereo typing of subject peoples was complex, ambivalent, and contradictory as a form of representation, as anxious as it was assertive. So, for example, in an analysis of mimicry, Bhabha (1984) argued that when colonized people become "European" the resemblance was both familiar and menacing to the colonists, and subverted their identities rather than confirming them. The hybrid that articulated colonial and native knowledges might reverse the process of domination as repressed knowledges entered subliminally, enabling subversion, intervention, and resistance. Similarly, for Baudet (1965: vii), "The European's images of non-

European man are not primarily, if at all, descriptions of real people, but rather projections of his own nostalgia and feelings of inadequacy."

Thus the term "postcolonialism" filled a gap left by the abandonment of the phrase "Third World" within (poststructural) progressive circles. As Shohat (1992: 101) noted, "The notion of the three worlds . . . flattens heterogeneities, masks contradictions, and elides differences." Historical, literary, and psychoanalytical postcolonial work was unified around an examination of the impact of colonial discourses on subjectivity, knowledge, and power. Postcolonial writing stressed the mutuality of the colonial process; rather than colonialism obliterating or silencing the colonized, distinctive aspects of the culture of the oppressed survived in the hybrid cultures of postcolonial societies. Postcoloniality marked a contemporary state, condition, or epoch, with the prefix "post" designating a movement beyond colonialism and Third World nationalist struggles in two senses: in terms of the chronologies of time and in terms of intellectual history. In particular, for Ella Shohat, of the College of Staten Island, the postcolonial

> forms a critical locus for moving beyond anti-colonial nationalist modernizing narratives that inscribe Europe as an object of critique, towards a discursive analysis and historiography addressing decentered multiplicities of power relations (for example, between colonized women and men, or between colonized peasantry and the bourgeoisie). . . . The foregrounding of "hybridity" and "syncretism" in postcolonial studies calls attention to the multiple imbrication of "central" and "peripheral" cultures. "Hybridity" and "syncretism" allow negotiation of the multiplicity of identities and subject positionings which result from displacements, immigrations and exiles without policing the borders of identity along essentialist and originary lines. (1992: 106–108)

Shohat usefully continued by noting that the key term "hybridity" could also become a catchall term that failed to discriminate between diverse types. She argued that while hybridity had to be examined in a nonuniversalizing manner, the cultural inquiry generated by this set of ideas needed relinking with geopolitical macrolevel analyses of, for example, the global ubiquity of Anglo-American informational media. Indeed, she found replacing the term "Third World" with "postcolonial" to be a liability, because the former contained a common project of linked resistance to neocolonialisms, whereas this sense of commonality was missing in the latter.

Other critics have found the term "postcolonial" overly fashionable and a mishmash of confusing elements that overemphasized textual (discursive) relations at the expense of other power relations (Goss 1996:

244). For Arif Dirlik (1994), of Duke University, the popularity of the term "postcolonial" "has less to do with its rigorousness as a concept or with the new vistas it has opened up for critical inquiry than it does with the increased visibility of academic intellectuals of Third World origin as pacesetters in cultural criticism." Even so, postcolonial projects have promoted agency and subjectivity, forces missing in many studies of colonialism. What some have called "the decolonization of the imagination" involved an act of exorcism for both the colonizers and the colonized, while the view of the world that emerged was less cast in terms of cultural imperialism than as a global melange (Pieterese and Parekha 1995: 1–19). Yet the term "postcolonial," while increasingly widespread, needs interrogating and contextualizing, historically, geopolitically, and culturally. This is a complex area of writing and research, one that nonetheless forms one of the mainsprings of a renewed (poststructural and anti-Eurocentric) criticism of key Western notions of progress and development.

Intellectual Dependency Theory

Additionally it has been argued that, since the colonial encounter, the economic hegemony of the West has been paralleled by academic dependence in which Third World intellectuals, trained in Western knowledge, spoke the colonial language, and stressed the history of the colonizer over that of the colonized—for example, African students studying British history for their A-level examinations. More than that, the Third World was made dependent on the First World for knowledge about itself. Academic dependency entailed the export of raw data from the Third World to the First, where its surplus (generalized knowledge) was released, fashioned into theories, and exported back to the Third World as pearls of wisdom (Weeks 1990). The conditions of this intellectual dependency system included control of global research funds and scholarly journals by center institutions, together with the prestige accruing to those who published in international journals, or were in contact with scholars in Europe or the United States.

Since the early 1970s, arguments have been made about the captive minds of Third World scholars, minds that were too uncritical and imitative of concepts coming from the West:

> Mental captivity . . . refers to a way of thinking that is dominated by Western thought in an imitative and uncritical manner. Among the characteristics of the captive mind are the inability to be creative and raise original problems, the inability to devise original analytical meth-

ods, and alienation from the main issues of indigenous society. (Alatas 1993: 308)

In response, some Third World scholars called for the "indigenization" of social science, indeed the indigenization of academic discourse as a whole. Social scientific indigenization went beyond modifying Western concepts and methods to make them more suitable for non-Western problems. It referred instead to deriving scientific theories, concepts, and methodologies from the histories, cultures, and consciousness of non-Western civilizations. For the University of Singapore sociologist S. F. Alatas (1993: 310–311) the eventual aim was to develop bodies of social scientific knowledge in which theories were derived from culturally and historically specific experiences. These, however, would not be restricted in application to the society or civilization from which they were drawn. He differentiated his approach from "nativism," the tendency for Western and local scholars to "go native" and reject Western science entirely. Instead, Alatas favored encountering, modifying, and combining Western theories with indigenous ones. For him, "the call to indigenization is simultaneously a call to the universalization of the social sciences" (Alatas 1993: 312; see also Amin 1989).

Positions such as this were not without problems, in particular because they did not point to a convincing array of examples (but see Abdel-Malek 1981). There were interesting contrasts with poststructural arguments about the resurrection of local knowledges. While highly critical of the West, indigenization theory does not advocate wholesale rejection of Western science, nor does it abandon notions of a common humanity, nor even of universal knowledge. Instead, it says that universal understanding must be based on universal experiences, and not on the false "universalization" of the experience of the West. The potential for recasting visions of a better life for Third World peoples based in a renewed, but critical, interest in local knowledge systems was clearly present.

Rethinking Development

In the context of the growth of postcolonial studies and the indigenization of knowledge, and with reference also to poststructural and postmodern social theory, the field of development studies has undergone a significant critique and rethinking. Indeed, the very notion of development has increasingly been challenged. As the Mexican activist Gustavo Esteva (1987: 135) put it: "In Mexico, you must be either numb or very rich if you fail to notice that 'development' stinks. The damage to persons, the corruption of politics, and the degradation of nature which until recently were only implicit in 'development,' can now be seen, touched, and smelled." For the former UNDP official Majid Rahnema (1997: ix), development has long been resisted at the grassroots level, by the "suffering poverty-stricken peoples" it is supposed to help. Organizations like the Centre for the Study of Developing Societies, founded by Rajni Kothari in Delhi in 1963, and the journal *Alternatives*, started in 1975, express these frustrations in institutional and intellectual terms. Additionally, in the 1970s and 1980s, a movement among many liberal and left-oriented Western practitioners began to criticize the legitimacy of development as it was then known. Some anthropologists reexamined their practice of producing the cultural knowledge that forms the basis for development projects. They thought that the features of an academic subculture (ethnocentrism, culturocentrism, elitism) contributed to making development "the greatest failure of the century." Now calls were made for "development from below." Voluntary groups, or nongovernmental organizations (NGOs), were seen as having greater diversity, credibility, and creativity than official agencies (the World Bank, United Nations, etc.) in producing a "just development" characterized by equity, democracy, and social justice as well as by economic growth (Clark 1991). Radical humanists, dissatisfied with 30 years of concerted international efforts that left more (rather than less) poverty, hunger, disease, and unemployment in their wake, likewise advocated local self-reliance as an alternative organizing principle (Galtung 1978), with participation advocated as research method. There was a turn by academics and development practitioners toward critical self-examination that focused on their research objectives and methods.

Participatory action research (PAR) came into prominence in the 1970s and early 1980s as an attempt to form an endogenous intellectual and practical research methodology for the peoples of the Third World. In Latin America, theories of dependence and exploitation, together with countertheories of subversion, liberation theology, and reinterpretations of ideas taken from Marx, Gramsci, and others on scientific commitment, were recombined with the aim of taking power rather than merely achieving economic growth. PAR was theorized as a total process of adult education, scientific research, and political action in which critical theory, situation analysis, and practice were all seen as sources of knowledge. Summarizing experiences from a series of participatory projects in Colombia, Mexico, and Nicaragua, Orlando Fals Borda said:

> Our objective was . . . to examine and test, in a comparative and critical manner, the idea that it was possible to produce a serious analytical work based on practical knowledge of the reality of both the ordinary

population and of the activists which would enrich not only the general
fund of science but also the people's own knowledge and wisdom. Our
idea was to take grassroots knowledge as a starting point and then to
systematise and amplify it through action in collaboration with external
agents of change—such as ourselves—in order to build and strengthen
the power of formal and informal rural workers' organisations. . . .
Our aim was not to carry out purely scientific or "integrated rural
development" work, objectives which no longer really satisfied us, but
to fashion intellectual tools for the ordinary working class. (1988: 5)

The overall political objective was to develop a more participatory,
direct, and self-managed form of democracy than in the representational
political systems. PAR defined peoples' power as the capacity of
exploited grassroots peoples to articulate and systematize their own and
others' knowledge so that they could become protagonists in defense of
their class and in the advancement of their society.

The idea derived from the Spanish existential philosopher José
Ortega y Gasset (1883–1955), who argued that through actual experience people intuitively apprehended the essence of things and placed
their beings in wider, more fulfilling contexts. This was complemented
by the sentiment expressed in Marx and Engels's statement that philosophers should change the world rather than merely explain it. So the
notion was to authentically participate in development as a real, endogenous experience, in the process turning the people involved into organic
intellectuals, but without creating hierarchies. Science, PAR said, was
not a fetish with a life of its own, or something that had absolute, pure
value. It was simply a valid and useful form of knowledge for specific
purposes, based in relative rather than absolute truths. A peoples' science might exist as an informal endogenous process that could correct
destructive tendencies in the predominant forms of science. A people's
science would converge with so-called universal science to create a total
paradigm. In this view, the forms and relations of knowledge production
had as much, or more, value as the forms and relations of material production. Ordinary people should be able to participate in research from
the beginning, deciding what the subject was, and should remain
involved at every step along the way. PAR preferred qualitative over
quantitative analysis, yet made use of explanatory scientific schemas,
like cause and effect. Its techniques included collective research, critical
recovery of history, valuing and applying folk culture, and the production and diffusion of new knowledge. PAR fulfilled Gramsci's objective
of transforming common sense into good sense or making critical
knowledge the sum of both experiential and theoretical insights. In the
words of Fals Borda, "This is a methodology for productive life and

work which differs from other more academic forms in that it can be assumed and practiced autonomously by oppressed peoples who need knowledge to defend their interests and ways of life. In this way, perhaps, it will help build a better world for everybody, with justice and peace" (1988: 97).

Yet even as the notion of PAR was formalized the critique of development passed into a new phase. Majid Rahnema (1990) argued that development had once appeared as a new "authority" for nationalist, well-educated, and modernized leaders of the colonial world. But the persistence of problems like poverty and malnutrition led to a serious crisis of confidence among the believers. Meanwhile "field work" among the poor changed the lives of idealists from privileged urban backgrounds. Participatory development grew out of these encounters. It promised a new, popular, bottom-up, and endogenous vision of development free from colonial and technoeconomistic shackles. Also a number of experts in the most responsible international organizations, such as the World Bank, began to recognize the importance of popular participation. Development gradually acquired a new face, "the face of a repentant saint, ready to amend, to work in a new fashion with the poor, and even to learn from them . . . [This was] the last temptation of development" (Rahnema 1990: 201). Rahnema argued that governments and development institutions became interested because participation was no longer perceived as a threat, was politically and economically attractive, was a good fundraising device, and was in keeping with a move toward the privatization of development as part of neoliberalism. There were real differences between institutional views of participation (in which local populations serve only as "extras" or "human resources") and the more radical views of the PAR theorists, who admitted that their knowledge was irrelevant if local people did not regard it as useful and believe in full participation. Yet despite their undoubtedly sincere intentions, Rahnema asked whether the change agents had really embarked on a learning journey into the unknown, or were they more concerned with finding ways of convincing the "uneducated" of the merits of their own educated views? In the latter case their scenario was hardly different from the conventional approach to development.

The PAR activists had their own ideological conception of people's power, thought that free dialogue would persuade the "oppressed" to share their own beliefs and ideologies, attributed lack of cooperation to the people's primitive consciousness, and believed their obligation to lie in transmitting science, as the work of the world's best minds, to the "nonconscientized." For Rahnema, this nourished endless schizophrenias, like "dialogical action," self-illusions he found beginning with the Brazilian educator Paolo Friere's writings on participation and dialogue (i.e., the notion that oppressed people did not yet have a critical consciousness and that progressive intellectuals needed to engage them in conscientization exercises). Rahnema saw most activists operating within a humanistic worldview, in which participation was viewed as a voluntary, free exercise among responsible adults, whereas millions of people lived under terroristic, repressive regimes; there were real differences between "us" and "them" and interactions were never innocent. According to Rahnema (1990: 222), participation, planned in advance to serve a particular cause, "can foster only chattering, frantic activism. . . . It is, ultimately, a dead tool . . . inevitably bound to fall into the hands of the highest bidder on the power market. It can never serve freedom, self-discovery, or creative action."

The Poststructural Turn in Development Studies

This dismissal of even the finest humanist, or most committed socialist, research and action pushed criticism of development to new heights. During the 1980s, poststructural critiques of modern, humanist endeavors like development, together with postcolonial skepticism about the continued operation of imperialism in new "benign" forms, entered development studies and changed it forever. Poststructural criticism brought two kinds of change to the field. First, there was a change in attitudes toward development. Progress, improvement, development—all had been assumed to be automatically good at the level of intuition. Yet, with poststructuralism, what previously had been assumed to be progressive, beneficial, and humane was now seen as powerful, controlling, and often (if not always) detrimental. More than this, the very notions "progress" and "beneficial" became suspect in terms not only of "Beneficent for whom?" but also, more revealingly, in terms of "Who determines what beneficial means?" To give a brief example, one contemporary critique of the effects of modern development, from Ivan Illich, read as follows:

> We have embodied our world-view in our institutions and are now their prisoners. Factories, news media, hospitals, governments and schools produce goods and services packaged to contain our view of the world. We—the rich—conceive of progress as the expansion of these establishments. We conceive of heightened mobility as luxury and safety packaged by General Motors or Boeing. We conceive of improving the general well-being as increasing the supply of doctors and hospitals, which package health along with protracted suffering. We have come to identify our need for further learning with demand for even longer confine-

ment to classrooms. In other words, we have packaged education with custodial care, certification for jobs, and the right to vote, and wrapped them all together with indoctrination in the Christian, liberal or communist virtues. (1997: 95)

For Illich, the rational human was decreasingly able to shape his or her environment because his or her energies were consumed in procuring new models of the latest goods. Rich nations, he said, imposed a straightjacket of traffic jams, hospital confinements, and classrooms on poor nations and called this "development." Yet more people, quantitatively and relatively, suffered from hunger, pain, and exposure than at the end of World War II. For Illich, underdevelopment was a form of consciousness rather than a deficient standard of living, a reified state of mind in which mass needs were converted into demands for packaged solutions forever beyond reach of the majority. Illich instead called for counterresearch on fundamental lifestyle alternatives. For Illich, the "benefits" of the modern world, even its medical systems, education, and democracy, were far from being obvious.

Second, there was a change in the methodology used in development studies. Again this involved reexamining that which previously had been taken for granted. Development had always been seen as a necessary dynamic of social life, something that occurred almost naturally in the modern world: development was to sociology what evolution was biology. Development happened as a necessary process, in the modern understanding, unless it was blocked by countervailing forces, which should be overcome and removed. For poststructuralists, by comparison, the term "development" was an invention, or social construction, and the concept had a discursive or a cultural (rather than a natural) history. From this view, economic agents acted as culturally produced identities. Economic rationalities were culturally created, took diverse forms, had distinct geographics, and produced specific forms of development as culturally embedded economic logics. As a cultural logic, development existed in two linked forms: as a set of ideas, forms of behavior, and social practices operating directly in the economic world; and as a discourse representing these real practices, but originating in academia, state bureaucracies, and institutions. The latter kind of development discourse did not merely represent economic practices already operating, in the sense of reflecting them in institutional thought, but also helped in forming them, directly through policy, indirectly by guiding the beliefs and ideas of economic agents. Representations were part of the "culture" forming economic identities. With these poststructural realizations, discourse analysis became a crucial component of development studies. Poststructural thought, especially in the tradition of Foucault, placed new emphasis on development discourses formed in the context of cultures and framed within power relations. Hence a new emphasis emerged: the history of ideas and discourses in the study of development.

Ideas about development—what it was, how it should be designed, who it served—were thus increasingly seen as deriving from modern cultural beliefs. The Swiss postdevelopmental theorist Gilbert Rist (1997) argued that development was the central belief in Western culture. Social beliefs, he said, were collective certainties continuously reproduced because of "the feeling of abandonment that wells up when one contemplates abandoning [them]" (1997: 22—24). The belief in development, Rist argued, was deeply rooted in the Western "religion" of modernity. Rist traced development to Greek antiquity. The Greek philosophers believed that the world was marked by a succession of "ages," with each age unfolding in the mode of a cycle. Aristotle theorized nature (which in Greek simultaneously means development) as the genesis of growing things. Reconciling this Greek theory with Christian theology, Augustine saw God's design behind natural necessity, while the multiple Greek cycles were reduced to one that culminated in the sacrifice of Jesus Christ, opening the way, Rist postulates, to a linear view of history and development in the Western imagination.

While this positioned development deeply in Western culture, there was a need also for explaining the use, or "deployment," of the discourse across global space. David Slater (1992, 1993), a professor of geography at Loughborough University in England, argued that the conceptualization of development was "enframed" by the West's geopolitical imagination. Modernization theory was a reflection of a will to spatial power, one "that sought to subordinate, contain and assimilate the Third World as other" (Slater 1993: 421). The political will fueling modernization had great difficulty accepting difference as autonomy; the "shadowy outsider" in the Third World had to be made safe through penetration and assimilation—hence the geopolitical domestication of global space. Slater saw modernization passing through a series of phases: the transference of Western democratic ideals and values, the maintenance of political order and stability, and counterinsurgency. Contemporary neoliberalism, he said, bears within it a supreme belief in the universal applicability and rationality of the Western development project. Slater saw the Third World "theorizing back" via dependency, with its stress on regional specificity, autonomy of thought, and the negative impacts of the modernization process. According to Slater (1993: 430), "The dependency writers constructed and deployed a geopolitical imagination which sought to prioritize the objectives of autonomy and difference and to break the subordinating effects of metropolis–satellite relations." Overall, Slater viewed the Western geopolitical imagination as a violation of other societies' rights to bear their own principles of social being. Insurgent ethnic–regional identities in peripheral societies refused, challenged, and formed another form of the geopolitical, as with struggles for the territorialization of democracy.

Encountering Development

Notions like these—the cultural embeddedness of development, its position in the Western geopolitical imagination, the deployment of development as power play—led to a new fascination with the origins of the idea in the modern mind. A new kind of poststructural critique of development emerged. Foucault's reappraisal of modern power, discourse, and knowledge was extended to Western development efforts as "uniquely efficient colonizers on behalf of central strategies of power" (Dubois 1991: 19). The pioneering ideas came from Arturo Escobar (1984–1985, 1988, 1992a, 1995), a Colombian anthropologist teaching at the University of Massachusetts. Following Foucault, Escobar contrasted reason's project of global emancipation with the dark underside of Western domination: reasoned knowledge, using the language of emancipation, created new systems of power in a modernized world. Development, he said, was one of these languages of power. Under the political conditions of the cold war (1945–1960), Escobar argued, the West's scientific gaze focused anew on Asia, Africa, and Latin America. The main concepts of development were the discursive products of a geopolitical climate characterized by anticolonial struggles in Asia and Africa and growing nationalism in Latin America, but more significantly by the rise to hegemony of the United States. In his 1949 Inaugural Address President Harry Truman proposed that the entire world should get a "fair democratic deal" via the intervention of a still youthful Uncle Sam eager to solve the problems of global poverty. This "Truman Doctrine" initiated a new era in managing world affairs. Yet Escobar saw the doctrine bearing a heavy price: the scrapping of ancient philosophies and the disintegration of the social institutions of two-thirds of the world's people. The Western dream of progress became a hegemonic global imagination. The Western discourse of development colonized reality so thoroughly that even opponents were obliged to phrase their critiques in developmental terms: another development, participatory development, socialist development, and so on.

Yet recently, Escobar claimed, poststructural social theories, offering accounts of how representations shaped the way reality was imagined, and thus acted upon, had been introduced by Foucault, Said, Mudimbe, Mohanty, Bhabha, and others. The poststructural account maintained the earlier Marxian theme of domination, but extended the range of social criticism into discourse, truth, imaginary and knowledge. Academic institutions, especially places like Harvard or Cambridge, together with large development organizations, like the World Bank, IMF, and U.S. Agency for International Development (AID), exercised power not only by controlling money flows, but also by creating the dominant ideas, representations, and discourses. These enframed the world in terms of European categories (Mitchell 1988), captured social imaginaries, and constructed identities. Western discourses of development were deployed through the practices of planning agencies, local development institutions, and health organizations. People thought and acted through Western categories, seeing the world not as it was but through a Westernized, developmental gaze. In brief, reality was socially constructed in the sense of being understood and re-created through Western ideas (Figure 5.1).

Escobar's creative move entailed applying poststructural and postcolonial notions to the postwar discourse of development, paying particular attention to economic development theory and the systematic production of knowledge and power in planning, rurality, health, nutrition, sustainability, and women and environment. The organizing premise of development as a postwar discourse was a belief in modernization through industrialization and urbanization. Its most important elements were capital formation, education in modern cultural values, and the need to create modernizing institutions at several scales (from international to national to regional). Development would result from the systematization of all these elements (in a synthesis of growth and modern-

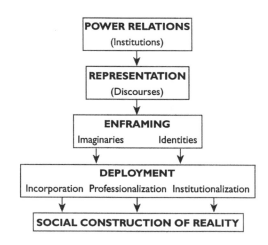

FIGURE 5.1. Escobar's model of developmental discourse.

ization theories). This system of thought defined the conditions under which objects, concepts, and strategies could be incorporated into development discourse. In Escobar's (1995: 41) words, "The system of relations establishes a discursive practice that sets the rules of the game: who can speak, from what points of view, with what authority, and according to what criteria of expertise." Under the hegemony of development, apparatuses of knowledge production (the World Bank, planning and development agencies, etc.) established a new political economy of truth, different from that of the colonial era. The template was Said's orientalism, a Western style for dominating, restructuring, and having authority over the East. A vast institutional network defined a perceptual domain, the space of development, that determined what could be said, thought, and imagined. From industrialization, through the "Green Revolution," to integrated rural development, policies repeated the basic "truth" that development consisted in achieving the conditions characteristic of the already-rich societies. The development discourse defined what could be thought, practiced, even imagined, in considering the future of Third World societies. According to Escobar:

> Development can be described as an apparatus . . . that links forms of knowledge about the Third World with the deployment of forms of power and intervention, resulting in the mapping and production of Third World societies. . . . By means of this discourse, individuals, governments and communities are seen as "underdeveloped" (or placed under conditions in which they tend to see themselves as such), and are treated accordingly. (1992a: 23; see also Sachs 1992)

The deployment of development, Escobar argued, operated through three main strategies:

1. The progressive incorporation of problems as *abnormalities* to be treated by specific interventions. This resulted in a "field of the intervention of power."
2. The *professionalization* of development, the recasting by experts of what otherwise would be political problems into neutral "scientific" terms, the aim being a regime of truth and norms, or a "field of the control of knowledge."
3. The *institutionalization* of development, the formation of a network of new sites of power/knowledge that bound people to certain behaviors and rationalities.

For Escobar, development proceeded by defining "problems" (poverty, population growth, archaic agricultural practices) and identifying "abnormalities" (the illiterate, the malnourished, small farmers) to be observed and clinically treated. The result was the creation of a space of thought and action, a perceptual–analytical field, that limited what could be included as legitimate development issues and practices. "Development was—and continues to be for the most part—a top-down, ethnocentric, and technocratic approach, which treated people and cultures as abstract concepts, statistical figures to be moved up and down in the charts of 'progress' " (Escobar 1995: 44). Escobar saw a spatial field of power/knowledge expanding outward from the West using development as its capturing mechanism. Within this field, networks of sites of power bound people into Western forms of thought and behavior. Development was particularly effective because it appealed to the finest ideals of the Enlightenment (often employing the most idealistic people in aid and development agencies) and to the aspirations for a better life by poor people. Development had been "successful" to the extent that it managed and controlled populations, that it created a type of manageable underdevelopment in a more subtle form than colonialism. In brief, progress was power. Escobar found this view of development as a modernist discourse different from analyses of political economy, modernization, or even alternative development, which proposed merely modifying the current regime of development.

For Escobar, all universal models, whether neoclassical or Marxist, denied peoples' capacities to model their own behaviors. Escobar favored, instead, autonomous peasant development strategies that opened spaces for peasants to struggle, that saw peasants not in terms of lacks but in terms of possibilities, and that modified social relations of production. Like the PAR activists, he thought that useful knowledge had to begin with peoples' self-understanding and build a system of communication involving peasants. In Taussig's (1987: 135) words, "From the represented shall come that which overturns the representation." Such local constructions, he said, could be investigated via ethnographies of resistance (e.g., Scott 1985) or the logics and actions of subaltern groups (Guha 1988; Comaroff and Comaroff 1991). Here local models "exist not in a pure state but in complex hybridizations with dominant models" (Escobar 1995: 96), that is, articulations between centric (dominant) texts and marginal voices. His best example was a "house model" of economy based in everyday peasant practice in Panama and Colombia (Gudeman and Rivera 1992). Rethinking development entailed two kinds of practice: making explicit the existence of a plurality of models of economies by placing itself in the space of local constructions—the notion of "communities of modelers"; and studying the processes by which local cultural knowledges were appropriated by global forces. In this latter case radical political economy needed to be supplemented by ethnographies of development and theories of hybrid cultures. Following the poststructural philosophers Giles Deleuze and Felix Guattari (1987), Escobar believed that global capital relied not so much on the homogenization of an exterior Third World, as on the consolidation of its diverse, heterogenous social forms: capital required "peripheral polymorphy." The global economy had to be understood as a decentered system employing manifold (symbolic, economic, political) apparatuses of capture in a process that, Escobar thought, still left room for localities to avoid the most exploitative mechanisms of capitalist megamachines. Modifying political economics involved the material, but also the semiotic, strengthening of local systems. While the main actors were social movements, Escobar also found a role for interpretive social theorists in helping form a conversational community across cultures.

Highly critical notions about development like Escobar's intersected with the profound sense of disillusionment, among progressive theorists and activists, about developmental practice (e.g., Edwards 1989) to produce a crisis of confidence in development studies—indeed, perhaps a crisis in progressive thought in general. As Escobar put it:

> For some time now, it has been difficult —at times even impossible—to talk about development, protest or revolution with the same confidence and encompassing scope with which intellectuals and activists spoke about these vital matters in our most recent past. It is as if the elegant discourses of the 1960s—the high decade of both development and revolution—had been suspended, caught in mid air as they strove toward their zenith, and, like fragile bubbles, exploded, leaving a scrambled trace of their glorious path behind. . . . Hesitantly perhaps, but with a persistence that has to be taken seriously, a new discourse has set in. (1992a: 20)

Brought on by critical thought's inability to leave behind the imaginary of development, the whole project of progress was said to be sick, dying, gone. Escobar compared this with a powerful social movements discourse which, while unclear about its possible directions, had become a privileged arena for intellectual inquiry and political action. Escobar aimed at bridging the two insights of the critique of development and social movements, believing (1) that a critique of the discourse and practice of development could clear the ground for a more radical, collective imagining of alternative futures; and (2) that thinking about alternatives to development required a theoretical and practical transformation that would draw on the practices of Third World social movements. Escobar claimed that a growing number of scholars were in agreement with this prescription, and, that rather than search for development alternatives they spoke about alternatives *to* development. These scholars shared a critical stance with respect to established science; an interest in local autonomy, culture, and knowledge; and a position defending localized, pluralistic grassroots movements. This tendency bears the name "post-developmentalism."

Postdevelopmentalism

Escobar's claim that a growing body of scholars shared a similar position on postdevelopmentalism was a little ambitious. But eventually a set of ideas promoted by a linked group of people circulated in publications and were put into practice by alternative institutions. These ideas coexisted with some degree of ease, if not yet as a fully coherent counter-discourse. These ideas stemmed from critics of development in Third World countries, especially in India; poststructural social theorists and a few development economists; and some political ecologists and environmentalists critical of the effects of development on nature. In *The Development Dictionary*, a manual of postdevelopmental thought, the modern age of development was proclaimed over and done with:

> The idea of development stands like a ruin in the intellectual landscape. Delusion and disappointment, failures and crimes have been the steady companions of development and they tell a common story: it did not work. Moreover, the historical conditions which catapulted the idea into prominence have vanished: development has become outdated. But above all, the hopes and desires which made the idea fly, are now exhausted: development has grown obsolete. (Sachs 1992: 1)

For the contributors to the *dictionary*, the main development credos were historically inadequate and imaginatively sterile. Development was a blunder of planetary proportions, an enterprise to be feared not for its failure, but in case it proved to be successful. The authors of *The Development Dictionary* wanted to disable development professionals by destroying the conceptual foundations of their practices. They wanted to challenge grassroots initiatives to discard their crippling development talk.

Likewise Serge Latouche's *In the Wake of the Affluent Society* (1993) argued that the Western dream of *la grande société* (the great society, the open society, the affluent society) promised affluence and liberty for all. Yet these possibilities were, like film star status, achievable only for a few, while the price, measured in terms of the reduction of real solidarities, was paid by everyone. Western civilization was confronted by the dark side of progress:

> The perception that power to create is also power to destroy; that power over nature is often more imagined than real; that market autonomy is often also an awful desolation, insecurity and simple nullity—numbness in front of the TV, or Lotto, walkman, glue sniffing, or some other virtual reality. What, in human life, is truly richness and progress? (O'Connor and Arnoux 1993: 12–13)

For Latouche, the West had become an impersonal machine, devoid of spirit, and therefore of a master, which put humanity to its service. For their own survival, Third World societies had to subvert this homogenizing movement by changing their terms of reference to escape the disempowerment inherent in underdevelopment. For Latouche, human practice was primarily symbolic; through the imaginary, material problems received distinctive definition and terms of resolution. Underdevelopment was primarily a cultural form of domination. Latouche saw the West coming apart, and the development myth collapsing. His main theme was the "post-Western world," an imagined future that could be explored via its early beginnings in the informal sectors of economies, in the practices of millions of people shipwrecked by development. The informal sector, for Latouche, was part of a whole social context involving neotribal peoples with residual and newly reinvented cultural identities, peoples with metaphysical or religious beliefs, peoples whose ensemble of daily practices were conducted under a different rationality that appeared from the outside to be deviant or irrational. All this he interpreted as resistances that were pregnant with another society. Latouche (1993: 26) described this vision as pushing speculation to the brink of science fiction, and in this lay a fundamental problem with many postdevelopmental approaches.

Given that postdevelopmentalists are not just destructive cynics, hopelessly caught in endless deconstructions, but do in fact believe in social change and political activism, the problem became: "What do they propose?" Based on reading *The Post-Development Reader* (Rahnema 1997), one of the main collections of essays in this field, three positions seem to recur:

1. *Radical pluralism.* Drawing on the ideas of Wendell Berry, Mahatma Gandhi, Ivan Illich, Leopold Kohr, Fritz Schumacher, and others, often expressed in the journal *The Ecologist*, postdevelopmentalists believe that the true problem of the modern age seems to lie in the inhuman scale of contemporary institutions and technologies. While people

are enmeshed in global structures they lack the centralized power necessary for global action. To make a difference, actions should not be grandiosely global, but humbly local. Thus Gustavo Esteva and Madhu Suri Prakash (1997) amended Rene Dubois's slogan "Think globally, act locally" to read "Think and act locally"—in their view, people could only think wisely about things they actually knew well. Esteva and Prakash urged support of local initiatives by small, grassroots groups—for example, growing food, in villages where collective or communal rights had priority over personal or individual rights. While local people needed outside allies to form a critical mass of political opposition, this did not call for thinking globally. Indeed, the opposite was the case. Esteva and Prakash believed that people thinking and acting locally would find others who shared their opposition to the global forces threatening local spaces and join in coalitions of thinkers and activists. Every culture had a cosmo-vision, an awareness of the place and responsibilities of humans in the cosmos, but this should not be twisted into cosmo-power.

2. *Simple living.* This appeared in two related versions: the ecological and the spiritual. In the ecological argument, demands made on nature by the industrial countries (20% of the world's people consuming 80% of the energy and raw materials) had to be reduced by between 70% and 90% in a half-century. This required more than efficient resource management; it required a "sufficiency revolution." A society in balance with nature required both intelligent rationalization of means, and (even more importantly) prudent moderation of ends (Sachs 1997). In the spiritual argument, the idea was that material pursuits should not be allowed to smother the purity of the soul or the life of the mind. Instead, the simple life self-consciously subordinated the material to the ideal—as with Zarathustra, Buddha, Lao-Tse, Confucius, and the Old Testament (Shi 1997). So, as set out by Gandhi (1997), a simple life entailed an economics of justice, decentralization, village life, and human happiness combined with moral, spiritual growth. In both versions of the simple living idea, ecological and spiritual, there was a notion of peace and harmony coming from simpler, less materially intensive ways of living, where satisfaction and happiness derived from spiritual sources (humanity or God) rather than consumption.

3. *Reappraising noncapitalist societies.* Here the basic idea was that life in the previous, nondeveloped world had not been so bad after all:

> They had no cars, no Internet and none of the consumer goods to which modern men and women are now addicted. They had no laws and no social security to protect them, no "free press," no "opposition party," no "elected leaders." But they had no less time for leisure, or,

paradoxically were no less economically "productive" for the things they needed. And, contrary to the racist cliches in vogue, they were not always governed by cannibals and tyrants. Effective personal and collective moral obligations often took the place of legal provisions. (Rahnema 1997: 379–381)

Into such societies poisonous development introduced a paraphernalia of mirages that dispossessed people of those things that had given meaning and warmth to their lives. The often hidden message of every development project was that traditional modes of thinking and practice doomed people to a subhuman condition from which nothing short of fundamental change could allow respect from the civilized world. The main argument in favor of development was that it was a generous response to millions who asked for help. But development had little to do with the desires of the "target" populations. The hidden transcript concerned geopolitical objectives. Requests for aid came from unrepresentative governments rather than from the people themselves. Thus postdevelopmentalism was not the end of searches for new possibilities of change. Postdevelopmentalism, instead, signified that the old self-destructive, inhumane approach was over (Rahnema 1997).

In general, postdevelopmentalism rejected the way of thinking, and the mode of living, produced by modern development, in favor of revitalized versions of nonmodern, usually non-Western, philosophies and cultures. From this view, modern, Western development was destructive rather than generative, a force to be resisted rather than welcomed. In a phrase, development was exactly the problem, not the solution.

The question remains, however, whether development can be both: problem *and* solution?

Critique

What might we make of sweeping condemnations, that seek to undermine the knowledge basis of all established notions about development, to deconstruct each optimistic expression of Western reason's intervention on behalf of the oppressed people of the world, to denigrate the accomplishments of modern life, and construct an alternative which, in many cases, celebrates mystical rather than rational understanding? Is reason to be rejected or *re*reasoned? Is development outmoded, or merely misdirected? These questions are so important that the postdevelopmental discourse must itself be deconstructed, not to synthesize its arguments in mild, sanitized forms into a recast conventional development model, but through critique to draw notions for use in a practice that might even retain some aspects of the idea of development.

Poststructural and postmodern theory favors fragmentation and difference except in its own treatment of modern development theory, which it portrays in terms of a monolithic hegemony. Hence, for Escobar (1992a: 26), "critiques of development by dependency theorists, for instance, still functioned within the same discursive space of development, even if seeking to attach it to a different international and class rationality." Thus critics gather under the rubric "modern development theory" notions regarded by their proponents as separate, different, even antagonistic. A typical statement lists, as essentially one contemporary development discourse, neoclassical growth theory, modernization, and radical political economy. These are said to share the following general positions:

1. A linear view of history in which the West is further along a given path of progress than Third World countries.
2. An agreement that the proximate cause of development is the exercise of human rationality, especially the application of science to production.
3. Advocacy of values like freedom, justice, and equality as experienced and defined in the West.
4. An instrumental assumption that means are separable from ends and that moral considerations apply more to ends than to means. (Banuri 1990).

These criteria describe an apparent similarity between what are taken to be merely different forms of Enlightenment thought. Beyond a vague similarity deriving from the Enlightenment, however, the question is whether the notion of a single developmental discourse creates an homogenous myth that destroys differences between, and within, theories crucial to their contents, visions, and intentions. Take historical materialism as a case in point.

This notion of a continuous modernist discourse sees Marx as a direct descendent of the Enlightenment. Thus in his "Preface" to a *Critique of Political Economy* Marx (1970) argued that societal transformation is driven by development of the material productive forces which, by coming into periodic conflict with the existing relations of production, create revolutionary ruptures that move society from one mode of production to another. What caused the development of the social forces of production? What propelled history? A rationalist version of Marxism (Cohen 1978: 150–157) found that Marx's "development thesis" rested on the proposition that humans were rational beings, who used their intelligence to relieve material scarcity by expanding their productive powers—that is, by increasing their ability to transform nature. In this rationalist version, Marx's theory of history could indeed be read as an elaboration of a central notion of the Enlightenment: history is the progressive achievement of human reason's control over nature.

But this is one reading of Marx, not the only reading, and not necessarily Marx's final position. Historical materialism was conceived as a critique of the very idea of beginning explanation with consciousness (of which rationality is a part), even in the form of an experientially based human imagination. Instead Marx argued that social analysis should begin with "real active life," that is, with labor and social relations of production. Marx's *Grundrisse* (1973: 479–498) set out a version of historical materialism in which social and natural relations were the basic categories of analysis, production had neither a single logic nor a single objective (such as capital accumulation), history took multilinear forms, and reasoning was of multiple kinds depending on social relations (Lefort 1978; Giddens 1981). Marx's multilinear, social relational theory does not rest easily in a supposedly singular discourse of development focused on Reason as cause and stretching from the Enlightenment to the World Bank.

Much the same can be said about "developmentalism" as a hegemonic discourse. There may be similarities between capitalist and state-authoritarian economic thought with regard to development. But developmentalism, as a mode of progressive thought, has long contained critical versions, which stem from various oppositions to the existing forms of development and emphasize the different trajectories of development of dependent societies (as with dependency theory), advocate different logics of development for different societies (as with democratic Marxism), and passionately favor the empowerment of poor people (as with PAR). Lumping these critical notions, and the radical practices guided by them, with neoclassical economics, modernization theory, and World Bank policy, into a broad, coherent, "developmentalism" denies fundamental differences and denigrates the efforts of theorist–activists, such as the dependency theorist Walter Rodney, who have been far more dangerously involved in praxis (Rodney was assassinated for his troubles) than are the poststructural philosophers who meet in the salons of Paris or the postmodernists who debate at annual meetings of the Modern Languages Association (for what are admittedly ferocious encounters)!

This prompts a first critical reaction to poststructuralism in general and to postdevelopmentalism in particular. Poststructural discourse theory argues for the social construction of meaning, elaborating the institutional bases of discourse, emphasizing the positions from which people speak and the power relations between these positions. This conception indicates constellations of discursive positions that persist over the long-term and take a multiplicity of forms. The problem is that in setting up a system of expectations about a theory, such that it may be part of a more general intellectual position, discourse analysis often denies what post-structural philosophy supposedly cherishes: differences of a fundamental kind. "Discourse" then becomes capable of reconciling even opposing tendencies in theorization. Indeed, there may be a kind of "discursive idealism," a process of reification in which the category "discourse" becomes an active force marshaling reluctant ideas into quasi-coherent, determining wholes. Perhaps, therefore, we need a more discriminating critique than discourse analysis. Reconstituted Marxist theories of ideology, as with Gramsci, might do a better job, as might some other conception more directly rooted in social, rather than discursive, relations.

The critical point is not to make the easy claim that poststructural critics of development theory overstate their position, but to argue that the analysis of discourse, with its linking of oppositional theoretical traditions because they "share the same discursive space" (i.e., oppose one another!) is prone to this kind of overgeneralization. Why? Exactly because it diverts attention away from the "international and class rationalities" and material contexts expressed in discourses, hence merging conflicting positions (PAR and World Bank) into a single developmental discourse, or condemning modernity as a whole rather than, for example, capitalist versions of modern consumptive life. True to its word about difference, poststructural theory would instead see development as a set of conflicting discourses and practices based in positions that contradict one another. These would have a variety of potentials rather than promoting a single copy of the experience of the West. In the following section this critique is extended into the Foucauldian concepts of power and knowledge.

Power–Knowledge–Discourse

In his later (genealogical) work Foucault tried to escape from a structuralist conception of discourses as lumps of ideas determinant in history (*epistemes*), and instead concentrate on the material conditions of discourse formation: social practices and power relations. Similarly Foucauldian postdevelopmentalists, like Escobar, are interested in the institutions that form and spread development theories, models, and strategies. Yet the power–knowledge–discourse trilogy still has problems. It is never clear what power is. "Power" alternates between a Nietzschean power, inherent in all human relations, and specific powers, such as those cohering in particular institutions or even individuals. And the positive aspects of power, the ability to get things done, get short shrift, in practice, compared with the negative aspects. Moreover, there is the poststructural critique of modern knowledge as oppressive, disciplining, normalizing, totalizing, essentialist, truth claiming, knowledge thought up in the pursuit of power, all of which are caricatures that fail to discriminate between types of knowledge production, different motives for thinking, the contestations between potentials, and the depositing in knowledge of competing politics. Finally, there is the product of power and knowledge in "discourse." Discourse (not capital) has to be abandoned; postdevelopmentalism attacks the *discourse* of development. Poststructural analyses often forget, in practice, the agency behind discourse, or overgeneralize agency as "modernity" or "power." Even in analyses following the later Foucault, strong reminders of discursive idealism remain. There is an overemphasis on representation, and the enframing of imaginaries, at the expense of practicality and action. Actually, intermediate conceptions, such as class, gender, and state, give more exact descriptions and yield more focused analyses. Let us take the power basis of development theory as an example.

As we have seen, the contemporary notion of "development" emerged most fully as Western policymakers reassessed their positions relative to newly independent states in the Third World during the post-World War II cold war. From the mid-1940s to the late 1950s the redefinition of foreign policy and the notions of development aid, assistance, food for peace, and so on, were repeatedly linked, especially in the newly hegemonic United States—hence the restatement of international control in American terms of the "rights of man," rather than in European terms of "the white man's burden." While initiated by Truman, the culminating triumph of this "development of development theory" is actually to be found in the various speeches of John F. Kennedy, president of the United States from 1960 to 1963. As Sorensen (1988: 329) correctly says, "No president before or after Kennedy has matched the depth of his empathy for the struggling peoples of Latin America, Africa and Asia, or the strength of his vow to facilitate their political and economic independence." Read a little more critically, the Kennedy administration managed to contain a fierce anticommunism within an overall framework of Western humanism in a development discourse that drew consciously on the latest in social science. Rostow's *Stages of Economic Growth* (1960) is obviously present in Kennedy's (in Sorensen 1988: 365–366) statement that "the only real question is whether these new nations [in Africa] will look West or East—to Moscow or Washington—for sympathy, help and guidance, in their great effort to recapitulate, in a few decades, the entire history of modern Europe and America."

Thus it quickly becomes apparent that the Kennedy statements on the Third World must be deconstructed to reveal their knowledge sources, motives, and power bases. There are excellent critical surveys by political scientists linking U.S. positions on development to broader domestic and foreign policy objectives (Higgott 1983; Gendzier 1985), although this literature largely predates the spread of poststructural notions into North American social science, *and* would benefit from Foucauldian techniques of discourse analysis. While necessary, however, the question remains: Is discourse analysis sufficient to the task? Take that culminating moment in postwar history, when an idealistic young president at last expressed the finest sentiments of American generosity toward the world in the one paragraph in Kennedy's Inaugural Address of 1961 dealing with U.S. relations with the Third World:

> To those peoples in the huts and villages of half the globe struggling to break the bonds of mass misery, we pledge our best efforts to help them help themselves, for whatever period is required—not because the communists may be doing it, not because we seek their votes, but because it is right. If a free society cannot help the many who are poor, it cannot save the few who are rich. (in Sorensen 1988: 12)

This speech initiated a renewed U.S. emphasis on development, using a modern rhetoric of equality, happiness, and social justice. But Kennedy justified "helping the many who are poor" as being morally right in terms of "saving the few who are rich." As Foucault would say, the language of development, helping and generous aid, expresses power relations. Kennedy's statement directly expresses class relations in the form of fundamental, modern beliefs. For Kennedy, scion of one of the richest families in the United States, representative of the New England liberal intelligentsia, supporter of the invasion of Cuba and the Vietnam incursion, development, antipoverty programs, and welfare are good philanthropic ideals but also, at the same time, preserve the continued possibility of wealth creation by the rich people of the world. Yet development, in the Kennedy statement, is not an expression of power in general, which universalizes the issue, nor is it an expression of power employed by a specific institution, such as the U.S. State Department, which confines the critique. The critical analysis of development as discourse is far more revealing in terms of motive forces when it is cast not in terms of power in general, nor the power of a specific institution, but in terms intermediate between these: class, gender, ethnicity, and state, on the one hand, and beliefs, ideals, and politics, on the other. In brief, while there is much to learn from discourse analysis, especially the serious attention given to statements and documents as symptoms of power relations, there are some real problems with it. These problems might be resolved, in part, through a dialogue with Marxism, socialist feminism, and other critical traditions which employ notions of class, gender, and ethnicity and speak in the language of ideology, hegemony, and fundamental beliefs.

Modernity and Science

These, however, are methodological skirmishes around the main issue: poststructuralism's negative assessment of modernism, especially its skeptical attitude toward material progress, the emancipation of humanity, empirical truth, and modern science. Beginning with the critique of progress, the poststructural literature rejects Western models of development altogether. As Escobar (1992: 27) puts it, "Rather than searching for development alternatives . . . [a growing number of Third World scholars] . . . speak about alternatives *to* development, that is, a rejection of the entire paradigm." In doing so, postdevelopmentalism denies the Third World what the First World already has—yet we must note that many critics of Western development live in the luxurious centers of Western modernity (Paris, New York, Geneva), and enjoy their benefits, while arguing that Third World people do not need them. In postdevelopmentalism, associating any trait with the West is sufficient to condemn it without further question, as though Western people are unique in one respect only: everything we do is perverse. As with Rahnema, there are tendencies to deny that poverty originally existed in the Third World, to romanticize local alternatives *to* development, to assume a reverse snobbery in which indigenous knowledge systems are automatically superior to Western science, to revel in spiritual mysticism as though gods and goblins are as "true" as gravity. Crimes committed in the name of religion at least rival those perpetrated for the sake of reason (although we would claim that many supposedly "modern" atrocities, such as Nazi Germany, were motivated primarily by mystical ideas—try listening to Hitler's speeches).

Most fundamentally the question of modern science must be debated with rigor and insight. In the *Development Dictionary* Claude Alvares (1992: 219–220) calls modern science "an epoch-specific, ethnic (Western) and culture-specific (culturally *entombed*) project, one that is a politically directed, artificially induced stream of consciousness invading and distorting, and often attempting to take over, the larger, more stable canvas of human perceptions and experiences." Gilbert Rist (1997: 3), in a wonderfully iconoclastic argument about development, dismisses scientific realism, the view that a world exists independently of the knowing subject and can be known with accuracy, with a single, overstated phrase: "As for objectivity, it is known to be a vain pursuit so long as we refuse to accept that the object is always constructed by the one who observes it." Yet even those who understand that objects assume shapes as ideas in the imagination through inexact representational processes refuse to accept that this mental shaping "constructs" these objects. Realists and materialists believe instead that objects in the world are already "there" before being encountered in thought and shaped (inexactly) into ideas. Realist science is an as yet incomplete project to found belief on evidence rather than faith. We can readily admit that evidence is inadequate, even misleading, and that reliance on the evidentiary is a belief. But science is a different order, a new kind, of belief, that radically questions everything, even the basis of its own knowledge claims ("epistemology"), rather than accepting the completely unknowable ("God's existence") on faith. Let it be clear that this is a response to Rist's (1997: 22) claim that Western beliefs in science and development are merely updated myths. Science conceived as evidence and radical questioning may advance understanding by enabling realistic appraisals of life and its circumstances—for example, by showing that lightening is a giant electrical spark passing from sky to earth, rather then an expression of anger from the gods in heaven, hence lightening conductors save lives, while prayer is ineffectual—without claiming omnipotence or total knowledge. Accuracy may be only the beginning of understanding, as existential philosophy argues. Accuracy may be a cultural invention of the West, as poststructural philosophy argues. But accuracy and evidence have this great difference from mystical blind faith: they liberate the mind from hallucinations of the supernatural. Science draws inspiration from a world of knowledge (China, Egypt, the Middle East), yet the West has contributed something that underlies technology, productivity, and greater material certainty: that "something" is "evidence."

We who try to base our beliefs on evidence rather than faith should look carefully at modernity's accomplishments: the fact that science has yielded productivity, has enabled back-breaking labor to be performed by machines, has yielded consumption above basic needs, does provide a margin of safety against natural catastrophes. A critique of development should discriminate between real advances like modern medicine, on the one hand, and the tragic misuse of scientific knowledge and technological productivity in support of frivolous consumption for a few rich people, on the other hand. Western science *has* demonstrated its positive power in improving material living standards, albeit at great environmental and social expense. Indeed, it is exactly the need for greater material security in Third World countries that empowers Western images and developmental models. Drawing on this tradition, development contains a real quest for improving the human condition, but one perverted by class power and ruling ideologies. There should be a struggle to reorient this practice rather than dismissing the entire modern developmental project as a negative power play. Therefore we need more discriminating class and gender analyses that show how potentials come to be misused, restricted, exploitative, and environmentally dangerous. We need to replace the critical category "modernism" with the more discriminating, more critical category "capitalism" as source of the perversion of the modern.

A more discriminating materialist poststructural critique sees development as a discourse and system of organized practices produced under definite social relations. Social relations rather than anonymous *epistemes* guide the discovery and use of knowledge, the writing of documents, and the structuring of practices. From this perspective, the social relations that undergird discourses have to be transformed by radical politics rather than the discourses themselves merely being deconstructed: it takes more than changing words to change the world. In this view also, development has unrealized potential, and radical analysis should be dedicated to extracting those notions from modern developmentalism that can be used to further the interests of peasants and workers, rather than dismissing the entire venture.

Let us give the final word, however, to the Delhi Centre for the Study of Developing Societies (Dallmayr 1996). In *Rethinking Development* (1989), Rajni Kothari, director of the Delhi Centre, argues that unfettered economic growth propelled by modern science and technology engenders a deadly arms race; a wasteful, consumption-driven civilization; and a pernicious class structure—all of which threaten democracy. The world, he says, is becoming overly dominated by a single conception of life. Yet Kothari also warns against simplistic versions of a counterview, like reactionary antimodernism, or rampant cultural relativism, that neglect the inextricable entwinement of North and South. He favors principles of both autonomy and integration. In terms of specific strategies, Kothari recommends fostering alternative lifestyles to high consumption and an ethic that discourages ostentatious living in favor of frugal limitation. In terms of the political organization of space, Kothari wants a Gandhi-style decentralization to promote a more equitable balance between urban and rural. He advocates a cultural attack on illiteracy and broad, popular participation in economic production and public life (a decentralized, participatory democratic structure that realizes social justice). For Kothari, the cultural, and especially the religious, traditions of non-Western societies offer alternatives to Western scientific and technological mastery: in the East, for example, science was based on a search for truth and was regarded as a means of self-realization and self-control rather than as a means of domination of nature. Yet, rather than dismissing Western modernity, Kothari calls for a process of critical interaction between civilizational traditions.

Likewise, Ashis Nandy (1987), a senior associate at the Delhi Centre, argues for a *critical traditionalism* that tries to marshal the resources provided by inherited cultural frames for purposes of social and political transformation. For Nandy, as with Gandhi, the recollection of cultural traditions has to recognize the fissures between oppressors and oppressed while privileging the voices and categories of victims. Nandy has a general distrust of the ideas of the "winners of the world," believing that the faiths and ideals of the powerless and marginalized are the way to freedom, compassion, and justice.

In these views we find a postcolonial postdevelopmentalism open to dialogue with a critical modernism.

Chapter 6

FEMINIST THEORIES OF DEVELOPMENT

M any of the issues raised by Marxist and poststructural theorists, themes like progress, modernity, development, and enlightenment, together with additional issues of gender relations, have also been raised by feminists. In the first wave of feminist activism and politics, which began as an organized movement in the latter half of the nineteenth century, the exclusion of women from suffrage (voting rights) revealed the partial and biased nature of modern, political democracy. In the second wave of feminist activism and theory, during the 1960s, capitalism was contested as biased, discriminatory, and unfair. The third wave of the 1990s is often associated with the entry of poststructural and postmodern ideas into a more differentiated feminism. During the second and third waves, feminists interested in inequality, poverty, and gender relations produced a significant body of critical ideas on development, and issues raised by feminists significantly impacted international agencies dealing with development problems—to the extent that feminist development theory now forms a recognizable system of concepts, discourses, and practices.

Feminist Politics of Development

Contemporary feminist practice among academics and activists has been particularly affected by debates begun by First World women of color and Third World women beginning in the late 1970s. An early statement from the Combahee River Collective (1984) questioned the notion of a common women's identity as a basis for political strategy. Poets and writers, notably bell hooks and Audre Lorde, criticized the women's movement for downplaying sexual, racial, and class differences. Works by Chandra Mohanty (1991a, 1991b) and Adrienne Rich (1986) signaled a move from a feminist politics of common identity—for example, the embrace of sisterhood, with its assumptions about similarly structured oppression for all women—to a feminist politics of location, which theorized that women were subject to particular assemblages of oppressions, and therefore that all women emerged with particular rather than generic identities. Women's movements became tied through networks into something resembling a common politics, but were no longer united by a belief in universal characteristics or led by progressive Western women in drive for global emancipation. In particular, Lorde, Mohanty, and others called for a dramatic shift in the practice of collective politics and in attitudes toward women in the Third World.

The United Nations Decade for the Advancement of Women (1975–1985) encouraged the growth of feminist groups worldwide (E. Friedman 1995; Miles 1996). As a result of pressure from feminist movements, virtually every development organization established projects and programs to improve the economic and social position of women. The almost universal assumption behind these projects was that women's problems stemmed from insufficient participation in an otherwise benevolent process of economic growth. The progressive, liberal idea was to increase women's participation and improve their share of resources, employment opportunities, and income in an attempt at effecting dramatic improvements in their living conditions. In the late 1970s, several studies documented facts about women's lives, such as the amount of unpaid labor women performed, while, at the same time, in-depth qualitative studies looked at women's roles in local communities. As a result of this research, the following summary prepared by the United Nations appeared:

- Women are half the world's people.
- Perform two-thirds of the world's working hours.
- Receive one-tenth of the world's income.
- Own only one-hundredth of the world's property. (Pezzullo 1982: 15)

Yet during the United Nations decade devoted to women their position actually worsened, in terms of decreased access to resources, health, nutrition, and education, and in terms of increased work burdens. This failure dramatized the limited efficacy of the integrationist approach, and radicalized the study of women and development (Sen and Grown 1987). At the International Women's Year Conference held in Mexico in 1975, and at a middecade Conference on Women held in Copenhagen in 1980, fierce debates erupted over women's issues and the relevance of feminist theory. By the time of the 1985 Nairobi Women and Development Conference, Third World women, by then a clear majority of those attending, defined the main issues, while most of the organizing and discussion occurred at alternative meetings held alongside the official UN program. The Alternative Forum at Nairobi attracted 16,000 women to discuss women's conditions; the main themes addressed were gender-based violence, the exclusion of women from control over vital resources, the feminization of poverty, and the need for more radical approaches that questioned the structures of existing societies. Feminism shifted from being primarily a Western women's concern to a more heterogeneous movement, with a more expanded definition reflecting greater involvement by regional organizations in Third World countries.

In the early 1980s Third World women called for new theories of development that embraced feminism, while women's conferences called for the empowerment of women as agents, rather than seeing them as problems, of development (Bunch and Carrillo 1990). A key event was the founding of DAWN (Development Alternatives with Women for a New Era) in Bangladore, India, in 1984. Grassroots organizing experiences led the founders of this organization to link microlevel activities to macrolevel perspectives on development:

> The experiences lived by poor women throughout the Third World in their struggles to ensure the basic survival of their families and themselves . . . provide the clearest lens for an understanding of development processes. And it is *their* aspirations and struggles for a future free of the multiple oppressions of gender, race, and nation that can form the basis for the new visions and strategies that the world now needs. (Sen and Grown 1987: 9–10)

Based on extensive research and debate, DAWN produced work on alternative development strategies that greatly influenced subsequent research and activism in the field. Basically, the group argued that short-term ameliorative approaches to improving women's employment opportunities were ineffective unless they were combined with long-term strategies to reestablish people's (especially women's) control over the economic decisions shaping their lives: "Women's voices must enter the definition of development and the making of policy choices" (Sen and Grown 1987: 82). The tendency since then has been to strengthen the voice(s) of Third World women and to promote an "empowerment approach" to women's development. At the fourth World Conference on

Women, held in 1995 in Beijing, the Platform for Action concerned the human rights of women: rights to education, food, health, greater political power, and freedom from violence (Bunch et al. 1995).

Women in the Third World have organized around economic, environmental, legal, military, cultural, and physical threats and resistance to dictatorship, militarism, fundamentalism, economic dependence, and violence against women. Women's movements are not necessarily organized around feminist agendas, but they do promote women's perspectives: examples include the Chipko Movement of the Himalayas, the Green Belt Movement in Kenya, the Self-Employed Women's Association in India, and Mothers of the Disappeared movements in Latin America (Miles 1996: 86). Increasingly, groups posit culturally specific feminisms as their political bases. Yet around the world feminists continue to unite around issues of economic justice, human rights, and degradation of the environment, the idea being unity through diversity.

Socialist Feminism

There has long been a socialist strain to feminism. Yet many left-wing feminist perspectives begin by criticizing Marxism. Socialist feminists pointed to deficiencies in classical Marxism—that its analysis missed activities and relations fundamental to women's existence—yet many also continued to admire the historical materialist form of understanding and shared Marxism's liberating intent. Socialist feminists have been particularly critical of classical Marxism's emphasis on the economy and its relative silence on the question of women (Mitchell 1966). An early feminist theorist, Heidi Hartmann (1984), argued that the analytical categories of Marxism were "sex-blind," in that the causes of gender inequality (male dominance over women) were lost during a structural Marxist analysis of class inequality (ruling class domination over workers). She called for a specifically feminist analysis to reveal the systematic character of gender inequalities. She also criticized most feminist analyses for being insufficiently materialist and historical. Hence both "Marxist analysis, particularly its historical and materialist method, and feminist analysis, especially the identification of patriarchy as a social and historical structure, must be drawn upon if we are to understand the development of western capitalist societies and the predicament of women within them" (Hartmann 1984: 3).

A main concern of socialist feminism has involved retheorizing the significance of women's work. Juliet Mitchell (1966), of Cambridge University, differentiated between the several structures affecting women's condition—production, reproduction, socialization, and sexuality—with the first involving women's work in the nondomestic economic sphere, and the others concerning women's work as wives and mothers. Each had different contradictions and dynamics, but all formed a unity in women's experience, with the family triptych of sexual, reproductive, and socializing functions dominant. Women performing domestic labor within the home and family created a different relation to the means of production than did men. These activities fulfilled the function of the maintenance and reproduction of labor power in (contradictory) relation to production. Mariarosa Dalla Costa (1973) emphasized the quality of life and relations in domestic work as determining women's place in society regardless of circumstances of place or class. Housewives were exploited workers, whose surplus was used most immediately by their husbands as an instrument of oppression. Under capitalism, Dalla Costa argued, women became the slaves of wage slaves.

In socialist feminism, as compared with Marxism, emphasis was placed on the sexual division of labor or on different types of social praxis (broadly interpreted) as bases of physical and psychological differences between men and women. Women were viewed as constituted by the social relations they inhabited and the types of labor they performed. Beginning with the Marxist notion of production for the satisfaction of needs, socialist feminism argued that needs for bearing and raising children were as important as material needs (food, shelter). So, too, were the needs of sexual satisfaction and emotional nurturing. All of these needs required (usually female) labor. Gender struggles over reproductive activity were fundamental, yet often ignored by traditional Marxist theory. Socialist feminist theories elaborated some of the implications of this basic position. Nancy Chodorow (1978), a sociologist at the University of California at Berkeley, argued that masculinity and femininity were constructed within the family, especially in children's relations with their mothers. Boys grew into achievement-oriented men adapted to work outside the home; girls grew into women adapted to emotional work inside or outside the home. Relations between economy, procreation, and male dominance were conceptualized by Ann Ferguson and Nancy Folbre's (1981) notion of "sex-affective production," the historically specific sets of activities that restricted women's options and remuneration. Socialist feminists in general theorized procreative activities and public sphere production as mutually interdependent, with neither ultimately determining the other, rather than the public determining the private. Public/private distinctions, socialist feminists thought, rationalized the exploitation of women. In general the idea was that women performed unpaid labor in reproducing labor power as a kind of subsidy for capital, as well as working directly for capital as employees in factories or producers of commodities. Thus women were the superexploited working class.

Two tendencies emerged from critical statements like these. First, there were those who wished to develop explicitly Marxian ideas in the direction of considering women (Vogel 1983). Hartmann's statement that Marx and Engels were analytically sex-blind was only three-quarters true: Engels had one eye half open. In a general statement similar to these quoted earlier (in Chapter 4), Engels said:

> According to the materialistic conception, the determining factor in history is, in the final instance, the production and reproduction of immediate life. This, again, is of a twofold character: on the one side, the production of the means of existence, of food, clothing, and shelter and the tools necessary for that production; on the other side, the production of human beings themselves, the propagation of the species. The social organization under which the people of a particular historical epoch and a particular country live is determined by both kinds of production: by the stage of the development of labor on the one hand and of the family on the other. (1972 ed.: 71–72)

Engels argued that the development of production was associated with the rise of private property, exchange, wealth differences, class antagonisms, and sexual relations; the position of women relative to men deteriorated with the advent of class society. In a significant elaboration of these insights, anthropologists Mona Etienne and Eleanor Leacock (1980) argued for the primary importance of social relations for understanding socioeconomic and sexual inequalities and hierarchies. In their opinion, the origins of all these inequalities were inextricably bound together. They developed a historical framework for considering relations between socioeconomic and sexual hierarchies by defining four broad types of production relations:

1. *Egalitarian relations among most gatherer–hunter and many horticultural peoples,* as part of which women had autonomy, multiplicity of economic roles, and decision-making power.
2. *Inequalities in tribal ranking societies* attributable to the growth of trade, specialization, and the reorganization of production relations. In particular, a "public" sector of the economy concerned with production for accumulation and trade was differentiated from a "private" household or lineage sector concerned with production for subsistence and sharing. Men's responsibili-

ties in hunting and warfare often led directly into trading and external political relations, and the growth of this public sphere undermined women's position.

3. *Stratified relations in preindustrial societies* in which the patriarchal household became an economically independent unit, and women's work was further privatized.

4. *Exploitation in industrial capitalist society* in which the subjugation of people generally was paralleled by the special subjugation of women (Etienne and Leacock 1980: 8–16).

The main point of this historical analysis was not formulating the details of gender inequality, but linking modes of production with social forms of gender relations. Not only did this begin to theorize the transition from earlier egalitarian relations to later male domination, it dispelled the myth that women have always ("naturally") been subordinated to men.

Second, however, some feminists had problems with this kind of work because it seemed to them that traditional Marxist analysis was simply being pointed in the direction of women in a kind of "add women and stir" formula. Instead, some feminist Marxists proclaimed that new analytical categories like "patriarchy" were needed. Thus Hartmann (1984: 14) defined patriarchy as a "set of social relations between men, which have a material base, and which, though hierarchical, establish or create interdependence and solidarity among men that enable them to dominate women." The material base of patriarchy lay in men's control over women's labor power. This control was maintained by excluding women from access to essential productive resources. Here the analytical potential lay in connecting the social institutions that coerced and legitimized unequal power relations with the personal processes of psychology and consciousness through which people, especially women, accepted and rationalized their positions in society.

Significant advances were therefore made by feminists in broadening the Marxian conception of the material reproduction of life. Socialist feminist theories of development stressed production and reproduction as inseparable aspects of the making of existence, and therefore as equally significant parts of development theory. This broader conception of development addressed gender as well as class relations, women's labor in the domestic and public spheres, child rearing and socialization, and the family as the particular locus of reproduction. For most of human history productive and reproductive processes occurred at the same time and in the same geographical location—as the barely distinguishable aspects of a whole way of life. More recently, and increasingly with "development," the various aspects separated into different social and spatial spheres. These spheres were bound together by relations of inequality and dominance. The entire surplus production system was underwritten by the unpaid labor of women. Sophisticated ideologies legitimated this exploitative system as natural ("women have always been the weaker sex"). Development therefore was gender-determined as well as a class process. Indeed, gender and class intersected to form the specifics of the developmental process. Contradictions between these various aspects of the life process have been a driving force in societal change. Class- and gender-dominated societies, characterized by exploitation, dominance, and unequal life conditions, developed in biased, dangerous forms. Socialist feminists believe in entirely different forms of development predicated on transformed gender relations. Socialist feminism remains committed to the Marxist notion of the historical and social creation of human nature in a process that includes gender, race, ethnicity, and other distinctions, as well as class. Socialist feminism calls for reproductive democracy, including collective, participatory control over family and procreative decisions, as well as control over commodity production (Jagger 1983: 148–163).

Feminist Epistemology

Questions of epistemology, many outlined for the first time in the late 1970s and early 1980s, became central foci of feminist concern by the mid- to late 1980s. In particular, the Enlightenment notions of reason, progress, and emancipation underlying modern development were subjected to feminist, as well as to poststructural, criticisms. In *The Man of Reason* Genevieve Lloyd (1984), a philosophy professor at the University of New South Wales, in Australia, argued that the ideal of rationality developed in the seventeenth century by Descartes, Spinoza, and other philosophers was characterized by "maleness," such that when philosophers spoke of "human" ideals they were really talking about ideals of "manhood." The seventeenth-century philosopher René Descartes separated clear and distinct thinking (reason), which he attributed to men, from the sensuous and imaginative faculties (emotions), which he attributed to women. Spinoza thought that emotions in their original states, as passions, were confused perceptions of reality that could be transformed into more intellectual emotions through a strong man's detached understanding of universality and transhistorical necessity. During the Enlightenment, passion and nonrationality in general were seen more positively, as wellsprings of action, Lloyd argued. Yet they were either to be transcended, or transformed, through the medium of reason, into "higher" modes of thought. Nineteenth-century romanticism, Lloyd thought, again revalued the passions, but put women on a pedestal, leaving "The Man of Reason" intact, preserving and indeed endorsing the modern dichotomy between reason and feeling. In poststructural feminist disaffection she found not only criticism of the Enlightenment notion that all problems could be solved by the progress of reason, but the more radical idea that many problems actually had their origin in (male) reason itself.

In a parallel argument, Sandra Harding, a professor of philosophy at the University of Delaware, argued that feminist criticisms of science moved from a position merely of improving science, to a position favoring transformation of the foundations of science and the cultures according it value:

> The radical feminist position holds that the epistemologies, metaphysics, ethics, and politics of the dominant forms of science are androcentric [male-centered] and mutually supportive; that despite the deeply ingrained Western cultural belief in science's intrinsic progressiveness, science today serves primarily regressive social tendencies; and that the social structure of science, many of its applications and technologies, its modes of defining research problems and designing experiments, its ways of constructing and conferring meanings, are not only sexist but also racist, classist, and culturally coercive. In their analysis of how gender symbolism, the social division of labor by gender, and the construction of individual gender identity have affected the history and philosophy of science, feminist thinkers have challenged the intellectual and social orders at their very foundation. (1986: 9)

Thus methodologies and transcendental truths taken to be humanly inclusive carried instead the marks of gender, class, race, and culture. Techniques of literary criticism, now employed to "read science as a text," revealed the hidden social meanings of supposedly value-neutral claims and practices. Feminist epistemologies laid the basis for an alternative understanding of the kinds of experience in which to ground the beliefs honored as knowledge. Such feminist critiques of science, Harding said, challenged personal identity to its prerational core.

Harding outlined three sets of feminist epistemological attitudes toward science: *feminist empiricism* argued that stricter adherence to the existing norms of inquiry by women scientists could correct social biases in science; *feminist standpoint theory*, originating in Hegelian and Marxian thought, argued that men's dominance resulted in partial, perverse understandings, whereas women's subjugated position gave the potential for more complete understanding; and *feminist postmodernism* challenged the universalizing assumptions of the other two positions, emphasizing the fractured identities created by modern life and the multiple nature of theorizing. Harding questioned whether feminists should give up trying to provide *one* true feminist story about reality when confronted by powerful alliances between science and sexist, racist social projects. She concluded that feminist epistemological notions had their own problems and contradictory tendencies, yet feminist criticism had already enhanced the understanding of androcentrism in science (Harding 1986: 29).

Yet even as these positions were being established, the entire (Western) feminist project was subjected to a devastating critique from women of color, lesbians, and Third World women. For Audre Lorde, a black lesbian scholar, the feminist claim that all women suffered the same oppression just because they were women lost sight of the varied tools of patriarchy, and ignored how these same tools were used by women against each other. For Lorde, differences between women should be seen as a fund of strengths—they were, she said, "polarities between which our creativity can spark like a dialectic" (Lorde 1981: 99). Without community, she thought, there was no liberation. But community could not mean shedding differences, nor holding to the "pathetic pretense" that differences between women did not exist. The failure of academic feminists to recognize difference as strength was a failure to reach beyond the first patriarchal lesson—"Divide and conquer"—which, for Lorde, had to be transformed into "Define and empower."

Lorde's notion of the place of knowledge, that is, differentials in the power to theorize difference, was expressed with particular force by Third World women. Trinh Minh-ha (1989) thought that difference should not be defined by the dominant sex, any more than it should be defined by the dominant (Western) culture. Under the aegis of "cartographies of struggle" Chandra Mohanty (1991a, 1991b), of Oberlin College, critically examined feminist writings that produced the "Third World woman" as a singular, monolithic subject as a consequence of what she called "discursive colonization." By this she meant the appropriation and codification of scholarship and knowledge by analytical categories that took feminist interests articulated in the West as their primary referents. For Mohanty, colonization implied a relation of structural domination involving suppression of the heterogeneity of Third World subjects. Feminist writers "discursively colonize the material and historical heterogeneities of the lives of women in the third world, thereby producing/re-presenting a composite, singular 'third world woman'—an image which appears arbitrarily constructed, but nevertheless carries with it the authorizing signature of Western humanist discourse" (Mohanty 1991b: 53). Much feminist work on women in the Third World, she said, was characterized by assumptions of privilege and ethnocentric universality, and was inadequately self-conscious about the effects of Western scholarship. Analyses based on cross-culturally singular, monolithic notions of patriarchy or male dominance led to a similarly reductive notion of "Third World difference," a systematization of the oppression of women that itself exercised oppressive power. Mohanty found disconcerting similarities between such feminist positions and the project of Western humanism in general. Humanism involved the recuperation of the "East" and "Woman" as Other in a binary logic where the first term (Identity, Universality, Truth), which in fact was secondary and derivative, was privileged over, and colonized, a second term (difference, temporality, error), which was in fact primary and originative—only because Woman and East were defined as peripheral or Other could Western Man represent himself as center or Same. As Mohanty put it, "It is not the center that determines the periphery, but the periphery that, in its boundedness, determines the center" (1991b: 73–74). French poststructural feminist theorists, such as Julia Kristeva (1980) and Helene Cixous (1980), had already deconstructed the latent anthropomorphism in Western discourse; Mohanty suggested a parallel strategy, a latent ethnocentrism in feminist writing on women in the Third World.

Mohanty's statement made from a position of feminism's Other profoundly disrupted the prevailing mode of feminist discourse, which had taken the form of competing political positions within an assumed Western and privileged realm. The notion of a singular progressive women's movement began to be questioned increasingly and insistently. Also, as the 1980s turned into the 1990s, the full force of the postmodern movement in philosophy and social theory began to affect feminist theory. Postmodern feminism found modern reason to be normalizing, Western, masculine prejudice whose "enlightenment" embodied a colonizing scientific rationalism. Postmodern feminists argued that Western reason made oppressive, universalizing, and dogmatically assumed truth claims by opposing the masculine knowing subject to a known (often feminized) conquered object. For some postmodern feminists, Enlightenment and feminism were opposed in principle; for others, the matter was not that clear cut. Jane Flax (1990: 42), professor of political science at Howard University, contended that feminist theory belonged on the terrain of postmodern philosophy: "Feminist notions of the self, knowledge, and truth are too contradictory to those of the Enlightenment to be contained within its categories. The way(s) to feminist future(s) cannot lie in reviving or appropriating Enlightenment concepts of the person or knowledge." Thus some feminist theorists began to sense that the motto of the Enlightenment, "Have courage to use your own reason" (Kant), rested on a gender-rooted sense of self and on self-deception. The suspicion spread that all transcendental claims reflected and reified the experience of a few persons, mostly white male Westerners.

Such positions, greeting postmodernism with "enthusiasm," were countered by other feminist social theorists who still found potentials in a critique of Western humanism (Johnson 1994). Thus Christine Di Stefano (1990) argued that feminism was firmly, if ambivalently, located in the modernist ethos with its insistence on the importance of gender. The feminist case against postmodernism consisted of the claims that

1. Postmodernism expressed a constituency (white, privileged men of the industrialized West) that already had an Enlightenment for itself and that was now ready and willing to subject that legacy to critical scrutiny.
2. The objects of postmodernism's various critical and deconstructive efforts have been the creations of a similarly specific and partial constituency (beginning with Socrates, Plato, and Aristotle).
3. Mainstream postmodernist theory (Derrida, Lyotard, Rorty, Foucault) had been remarkably blind and insensitive to questions of gender in its rereadings of history, politics, and culture.
4. The postmodern project, if seriously adopted by feminists, would make any semblance of a united feminist politics impossible.

Thus many left feminists urged skepticism about anti-Enlightenment criticisms. Luce Irigaray (1985) asked, Was postmodernism the "last ruse" of patriarchy? Nancy Hartsock (1985) said that postmodernism appeared to side with marginal groups, but she found postmodern theory hindering rather than helping; postmodern theories gave little guidance at their best, and at worst merely recapitulated the effects of Enlightenment theories.

Many other feminist theorists, like Flax and Di Stefano, were ambivalent about the choice between modernism and postmodernism. However, rather than attempting to resolve this ambivalence (by favoring one side over the other), Sandra Harding (1990: 86) argued that "such an ambivalence should be much more robust and principled"— that is, she argued for a self-conscious and theoretically articulated ambivalence that derived originally from the tensions and contradictions in the worlds inhabited by feminists. Even so, Harding concluded, feminism stood on Enlightenment ground in its belief that improved theories contributed to social progress. She thought that feminist inquiry could produce less-partial representations without asserting their absolute, universal, or eternal adequacy. Thus both feminist science theorists and their feminist postmodern critics "stand with one foot in modernity and the other in the lands beyond" (Harding 1990: 100). She thought that feminism needed *both* Enlightenment and postmodern agendas.

Located in such an in-between position, Donna Haraway (1991), of the University of California at Santa Cruz, argued for a usable doctrine of feminist objectivity she called "situated knowledges." In this conception, objectivity was concerned with particular and specific embodiment, and not the false vision of transcendence: "Only partial perspectives promise objective vision. . . . Feminist objectivity is about limited location and situated knowledge, not about transcendence and splitting of subject and object. In this way we might become answerable for what we learn how to see" (Haraway 1991: 190). For Haraway, feminism attempted to theorize the grounds for trusting the vantage points of the subjugated (seeing from the peripheries and the depths). The positionings of the subjugated were not exempt from critique, but should be preferred because they were least likely to deny the critical, interpretive core of knowledge (in this we see the remnants of a feminist standpoint). The question, for Haraway, was *How* to see from below? Such a preferred positioning was as hostile to relativism as it was to totalization and single vision. The alternative was partial, locatable, critical knowledges sustaining webs of connection in politics, and conversations in epistemology, whereas relativism was being nowhere, yet claiming to be everywhere (a "god-trick"). With other feminists, Haraway argued for a practice of objectivity that privileged contestation, deconstruction, construction, webbed connections, transformation, mobile positioning, and passionate detachment:

> I am arguing for politics and epistemologies of location, positioning, and situating, where partiality and not universality is the condition of being heard to make rational knowledge claims. These are claims on people's lives; the view from a body, always a complex, contradictory, structuring and structured body, versus the view from above, from nowhere, from simplicity. Only the god-trick is forbidden. (Haraway 1991: 195)

So the only way to find larger vision was to be somewhere in particular (cf. "thinking locally" in Chapter 5). The feminist science question revolved around objectivity as positioned rationality. Its images were made from joining partial views and halting voices into a collective subject position, a series of views from somewhere.

Feminist Criticism of Development Theory

Feminist incursions into the heart of modern epistemology, together with
the growth and differentiation of radical and socialist feminist thought
in general, led to a critical reexamination of development theory as a
masculinist enterprise. In one leading example, Catherine Scott (1995), a
professor of political science at Agnes Scott College, saw modernization
and dependency theories conceptualizing themes like modernity, development, self-reliance, and revolution within a vision informed by
gendered preoccupations and conceptions; these extended to the dominant policies and practices of international agencies and revolutionary
governments alike. In modernization theory, Scott (1995: 5) argued,
modernity and a rational, forward-looking, male-dominated public
sphere were contrasted with a "feminized," backward traditional society, while the achievement of modernity was seen as a power struggle
with the feminine on the way to "maturity." In modernization, development required the emergence of rational industrial man, receptive to new
ideas, punctual, optimistic, and universalistic, with a counterpart in the
modern efficient state with its new mechanisms of domination and
power. For Scott, the universal model of the modernization process was
in fact based on an often idealized version of masculine modernity. In
this approach, women were alternately invisible, treated paternalisti-
cally, or used as a "litmus test" for determining the degree of a country's
backwardness. Modernization required self-propelled men to leave the
household, abandon tradition, and assume their place among other
rational men. Women and the household were conceived as part of the
past, representing a dangerous worldview that nature was unalterable
and people powerless to control it. Modernization involved the subordination of tradition, nature, and the feminine. For Scott, theories of modernization also replicated the public/private dichotomy prominent in
Western thought: the private and females sphere was inferior and derivative or at best complementary to the public and male sphere.

Dependency theory opposed modernization as representing the
spread of capitalism and the intensification of exploitation. Scott argued
that dependency, in its U.S. version especially, did not challenge the
notion of an inherently dynamic and progressive capitalism eventually
enabling an end to the pressing requirements of material necessity. As
with Marx in his notions about an unchanging Asia, dependency theorists saw precapitalist social formations as obstructions to the realization
of autonomous development in the peripheries. Hence dependency theory, she thought, shared with modernization theory dichotomous
oppositions between the rational sphere of social production and the private, precapitalist realm in a binary logic of center and periphery.

Dependency theory also portrayed industrialization of the public sphere as the paradigm of economic development with stagnant precapitalist social structures as obstructions. Dependency theory shared with Marxism a definition of development as the mastery and transformation of nature, centering conceptualizations of social struggles around productive activity, excluding struggles between men and women, and retaining (however implicitly) notions of nature as feminine.

Scott thought that both modernization and dependency theorists could learn much from such a critical rereading of their ideas. This could lead to a reconsideration of the meaning of modernity, industrialization, work, and development. Rereading allowed development theory to be placed within the crisis affecting Western social theory in the sense of questioning the subjects of theory; masculinist dichotomies, like modern and traditional, center and periphery, First and Third Worlds; and the role of theory in maintaining the essentialist categories that made dominance possible. Scott preferred feminist standpoint theory as perspective. This allowed a sensitivity to the ways systemic power structures lives that had possibilities for rewriting the meaning of development in terms of peoples' continuing efforts to realize their aspirations.

Women, Development, Theory

In response to such criticisms, feminists and development activists made a series of attempts at reformulating development theory. The basic issue was this: Given that women performed most of the labor in many, if not most, Third World societies, why had they been excluded from development theory, and what difference would it make if theory was reformulated to center around women's experiences and gender relations? Placing gender relations at the center of theorization, feminist development theorists argued, reoriented developmental discourse. The traditional areas of developmental concern were seen from a different vantage point in which aspects previously treated as marginal become instead the main foci of interest—for example, Third World industrialization employed not labor (assumed to be male) but women workers, while gender relations, previously relegated to the sidelines, became essential to understanding productive activity. As a consequence, new aspects of development were brought into focus; for example, the informal and rural sectors of the economy, the reproductive sphere as a vital component of development, or the relations between production and reproduction. Proponents of this new view claimed that it did more than change development theory: it actually improved or transformed it.

To make this more concrete, we might consider rethinking development from the position of the feminist standpoint theory outlined in *Money, Sex and Power* by Nancy Hartsock (1985), a professor of political science at the University of Washington. In Hartsock's work, standpoint theory posited a series of levels of reality, in which the deeper level included and explained surfaces or appearances. Feminist standpoint theory amplified the liberatory possibilities embodied in women's experience. The feminist standpoint was related to the working-class standpoint, but was more thorough going, particularly because women did most of the work involved in reproducing labor power. The male worker's contact with nature outside the factory was mediated by women; hence the female experience of nature was deeper. For Hartsock, women's experience in reproduction represented a unity with nature that went beyond the proletarian experience of material/metabolic interchange. Motherhood resulted in the construction of female existence centered in a complex relational nexus and focused on the woman's body. The man's experience was characterized by a duality of concrete versus abstract deriving from the separation between household and public life. Such masculine dualism marked phallocentric social theory, a system of hierarchical dualisms (abstract/concrete, mind/body, culture/nature, stasis/change, developed/underdeveloped, First World/Third World, etc.) By comparison:

> Women's construction of self in relation to others leads in an opposite direction—towards opposition to dualisms of any sort; valuation of concrete, everyday life; a sense of variety of connectedness and continuities with other persons and with the natural world. If material life structures consciousness, women's relationally defined existence, bodily experience of boundary challenges and activity transforming both physical objects and human beings must be expected to result in a world view to which dichotomies are foreign. (Hartsock 1985: 242)

A feminist standpoint, Hartsock thought, might be based in the commonalities within women's experiences, but it was not obvious or self-evident—it needed reading out, developing, and propagating. Hence, for Hartsock, women's life activity formed the basis of a specifically feminist materialism and, we might add, a specifically feminist development theory. Generalizing the human possibilities present in the life activity of women to the whole social system might raise for the first time in history "the possibility of a fully human community, a community structured by a variety of connections rather than separation and opposition" (Hartsock 1985: 247). Extending this, socialist feminists want to reformulate development in a way that combines, rather than separates, everyday life and its societal dimension, productive activities of all kinds considered as a totality rather than split into hierarchical types, and relations with nature placed at the heart of decisions on what, and how much, to produce.

The interaction between feminist theory and development has taken five main forms in the literature: Women in Development (WID); Women and Development (WAD); Gender and Development (GAD); Women, Environment, and Alternatives to Development (WED); and Postmodern and Development (PAD) (Rathgeber 1990; Young 1992; Visvanathan et al. 1997). Each of these trends is discussed below in terms of their origins, position within feminist and development theories, their underlying assumptions, strategies, and problems (see Figure 6.1).

Women in Development

This school of thought originated with the publication of Esther Boserup's *Women's Role in Economic Development* (1970), an early analysis by a Western feminist of the sexual division of labor in the

WID	WAD
WID **Women in Development** Liberal Modernization Theory Restructuring development programs Welfare, Equity, Anti-poverty, Efficiency Empowerment	**WAD** **Women and Development** Socialist Feminism Alternative Development Dependency, Global Capitalism Patriarchy

GAD
Gender and Development
Radical Feminism
Women's Emancipation

Capitalism, Patriarchy, Racism

WED	PAD
WED **Women, Environment,** **and Development** Feminist Political Ecology Sustainable Development Gendered knowledges, Rights, Politics	**PAD** **Postmodernism and** **Development** Postmodern Feminism Postdevelopment, Different Development Representation, Discourse, Local Knowledges

FIGURE 6.1. Forms of feminist development theory.

Third World and its relation to the negative impact of development strategies on women. Boserup argued that women in agricultural societies earned status as food producers. The modernization process, supervised by colonial authorities imbued with Western notions of the sexual division of labor, placed new technologies under the control of men, thereby marginalizing women, reducing their status, and undercutting their power and income. Modernization was not automatically progressive. However, more enlightened policies by national governments and international agencies might correct these mistakes. As Jane Jaquette (1990: 55) says: "Boserup's path-breaking work defined a new arena of policymaking and marked out a new area of professional expertise. The United States and other countries that are major donors of development assistance took steps to promote the integration of women into the development process."

The term "Women in Development" was first used by the Women's Committee of the Washington, DC, chapter of the Society for International Development as part of a strategy to call attention to Third World women's situation (Rathgeber 1990: 490). In the United States, the Percy Amendment to the 1973 Foreign Assistance Act called for particular attention to projects that integrated women into the national economies of foreign countries, thereby improving their status and assisting the development effort. An "Office for Women in Development" was established in the U.S. AID organization in 1974 and moved to the U.S. Bureau for Program and Policy Coordination in 1977. This office served as focus for a network of researchers and practitioners in the universities, the research institutions (e.g., the International Center for Research on Women), and the major foundations interested in development (of which the Ford Foundation stands out). Also, after the 1975 International Women's Year Conference in Mexico, the United Nations established UNIFEM (the United Nations Development Fund for Women) as a way of reaching out to the poorest women in the world. When asked what they needed most, women replied income to provide for themselves and their children (Snyder 1995). At this time, the main idea was bringing women into the development process (Mueller 1987). WID accepted the prevailing modernization theory of the time—that is, development as a linear process of economic growth. Modernization's argument was that differences between the modern and the traditional resulted from lack of contact. Applying this idea to women, WID theorists argued that Third World women were left out of the development process; Kate Young (1993) calls this recognizing women's "invisibility." By the mid-1970s donor agencies were implementing "intervention programs with the transfer of technology, extension of credit and services that would improve women's workloads" (Rathgeber 1990: 491).

Caroline Moser (1993) has noted five variations within the WID school reflecting changes in the policies of the western development agencies:

1. The "welfare approach" prior to 1970 focused on women's reproductive roles and related population issues, with programs initiated on birth control; Chowdry (1995) argued that this approach illustrated WID's representation of "Third World" women as *zenana* (private, domestic world).
2. The "equity approach" reflected calls for equality coming from the UN Decade for Women. This met with considerable resistance from men.
3. The "antipoverty approach" focused on women entering the workforce, or having access to income-generating activities; Chowdry (1995) pointed out that women were still seen as occupying the domestic, private sphere, removed from the political and economic affairs of society.
4. The "efficiency approach" was aligned with IMF structural adjustment programs and stressed women's participation in newly restructured economies.
5. The "empowerment approach" reflected Third World feminist writings, grassroots organizing, and women's need to transform laws and structures through a bottom-up approach.

In all these approaches women were represented as victims.

Chowdry (1995: 26) argued that WID, as implemented by international development agencies, originated in two modernist discourses the colonial discourse; and the liberal discourse on markets. The colonial discourse homogenized and essentialized Third World people, especially by using the image of the "poor woman." The liberal discourse promoted free markets, voluntary choice, and individualism, which disempowered Third World women. WID aligned itself with liberal feminism, although it also used the poor woman image at times to evoke sympathy and obtain funds. Many WID practitioners were well-educated liberal feminists; within WID the liberal feminist view of rationality and individual self-improvement prevailed. There was an emphasis on "role models" or "outstanding women who have gained social recognition in the public sphere" (Young 1993: 129). WID tended to accept the existing social and power structures, working within them for improvement. Hence the sexual division of labor was taken for granted or as natural without theorizing how women became oppressed by men. Ideological aspects of gender, unequal responsibilities between men and women, and the unequal value placed on men's and women's activities were all ignored.

As an ahistorical approach, WID did not consider influences on women such as class, race, or culture. WID's exclusive focus on women and its avoidance of gender relations made for a shallow analysis. WID avoided questioning women's subordination as part of a wider global system of capital accumulation. WID emphasized poverty and not oppression; moreover, poverty was not seen as an outcome of male oppression over women. Hence development strategies based on WID would be flawed, severely limited in their ability to bring about change. WID focused solely on the (formally) productive aspect of women's work, ignoring or dismissing reproductive activities. Mirroring modernization theory, development in WID was seen as economic growth that could only occur in (formally) productive activities. This led to a partial analysis of women's roles and relations. For example, WID-supported activities provided income-generating opportunities for women, but WID offered no strategies for reducing the burden of household tasks or improving reproductive technologies. WID adopted a nonconfrontational approach that sidestepped women's subordination and oppression. This emphasis on poverty also created a division between the demands of First World and Third World feminists as WID became involved with the needs of women "out there" in the developing world, while the feminist theorists themselves remained part of Western culture—hence a new kind of maternal, sorrowful gaze. More generally there was a neglect of questioning the whole assumption and goal of the dominant development paradigm of modernization theory (Rathgeber 1990; Young 1993).

Postmodern feminists claimed that theorists and practitioners working in the WID school tended to represent women in the Third World as backward, vulnerable, and in need of help from the First World. Jane Parpart, of Dalhousie University, and Marianne Marchand, of Middlebury College (1995: 16), argued that "WID discourse has generally fostered development practices that ignore difference(s), indigenous knowledge(s) and local expertise while legitimating foreign 'solutions' to women's problems in the South." The outstanding poststructural critique of WID came from Adele Mueller (1987). Employing Foucault's (1980a) notions of the connections between power and knowledge, and Dorothy Smith's (1990) ideas about the social construction of documentary reality, Mueller concluded that the documentary procedures used by WID programs functioned to shift control from the Third World setting to centralized development agency headquarters in Washington, Ottawa, and Geneva. Development was defined as a technical problem requiring sophisticated methodologies available only in the First World. Accounts of Third World women were written in a policy language amenable to the ongoing practices of development agencies. "Integrating women into development" basically involved WID professionals learning to speak bureaucratic policy language. Mueller's (1987: 2) main finding was that "far from being a liberating force in the worldwide women's movement, Women in Development discourse is produced in and enters into the procedures of the Development institution in order to manage and otherwise rule the hierarchical divisions of the capitalist world order." As a response to these and many other theoretical, political, and practical inadequacies of the WID school, a new paradigm opened to the left, Women and Development.

Women and Development

The WID approach argued that women should be brought into modernization. The WAD perspective argued that women have always been part of the development process and that it was exactly their link with modernization that had impoverished them. WAD drew much more from dependency theory and neo-Marxist approaches to underdevelopment. Issues such as the origins of patriarchy, the intensification of patriarchy with the spread of capitalism, and Engels's (1945 ed.) analysis of the rise of private property (alongside the agricultural revolution and the domestication of animals) formed the historical background for this school of thought (Bandarage 1984; Mies 1986). Rathgeber (1990) pointed out that the WAD perspective focused on relations between men and women. Women always played important roles in the economies of their societies as both productive and reproductive actors. It was precisely how women were integrated into global capitalism by the core countries that explained their marginalization and oppression—for example, women used as cheap labor for multinational corporations in export-processing zones (Visvanathan 1997).

Here the classical analysis of women in the international division of labor was presented by Maria Mies (1986). For Mies, a German sociologist, the historical development of the division of labor (the system of specialization in types of work) was a violent, patriarchal process in which a certain class of men, by virtue of arms and warfare, established an exploitative relationship with women, other classes, and other peoples. The quick accumulation of wealth produced a conception of progress that made satisfying the subsistence needs of the community appear backward and outdated. This predatory, patriarchal division of labor was based on a structural separation and subordination of human beings, men from women, or local people from foreigners, that was extended to include a separation of men from nature. Science and technology became the main productive forces through which men could emancipate themselves from both women and nature. The colonial division of labor, that is, exchanging raw materials for industrial products to the detriment of colonial labor, was linked to the establishment of an internal colony composed of the nuclear family and the "housewifization" of women. Under the new international division of labor, formed by the partial industrialization of selected Third World countries since the 1970s, the use of docile, cheap female labor (housewives rather than workers) in the Third World was linked with the manipulation of women as consumers in the First World. Hence a feminist strategy for liberation should aim at the total abolition of all these relations of retrogressive progress: the end of exploitation of women and nature by men, the end of the exploitation of colonies by the First World, and of classes by the elite. In particular Mies developed a feminist conception of labor that took as its model not the male wage earner, but the mother, for whom work was always both burden and enjoyment. For mothers, peasants, and artisans, work processes were connected with the direct production of immediate life, rather than with production of mere things and wealth. A feminist conception of labor was also oriented toward a conception of time in which work, enjoyment, and rest were interspersed and balanced. Work could be a direct and sensuous interaction with nature, organic matter, and living organisms, yet was also useful and necessary for the people who did it and for those around them: this means bringing together processes of production and consumption within regions. All this amounts to an alternative economy that was self-sufficient.

Naila Kabeer (1994) distinguished between two groups within the WAD school. Dependency feminism used the traditional Marxist–feminist framework and saw inequalities between men and women produced by the larger global economy; this analysis extended the WID critique of mainstream development theory. A second grouping focusing on "global capitalist patriarchy and male violence" was aligned more with radical feminism, which saw gender having precedence over class. The international network of Third World women researchers DAWN mainly adhered to the WAD perspective.

In one of the main research documents produced by DAWN, Gita Sen and Caren Grown (1987) argued that the perspective of poor, oppressed women provided a powerful vantage point for examining the effects of development programs and strategies. This was so because oppressed women knew poverty, yet women's undervalued work was nevertheless vital to social reproduction. Such experiences with economic growth were determined by gender and class. The existing economic and political structures, often the legacy of colonial domination, were highly inequitable between nations, classes, genders, and ethnic groups. Fundamental conflicts arose between women's economic well-being and mainstream development processes. Because economic growth was harmful to the needs of poor people and basic needs were marginalized from the dominant production structures, survival became increasingly difficult:

> Systems of male domination ... on the one hand, deny or limit [women's] access to economic resources and political participation, and on the other hand, impose sexual divisions of labour that allocate to them the most onerous, labour-intensive, poorly rewarded tasks inside and outside the home, as well as the longest hours of work. Thus when development programmes have negative effects, these are felt more acutely by women. (Sen and Grown 1987: 26)

Women were controlled through sexual violence. For example, public spaces were physically dominated by men, making it difficult for women to make a living in the formal ("public") sector. Modern education and mass media perpetuated sex-biased stereotypes. A series of interlinked crises (growing impoverishment, food insecurity, financial disarray, environmental degradation, demographic pressure) worsened the problem, so that the majority of the world's people found survival almost impossible. Rather than channeling resources into antipoverty programs, and reducing the burden of gender subordination, nations militarized while donor agencies expressed hopelessness and lack of concern. Agencies like the World Bank deemphasized basic needs in the 1980s and espoused structural adjustment instead.

By comparison, an approach that began from the perspective of poor Third World women (in a version of feminist standpoint theory) would reorient development analysis to critical aspects of resource use and abuse, to the dominance of women's labor in satisfying needs, with attention focused on poverty and inequality, and pointing to new possibilities for empowering women (there were many examples of organizing efforts among poor, self-employed women). The basic needs approach of agencies like the World Bank in the 1970s involved loans for urban sites and services, social forestry, and support of small farmers, but only under a methodology of commercialization and market integration, and in the context of inequality, which led to exacerbations of the problems that were supposed to be solved. Development programs used a top-down approach to project identification, planning, and implementation. For Sen and Grown (1987: 40–41), policies had to be oriented toward meeting people's basic needs. They deemed the absence of local participation not only undemocratic, but inefficient. The approach of "integrating women in development" used during the UN Decade for Women had basic flaws, not only because of the difficulties in overcoming ingrained cultural attitudes and prejudices, but because of the nature of the development programs into which women were to be integrated. Sen and Grown (1987: 82) argued that "short-term, ameliorative approaches to improve women's employment opportunities are ineffective unless they are combined with long-term strategies to reestablish people's—especially women's—control over the economic decisions that shape their lives." By the latter they meant breaking the structures of inequality between genders and classes and planning changes to reorient production to meeting the needs of the poor. This means national liberation, a shift from export orientation meeting to internal needs, reducing military expenditures, and controlling multinational corporations—that is, structural transformation rather than structural adjustment.

Nevertheless, according to a critique by Eva Rathgeber (1990), of the International Development Research Center in Ottawa, Canada, WAD neglected social relations of gender within classes and did not completely take into consideration variations in patriarchy in different modes of production and how these impacted women. Rather than patriarchy, the WAD approach stressed women's relations within international class structures of inequalities. Kabeer (1994) argued that Marxists working in this school gave insufficient attention to reproduction. Also, when it came to the creation and implementation of development projects, critics claimed that WAD, like WID, tended to group women together without much notice given to race, class, or ethnicity—although, we might add, this seems to neglect Sen and Grown's clear emphasis on poor women. There was also the difficulty of changing fundamental structures. Kabeer (1994) argued that Marxists and dependency feminists took uncompromising stands that prevented them from making realistic, effective changes. Furthermore, poststructural critics saw analyses such as Sen and Grown's (1987) universalizing the Western sexual division of labor and employing categories like "labor" and "production" rooted in the culture of capitalist modernity that were inadequate for describing "other" societies. Such concepts were abstracted from the historical experience of the European Man who repressed not just women, but also "other" people. Feminists using the Marxist paradigm had not overcome its limitations. Extending this paradigm repressed, distorted, and obscured many aspects of women's existence. Additionally, Sen and Grown were said to construct poor Third World women in feminism's own narcissistic self-image. Instead of patronizing "poor Third World women," it was argued, we must learn to learn from them, which means appreciating the immense heterogeneity of the field. First World feminists should learn to stop feeling privileged as women (Spivak 1988: 135–136). Consequently Sen and Grown's "alternative visions" were said to be mired in androcentric Western thinking; they failed to provide a genuine alternative to mainstream development (Hirshman 1995).

Gender and Development

The origins of the GAD perspective lie with women working in the mid-1970s at the Institute of Development Studies, at the University of Sussex. This feminist group was interested in analyzing women's subordination within the development process from the vantage point of gender relations between men and women. They initially drew on Marxist analyses of social change and feminist analyses of patriarchy (Young 1993: 134). GAD differed from WID in its conceptualization of the sexual division of labor. Whereas WID tended to accept the sexual division of labor, but argued that more value needed to be placed on the tasks women did, GAD rejected the sexual division of labor, arguing that it was a system whereby men and women became dependent on each other, and concluded that the allocation of tasks should be changed. DAWN's work also contributed greatly to the GAD approach (Chowdry 1995; Rathgeber 1990).

However, in the GAD approach, gender relations rather than "Women" became the main analytical category, while a number of assumptions ignored by WID and WAD were explored in greater depth. For example, GAD argued that women were not a homogenous group, but were divided by class, race, and creed. Women's roles in society could not be seen as autonomous from gender relations. This became a way of looking at the structures and processes giving rise to women's disadvantaged position. Disadvantage came from the globally pervasive ideology of male superiority: men had power and control over women. Kate Young (1993: 134–135), executive director of Womankind World-wide, has said that GAD was a holistic approach in which gender was not assumed to be the main ordering principal of social hierarchy; other culturally specific forms of inequality and divisions occurred, and gender was interrelated with this overall, socially created hierarchy. Consequently, gender had to be acknowledged as part of a wider international system. For example, capitalism used gender relations to produce a reserve of labor, while women's unpaid labor in the household was a way of creating wealth for global corporations.

When it came to developmental practice, GAD was seen as opening doors for women as social actors among wider structures of constraints:

> It is therefore necessary to analyze how these other forces (political, religious, racial and economic) intersect with and dynamize gender relations, provoking in some instances structural rather than individual responses to produce rational configurations which may be reinforcements of old forms or may be quite new ones. Alternately, individual responses may take on a momentum and massification which leads to structural change. (Young 1993: 139)

Unlike WID and WAD, GAD saw the state as an important actor promoting women's emancipation. Rathgeber (1990) has argued that GAD went further than WID or WAD in questioning underlying social, economic, and political structures. This made its recommendations difficult to implement, since they depended on significant structural change. However, Kabeer (1994) argued that GAD also opened new strategies for feminist intervention. GAD's multifarious approach distinguished between capitalism, patriarchy, and racism, and enabled feminists to identify places in official policies for strategic interventions. While some saw these strategies as necessary for feminists to respond to the needs of poor women (Visvanathan 1997: 24), others argued that GAD did not get rid of its modernist tendencies, while still essentializing poor women:

> The poor, vulnerable Southern woman is a powerful image, and its easy adoption by both mainstream and alternative development theorists and practitioners is understandable. . . . Yet this very image reinforces and maintains the discourse of modernity so essential to Northern hegemony and development practices. (Parpart and Marchand 1995: 16–17)

This focus on image and discourse resulted from the influence of poststructural and postmodern ideas on the gender debate. But before we discuss postmodernism, we turn to an important offshoot of the WAD and GAD approaches, one that focuses more on relations among women, development, and the natural environment.

Women, Environment, and Development

This perspective originated in the 1970s as feminists drew parallels between male control over nature and men's control over women and connected masculine science and industrialization with assaults on the ecological health of the planet. Carolyn Merchant (1980) traced the roots of the world's environmental dilemma to the worldview developed by the founding fathers of modern science (Francis Bacon, René Descartes, Isaac Newton) that conceptualized reality as a machine rather than as a living organism. She argued that this conceptualization had resulted in the death of nature as a living being and an acceleration of the exploitation of human and natural resources in the name of culture and progress. Likewise, ecofeminists interested in the contemporary Third World, such as Vandana Shiva and Maria Mies, adopted a radical feminist perspective on the exploitation of nature. Shiva (1989) argued that science and development were not universal categories but were instead special projects of Western patriarchy that were killing nature. Development activity in the Third World superimposed the scientific and economic paradigms created by Western, gender-based ideology on communities previously immersed in other cultures with entirely different relations with the natural world. As victims of the violence of patriarchal development, women resisted "development" to protect nature and preserve their sustenance:

> Indian women have been in the forefront of ecological struggles to conserve forests, land and water. They have challenged the western concept of nature as an object of exploitation and have protected her as Prakriti, the living force that supports life. They have challenged the western concept of economics as production of profits and capital accumulation with their own concept of economics as production of sustenance and needs satisfaction. A science that does not respect nature's needs and a development that does not respect people's needs inevitably threaten survival. (Shiva 1989: xvii)

Thus ecological struggles simultaneously liberated nature from ceaseless exploitation and women from limitless marginalization. In an analysis of the effects of the Green Revolution in the Punjab region, on India's border with Pakistan, Shiva argued that the assumption of nature as a source of scarcity, with technology as a compensating source of abundance, created ecological and cultural disruptions that ended in diseased soils, pest-infested crops, waterlogged deserts, discontented farmers, and unprecedented levels of conflict and violence.

For Diane Rocheleau, Barbara Thomas-Slayter, and Esther Wangari (1996), development theorists at Clark University, there were real gender differences in experiences of nature and responsibility for the environment that derived not from biology but from social constructions of gender that varied with class, race, and place. They saw feminist scholarship on the environment taking a number of forms. Some schools of thought, such as socialist feminism, disagreed with biologically based portrayals of women as nurturer, and saw women and the environment more in terms of reproductive and productive roles in unevenly developing economies. For example, Bina Agarwal (1991) argued that women in India have been active not because of some "natural" relation with the environment (as with Shiva) but because they suffered more in gender-specific ways from environmental destruction. Feminists thus drew from cultural and political ecology's emphasis on unequal control over resources (Peet and Watts 1996), but treated gender as a critical variable in interaction with class, race, and other factors shaping processes of ecological change. Three themes were pursued in feminist political ecology: gendered knowledge, reflected in an emerging science of survival in healthy homes, workplaces, and ecosystems; gendered environmental rights, including property, resources, and space; and gendered environmental politics, particularly women's involvement in collective struggles over natural resources and environmental issues (Rocheleau et al. 1996).

"Sustainable development" became a central issue in the WED perspective. This notion linked ideas of equity between generations, maintaining a balance between economic and environmental needs to conserve nonrenewable resources, and reducing industrialization's waste and pollution. Sustainable development was seen as an opportunity for challenging the Development = Economic Growth equation from the perspective of a feminist methodology. This meant differentiating feminism even from other alternative notions of economics and development. Thus, according to Wendy Harcourt (1994), the alternative "real-life economics" (Ekins and Max-Neef 1992), which wanted to expand the notion of development to consider environmental degradation, poverty, and participation, still needed demystifying to disclose its sexism. For example, economics in the form of mathematical models was reductionist and inadequate for expressing ambiguities and contradictions in complex processes. For Harcourt, also, "people-centered economics," an attack on self-interestedness, an economics to make the world a better place, the advocacy of local-scale development and investment in people, started from a Eurocentric point of view, was a universal model (with variations), and used residues ("investment in people") of the language of economic growth. Likewise, postdevelopmentalism idealized traditional societies' relations with nature and was overly pessimistic, seeing no role for Western modernity, whereas instead we must deal with the contradictions of a process in which we are inevitably immersed. Harcourt favored work on culture, economics, and modernization that pointed to the breakdown of cultures with industrialization (Mazlish 1991).

Similarly Frederique Apffel-Marglin and Steven Marglin (1990), of Smith College, saw economics as part of an *episteme* (a system of ideas and discourses) based on logic and rationality disembodied from contexts (an instrumental logic of calculation); *techne* knowledge by comparison was embedded in practice and was gained through process within a community; but Western civilization considered only *episteme* as pure knowledge. For feminists, the historical replacement of *techne* by *episteme* in the West and the contemporary process of replacement in the Third World undervalued women's nurturing and sustaining the environment. Western development economics, with its devaluation of nature, and failure to treat other cultures with dignity, could learn from other modes of social organization rather than always assuming superiority (Harcourt 1994a).

Postmodernism and Development

The PAD perspective reacted to the controversial entry of poststructural and postmodern critiques into feminist theory by asking whether a more accessible and politicized postmodern feminism had relevance for the problems facing women in Third World societies. The PAD perspective criticized the GAD view as representing Third World women as "other" or, in the case of WID, using three images, women as victims, women as sex objects, and women as cloistered beings. Postmodern feminists found the WID view embedded in colonial/neocolonial discourse and enshrined in the liberal discourse on markets, both of which disempowered women. Particularly appealing for PAD theorists was postmodernism's emphasis on difference, which provided space for the voices of the maginalized (hooks 1984), or disrupted the representation of women in the South as an undifferentiated "other" (Mohanty 1991). Also, the postmodern critique of the subject and truth suggested an alliance between postmodernism and feminism based on a common critique of the modernist *episteme*. Specifically, postmodern critiques questioning the certainty of Eurocentric development studies, and criticizing the silencing of local knowledges with the propagation of Western expertise, were relevant for the development of women. Some of the themes coming from the encounter between feminism, postmodernism, and development included: a critique of colonial and contemporary constructions of the "Third World" woman—what Apffel-Marglin and Simon (1994) call "feminist orientalism"; an enhanced deconstruction of development discourse, which disempowered poor women in particular; the recovery of women's knowledges and voices; the celebration of differences and multiple identities; and a focus on consultative dialogue between development practitioners and their "clients."

An example would be Jane Parpart's (1995) deconstruction of the development "expert," that is, the person with special, technical knowledge of the modern world who could solve the problems of the developing countries. The notion of expertise, Parpart argued, was embedded in Western Enlightenment thought, with its specialization of knowledge—for example, development economics, as the "science of economic progress." Yet it was also recognized that postmodern feminism, taken to extreme, could stymie collective action among women, while the impenetrable jargon of postmodern writing was an insurmountable obstacle for people mired in illiteracy and economic crisis (Parpart and Marchand 1995). Rather than rejecting development altogether, most postmodern feminists in this field recognized the real problems faced by poor women and the need for addressing developmental issues. They favored an approach "that accepts and understands difference and the power of discourse, and that fosters open, consultative dialogue [which] can empower women in the South to articulate their own needs and agendas" (Parpart and Marchand 1995: 19).

Critique

What distinguishes the feminist perspective on the modern development process? Development as a conscious practice, as a set of policies, alters gender relations in favor of men, shifting resources to the male sphere of control, making women more vulnerable to disasters, whether natural or social in origin. As feminist scholarship deepened, attempts to delineate the causes of these problems likewise went from considering deficiencies in the distribution of material benefits, to addressing inequalities in control over productive resources, to attacking the androcentrism of the founding Western cultural ideas about science and values. Carolyn Merchant (1980: 11) says that feminist history turns society upside down. And at first sight feminist critiques of development appear to view the world in reverse, seeing the normal as abnormal, the praiseworthy as abhorrent, and the apparently just as unjust. In this sense, criticism from a feminist standpoint tends to reverse the dominant trend, move in support of the antithesis, see things as opposites. So a feminist-inspired "development policy" (if that is not a contradiction in terms) would see productive labor as reproductive work.

Yet this would imply mere reversal as feminism's contribution to development theory. More than this is going on beneath the ever-shifting feminist perspectives (from WID to PAD). Theoretical viewpoints derive from thinking about the experiences of particular groups of people, and these histories are far more than Western feminist reactions to male domination in the West. As feminist thought changes, under the constant pressure of critique and countercritique, attempts are increasingly made to recognize, and even think from, the quite different experiences of a world of peoples (especially different groups of women), from experiences that, while comparable in some respects, are incomparable in others. Incomparability means that Western women theorists cannot just reverse Western male-centeredness, but rather must invent new things. More importantly, Western women's reversals are but one tradition in feminist critical thought. There is a world of different experiences waiting to be recognized, drawn upon, criticized, but also appreciated. Likewise, interventions into the development process take many forms, some of which are not only incomparable but even in opposition, one to the other, so that "global feminism" is at best a network of tolerance, and at worst a barely contained squabble. This means that "development" even conceived as reproduction-centered improvements takes forms so multiple that continuity or similarity of project becomes difficult and, for some, impossible. Even the words "project" or "improvement" imply, for adherents to the PAD perspective, immersion in Western thinking, a capturing of the imagination by Western themes of progress. For others, in the WAD school for instance, immersion in western thinking involves instead interaction between traditions, so that anticolonial struggles (at home and in the colonies) are also parts of the "Western" theme of progress. Are there emancipatory and developmental themes common to all oppressed peoples? And is it possible to synthesize difference and similarity through a dialectic that does not submerge difference in similarity? We think that something like this was attempted by the WAD position in feminist developmentalism. We find the criticisms of WAD overdrawn and would like this discourse to return to the agenda set by Sen and Grown (1987)—breaking structures of inequalities; reorienting production to meet the needs of the poor; combining immediate, ameliorative improvements with long-term strategies that establish women's control over decisions—themes that we raise again in our concluding chapter, which derives from a feminist socialism.

However, while reading the recent literature on feminism and development, we could not help noticing the hesitancy of the ideas expressed, the tendency to repeat a few established themes, the incomplete nature of conclusions. Virtually the entire discourse on women and development consists of collections of essays, most of which are case studies exemplifying general themes scarcely or never stated. This is particularly the case with concrete proposals for change: studies that cry out for some proposal of what to do in desperate situations suddenly end where they should propose, or call (safely) for "further research." At first glance, the problem involves feminist reluctance to "speak for others," not just in terms of Western women prescribing for non-Western women what they should want from social change, but also from non-Western elite women speaking for non-Western peasant women. Yet there is more than problems of "speaking for others" involved here. Feminist thought, taken to the extreme, involves restructuring the imagination to think in entirely new ways. But how are new ways of thinking imagined when the imagination is already structured, either by male-dominated educational processes, or negatively by critiques of androcentrism in science, theory, and culture? How can development be imagined anew by feminist theorists trained in Western notions of progress or by feminists immersed in critiques of these same notions, and trapped in their reversals? Well, for one thing, feminists from nonelite or non-Western backgrounds can remember their pasts. For another, the dialectical mode of thought is only caricatured by a simple progression from thesis (development) to antithesis (critique of development) to synthesis (modified kinds of development). Dialectical thought is far more innovative than this, allowing the results of many experiences of quite different kinds to be drawn into synthetic statements that allow for diversity. So alternative, feminist conceptions about developmental thought are difficult, but not impossible. It is time to raise again fundamental issues of real socialist feminist alternatives. We are at an early stage in relating feminism to development.

Chapter 7

CRITICAL MODERNISM, RADICAL DEMOCRACY, DEVELOPMENT

In capitalist modernity progress is conventionally understood as economic growth. From this perspective, an increase in the total volume of goods and services is the best thing that can happen to a society. Again conventionally, the causes of growth are understood in terms of efficiency and modernization. While there are several different versions—modernization theory, neoclassical economics, and neoliberalism, to name but three—the basic idea behind all such theories is that modern, competitive behavior and technological improvements coordinated through free markets lead to economic growth and, eventually, material benefits for everyone. "Development" is often conceived as the pleasant face of this kind of consumptive modernization; economic growth is merely recast in terms of "sustainability," "redistribution," or some other liberal agenda, to make it more palatable. Third World countries "develop" by copying the model of industrialization already set by the example of the First World countries. Thus modernization and development are captured by a single historical experience repeated eternally at the "end of history" (in terms of lack of temporal change) and the "end of geography" (in terms of lack of spatial variation).

Yet it is clear that neither history nor geography have really "ended." The existing process of modernization cannot possibly continue. If successful, it would lead to a five- or sixfold increase in global incomes, consumption, resource use, and pollution of natural environments already strained beyond capacity. Such an increase shows the natural impossibility of endlessly copying the Western model—continue the process and human history will really end! So, too, the fact that capitalist modernization leaves 200 million people in poverty at the very heart of modernity (in the so-called advanced countries) shows its social implausibility and ethical irresponsibility. Yet such is the dominance of neoliberal theory that crises in the global economy, such as the massive bailout of South Korea, Thailand, Indonesia, and other countries by the IMF in the late 1990s, lead only to slightly revised versions of the same modernization approach—models involving even less redistribution of wealth and even more "incentives" (for the already rich) are intoned as deep wisdom by "economic experts" (the high priests of conventional development theory). Conventional thinking about modernity, growth, and development, so defined, is hopelessly, dangerously blind to its own deficiencies. Moreover, alternatives to conventional thinking are not taken seriously in the centers of power. The future existence of the world's peoples depends on breaking this style of developmental thought.

Critical Modernism

Neoliberal orthodoxy is challenged by theoretical alternatives, for here, in the realm of the critical mind, opportunities still exist for speaking from other positions. Marxist and neo-Marxist theories argue that modernization is perverted by capitalist social relations to yield high material standards of living for a few at the expense of poverty for the many, while the environment is degraded and nature destroyed to satisfy the consumptive whims of the richest 5% of the world's people. Marxists and neo-Marxists offer an alternative: to rationally control the development process through social means like collective ownership and democratic reasoning. Poststructural theory argues that the reason, knowledge, and ideas of progress underlying the modern project are saturated with Western power, to the extent that "development" is the source of our problems rather than their solution. Poststructuralists contend that we should abandon the developmental problematic and find simpler lives in material and spiritual terms. Feminist theories find modern reason to be masculinity in logical disguise, with development practices subjugating women while pretending humanitarianism. For most feminists, the idea is to rethink the meaning and practice of development from a critical, gendered perspective; a few postmodern feminists go so far as to advocate abandonment of development altogether. All three approaches find development, as presently understood, to be a mistake of (natural and social) geographic proportions. They differ mainly on what to do about it: Marxists want to rescue modernity's beneficial aspects in new sociopolitical forms; postmodernists want to hasten the downfall of the modern project altogether through deconstructive critique in favor of support for subjugated knowledges and oppositional social movements; most feminists want to reconstruct development along reproductive–democratic lines.

In the present political and intellectual climate, dominated on the right by neoliberalism (the market solves all problems), and on the left by postmodernism (development is a dead issue), statements about alternative development, understood as organized, collective interventions into social, cultural, and economic processes on behalf of defined political goals, have been silenced to the point almost of disappearing from memory. Yet given the momentous problems faced by some two billion desperately poor people, this kind of instant amnesia, typical of the postmodern age, is a tragedy of politics, in terms of the loss of direct engagement, and a travesty of justice, in terms of forgetting about others, or losing sight of urgency in the desperate pursuit of theoretical complexity, academic reputation, or the latest exaggerated intellectual trend. This is true no matter the source, whether mainstream neoliberal selfishness or postmodern romanticism about indigenous peoples.

Here we reach a different conclusion: there is a need to rethink the development project rather than to discard it. We want to reconsider development in the full knowledge of the postdevelopmental and feminist critiques. Indeed, we want to employ these criticisms to elaborate a more powerful, more persuasive, critical yet still modernist approach. We believe that democracy, emancipation, development, and progress are fine principles corrupted by the social form taken by modernity—that is, capitalism as a patriarchal, class system, a type of society operated in the interests of a male elite, based on the profit motive to the exclusion of everything else. In our view, the main problem with democracy is that it has never been achieved. In which society do people directly control the basic institutions, the places (work, family, neighborhood) where they spend most of their lives? Likewise, the trouble with emancipation is that it applies to the privileges of the few rather than to the rights of the many. So, too, the deficiency of development lies in its limited aims (an abundance of things) and the timidity of its means (copying the West). And as for progress, it is little more than a cliché, recounted daily in the eternally optimistic chatter of television "personalities" and company executives forever "coming on board" and "moving forward." As poststructural theorists rightly claim, these modern terms are beyond redemption, if considered as statements divorced from ideas (i.e., as signifiers relating only to other signifiers). But to concede "progress" to the mindlessly optimistic is to give up on an idea held by the seriously optimistic at that level of belief that still finds reasoning, science, technology, and democracy to be potentials that could make possible a better life for all people. And while a better life, in terms of material sufficiency, may easily be denigrated by those who already lead lives of abundance, it is a dream full of hope for those who have never known security of existence. Thus, for us, "development" is a term still full of positive meaning.

A critical modernist developmentalism learns from the Marxist, poststructural, and feminist critiques of modernity, but retains belief in the potential, rather than the present practice, of development. Critical modernism entails a critique of capitalist power systems in traditional Marxist terms of class ownership of productive resources, in feminist terms of male dominance, and in poststructural terms of the hegemony of elite discourses. Yet different from postmodernism, it converts these negative criticisms into positive political proposals on how to change the meaning and practice of development. Critical modernism distrusts any elite, be it entrepreneurial, bureaucratic, scientific, intellectual, racial, geographic, or patriarchal. Critical modernism favors instead the views of oppressed peoples of all kinds, from peasant social movements, to indigenous organizations, to women organizing for reproductive rights, to working-class movements. Even so, "favoring" the ideas of oppressed peoples does not mean believing everything they say in a kind of New Age romanticism that finds eternal wisdom in every shaman's prayer. And while poor peoples' movements have to be seen in their own terms and contexts, critical modernism favors alliances that draw together the powers of the oppressed majority to counter what is otherwise the overwhelming power of the exploiting minority. Critical modernism listens to what people say. Yet, controversially, it wants to combine the popular discourses of social movements with the liberating ideas of modernism, especially in the form of a people's science. Critical modernism finds wisdom and worth in all experiences. But it insists that this principle applies to the Western experience of modernity as well, despite postmodernism, except that critique is all the more necessary. We can learn a lot from the modern experience of the West, and not all we have to learn is negative.

Criticize everything, convert critique into proposal, criticize the proposal, but still do something—that is the critical modernist credo.

Critical modernism should focus on the question of development, understood as the social use of economic progress, as a central theme of our age. On the one hand, development seen simply as aggregate economic growth cannot continue much longer—natural constraints prevent this, and there are abundant natural signs of approaching catastrophe. On the other hand, development seen as material transformation for the world's hungry people is an ethical and practical necessity, one just as pressing as the natural constraints on growth. Unless we can find far better systems under which a much fairer life for all can be led, then let nature take its revenge on a greedy species! "Development" has to be transformed, as a term with meaning, as a belief in better things, as a practice employing millions of altruistic people, and as the main hope for a saner world. Here we offer five ideas to help transform the concept of development: the critique of modernity as capitalism, the promise of an ethical development, the growth of new social movements, the premise of radical democracy, and some initial notions of a truly alternative development.

The Critique of Capitalist Modernity

The will to find a better life is founded on criticism of its present social forms. Criticism can be an active, creative endeavor, in which negativity is transformed into positivity by showing what most needs changing in which particular ways. Two kinds of critique contend on the left: critical modernism (sometimes called radical humanism or socialist feminism, both generally inspired by socialist ideas); and postmodernism (including many poststructural ideas, much of postcolonialism, and parts of feminism). The two radical criticisms differ fundamentally in their mode of criticism: critical modernism criticizes material power relations in order to change them; postmodernism criticizes discourses and ideas to under mine their modern certainty. The two differ also regarding the possibilities of development: critical modernism hopes to transform development, postmodernism intends to abandon it. These differences derive not only from the nature of the respective critiques, so that postmodernism focuses on development as discourse, while critical modernism emphasizes development as a class and gendered practice, but derive also from differences concerning the social object that forms the target of criticism: modernism or capitalism. Modernism is understood mainly in discursive terms, capitalism as a system of class power.

A critical modernism learns from the poststructural critique, but is not entirely persuaded by it. The poststructural critique overemphasizes representation at the expense of practice, as though words were the main problems in life: Change the word, and the world will change. As a result of overvaluing words, too many postmodern critiques end in a nihilistic never-never land, where nothing is proposed, and little gets done in anything approaching real terms. Nor is critical modernism willing to abandon the political principles of an older radicalism, such as democratic Marxism or socialist feminism—especially their ideas about social control of the reproduction of existence. Most importantly, critical modernism remains modern, in terms of favoring a scientific attitude toward the world, that is, in requiring some kind of evidence before believing, rather than accepting purely on faith, as with premodern understanding, or denying any validity to evidential truth, as with postmodernism. Given a choice between the Catholic "inner eye of faith" and the modern "inner eye of reason," critical modernism prefers the second, except that the inner eye "sees" as a result of practice and discussion.

Critical modernism centers on a critique of capitalism, as the social form taken by the modern world, rather than on a critique of modernism as an overgeneralized discursive phenomenon. The radical critique of capitalism, as a corrupt form of modernism, allows space for the retention of modernist discoveries in new forms: science, technology, medicine, hospitals, as one stream; emancipation, democracy, reasoning, planning, as a second; technology, productivity, machines, material certainty, to mention a third. The idealistic aspect to this (selective) retention of the modern is that the project contains ethical intentions worthy of respect and support. The material aspect is that modernism results in benefits for large numbers of people who live far better lives than they otherwise would live. And the practical aspect is that science and democracy are now endemic in the very structure of Western meaning and will not disappear simply because postmodern theorists are tired of them— yet benefit from modernity all the more by criticizing it (postmodern theory is a growth machine for a few academics). Hence there is a need for a more active, critical engagement with modernity as a form of capitalist practice guided by social relations rather than criticizing modernity as a discursive formation. We should learn to live with modernity by criticizing and changing it!

Let us repeat the classical Marxist critique of capitalist modernity, lest it be too easily forgotten, and let us emphasize relations between social reproduction and nature as the basic, fundamental contradiction that threatens an end to the premodern, modern, *and* postmodern worlds. Marxism's thesis is that capitalism is a class and patriarchal society in which a minority owns and controls the means of the reproduction of existence, determining thereby the character and direction of development, the social relations with nature, and the way people are created as kinds of human beings. Production is organized not as a social activity that directly satisfies needs, but as a profit-making endeavor in which needs are met only when profit can be made. Profits are driven by an elite's desire for conspicuous consumption (a dress that costs $150,000, made to be worn once; a string of pearls costing $3 million), but also by the constant need for reinvestment inherent in competitive market relations. In Fordist capitalism, mass consumption becomes the main source of pleasure: more consumption means a better life. Elite desire, the competitive need for profit, the substitution of machines for human labor power, the pursuit of the latest style or gadget—all are endlessly expansive. Economic growth becomes a necessity rather than a choice. Under growth's driving force, production is escalated but the natural consequences are depleted resources, used-up energy sources, and ever-growing pollution, while all the time poor peoples' needs remain tragically unmet amid landscapes of casual overabundance. Profit is made each time a commodity is sold, so rapid changes in fashion, or built-in obsolescence, are integral parts of the capitalist lifestyle. Endless waves of consumer subcultures speed the resource cycle from natural material, through commodity, to the garbage heap. As material objects become valued for their powers of signification, rather than for their direct utility, consumption becomes as endless as the need for status (the more you have, the more you want), while nature is used to provide the commodity platform for the signs of prestige or sexuality. In a phrase, the culture of advanced capitalism is driven by the logic of profit rather than by the satisfaction of needs or natural renewability.

Additionally, while markets provide links between supply and demand that are so efficient in the short run that alternative forms of economic integration seem absurd, market-driven production is disastrous for nature, culture, and social relations in a long run that becomes increasingly unimaginable. The market is an anonymous institution, masking the resource origins of supply, so that consumption occurs in ignorance of its long-run environmental and social consequences. Hence it is "normal" for even environmentally conscious consumers to destroy the natural conditions of existence even as they consciously try to care for nature in their everyday practices. Hence, people do not directly make decisions about resource use, employing ethical means of need satisfaction, or natural–geographic principles of renewability. Instead, decisions are made indirectly via market mechanisms that sideline environmental considerations as "externalities." Meanwhile, companies profit from social resistance to the rape of nature through the sale of green-friendly products (the new marketing frontier). Further, capitalist societies employ high technology to immediately remove resource blockages to profit making, which in turn poses long-term threats to the environment—chemical technologies are leading examples. In such ways are the contradictions embedded in capitalist social relations released in the developmental tendency toward environmental catastrophe. In such ways are capitalist societies meshed into contradictory relations with a nature they increasingly are capable of completely destroying. Exactly the mechanisms that make capitalism so efficient a provider of a high-consumptive lifestyle make it effectively destructive of the natural world.

But now, after 200 years of plundering the natural world and discharging poisonous effluents and pollutants with reckless abandon, we see signs that natural limitations may impose, at the risk of humanity's annihilation, a transformation in social relations, modes of thought, lifestyles, and systems of ethical morality. These relations between economic growth and the natural environment are basic, structural contradictions necessitating fundamental human and societal change. If it is indeed the case that disastrous natural relations derive from unequal social relations, "fundamental transformation" must involve new forms of social organization at the level of control over the bases of power. In the absence of some cataclysmic moment of last-minute self-realization, how might this transformation occur?

Ethical Development

Ethics are principles of right and wrong, good and bad, that human beings following their best intentions try to exercise in their relations with others and with the natural world. Humans differ from animals in the fundamental sense of being conscious of existing, but also in having conscience about our actions. That is, we make moral and ethical judgments about intentions and behaviors in which our actions are related to broader contexts, something greater than the particular, something long lasting, perhaps even eternal. This relationship to wider meanings occurs at the level of belief—that is, principles of existence held at the emotional level so that ideas are felt in a bodily way. For religious people, this greater thing is God, the originator of life and guardian of its purposes. Ethical principles by which to live were set down once and for all by the prophets who established a direct connection between themselves and the heavens. But religion can also be seen as a cultural form for legitimating ethical principles actually derived from contemplation of the lessons of life's experience. And ethics can be discussed far more directly in historical terms of human experience, for example, the conditions under which people are happiest, or the forms of life that are environmentally sustainable—although there remains a dimension seemingly beyond direct analysis, for example, What constitutes "happiness"? or Is sustainability the only natural basis for ethical principles? In other words, when we ask the questions, How should we live? and Why should societies develop in certain ways?, the only sure guide is what we have done, and what we can learn from history, practice, and experience through eternal discussion.

In the case of development, however, the ethical problems of what and how much to produce are made less intractable by the obvious needs of the world's two billion poverty-stricken people. There is a disturbing tendency for poststructural discussions to see poverty in terms of the social construction of a deficient term, rather than in terms of the material reality of massive and absolute deprivation. This tendency is accompanied by the ethical advocacy of "convivial poverty" and the spiritual ideal of simplicity and frugality (Rahnema 1997). Support comes from proverbs like: "You are poor because you look at what you do not have. See what you possess, see what you are, and you will discover that you are astonishingly rich" (Rist 1997: 294). If poverty is considered purely as a social construct, or something that has entirely different meanings depending on the cultural context, then simplicity, dignity, and the discovery of inner richness may have some validity as responses. But if poverty is considered materially as the absolute lack of inputs vital to continued existence, such as not enough food (of any kind) to keep people alive, as a far too universal reality, then postmodern ethical advocacy is a cruel hoax: it amounts to telling those who are about to expire that they are (astonishingly!) rich, that they should die with "dignity" rather than struggle for life. Here "dignity" is the postmodern equivalent of the myth of heaven, "put up and shut up." But poor people are not quietly dignified, they are actively so. The poor have spoken, and they want what they need: food, shelter, services. These are authentic needs that satisfy any ethical principle, whether of happiness or resource scarcity. The ethical question is not *whether* but *how* to provide these basic needs. And the means of providing for needs is called development. This principle of the ethical satisfaction of urgent needs lies at the core of most social movements. While universal in its essence, it emerges in quite different forms depending on circumstance.

New Social Movements

Rather than structural contradictions, such as resource deprivation and poverty, producing societal transformation directly through ethical realization, the linkage with social action seems to occur indirectly: contradictions provoke crises, the people directly affected build social movements, and these accumulate into widespread popular opposition to the existing forms of social life. The new thinking about social movements stresses the social and cultural creation of organized opposition through mediations of at least five types:

1. Perceptions and interpretations place the specific adverse situations faced by people into their cultural meaning systems.
2. A sense of collective identity or commonality with others is often place-based or environmentally structured.
3. Deprived conditions spur injured or aggrieved people to different

levels or types of actions, ranging from sullen individual resistance to organized social movements.

4. Social, cultural, and spatial linkages of many kinds between social movements create broad-based political forces.
5. "Old" social movements, such as unions and leftist parties, can find solidarities with "new" social movements, such as organizations advocating popular development.

Recent theory, often focused on the Third World, stresses the rise to prominence of the new social movements, independent of traditional trade unions or organized political parties: squatter movements and neighborhood councils, base-level communities within the Catholic Church, indigenous associations, women's associations, human rights committees, youth meetings, educational and artistic activities, coalitions for the defense of regional traditions and interests, self-help groupings among unemployed and poor people (Evers 1985). Radical theorists find potential for direct action by the peoples in movements to construct a new political power base and initiate popular social change. Some of the ideas relevant here include the notion of everyday resistance (Scott 1985, 1990); de Certeau's (1984) notion that the "marginal majority" effects multiple, infinitesimal changes in power structures; social movements as cultural struggles over meaning as well as over material conditions and needs (Touraine 1981, 1988; Melucci 1988; Escobar 1992b); and the notion of politics as a discursive articulatory process (Laclau and Mouffe 1985). Putting this more directly, the new social movements oppose more than deprivation; issues of culture, ideology, ethics, and way of life are contended as well.

This widening of the scope of attack is paralleled by poststructural analyses of the thoughts, imaginaries, statements, and institutions of both dominant and subaltern groups. The social imaginaries and discourses that social movements contend do not arise from a denatured ivory tower. Rather, the environment is an active constituent of imagination, and discourses assume regional forms organized by natural contexts. In other words, there is not an imaginary made in some separate "social" realm, but an environmental imaginary, or rather whole complexes of imaginaries, with which people think, contend the threats to their livelihoods, and devise alternative strategies. Each society carries an "environmental imaginary," a way of imagining nature, visions of social and individual practice, including forms of development, that are ethically proper and morally right with regard to nature. This imaginary is typically expressed and developed through regional discursive formations, which take as central themes the history of social relations to a particular natural environment. Environmental imaginaries are frequently, indeed usually, expressed in abstract, mystical, and spiritual lexicons. However, they contain at least to some degree reasoned approaches that "work out" the consequences of actions on environment, like agricultural or industrial production.

A liberation ecology would borrow from poststructuralism a fascination with discourse and institutional power, yet remain within that tradition of Marxist political ecology that sees imaginaries, discourses, and environmental practices as grounded in the social relations of production and their attendant struggles. The environmental imaginary emerges, therefore, as a primary site of contestation; critical social movements have at their core environmental imaginaries at odds with hegemonic conceptions. An environmental imaginary is a particular kind of situated knowledge (Haraway 1989). But perhaps most importantly, through the concept of environmental imaginary, liberation ecology sees nature, environment, and place as *sources* of thinking, reasoning, and imagining about social and economic practices. There is an active interaction between practice and idealization in which imaginaries are constantly rebuilt and refigured, accumulate and change, during practical activities that imagination has previously framed. Yet the word "imaginary" is meant in the full sense of creativity—the projection of thought into the scarcely known—so that it is a vital source of transformational, as well as merely reproductive, dynamics: the imaginary links natural conditions with the construction of new social and economic forms (Peet 1996; Peet and Watts 1996).

In the sense of forming linkages and joining movements old and new together, there remains a need for ethical, critical, and political principles that transcend the local so that particular movements, with environmentally based imaginaries, can coalesce into regional and global oppositional movements organized around at least quasi-universal principles. Why is this important? Because most social movements can be obliterated in the absence of outside support (e.g., the Zapatista movement in Chiapas province, Mexico). Because local social movements face opponents embedded in global power structures. And because local success often entails changing these broader power structures, for example, changing property rights at the national level, or removing international threats to common property resources. After the postmodern recognition of difference comes the critical modernist rediscovery not of sameness, but of similarity. Social movements, old and new, are united in their oppositions to resource deprivation, by which is meant, primarily, the lack of material necessities and the capacity to produce these. They are united also in their resource demands, to get back what once they had, to recover their share, or more simply to get more so that old people can live and children survive. The dignity of the poor lies not in accepting their lot, learning to live simply with the constant possibility of death, but in the possibility too of life and resistance, silently or openly, locally and regionally, particularly and universally. Liberation ecologies, in the sense of environmentally based differences in conceptions of resource use, are also liberation ecology, in terms of similarity of resource deprivation. Are there political principles that combine the universal with the particular?

Radical Democracy

Radical democracy believes in direct popular control over all the resources and institutions used and inhabited by people, from field to forest, factory to family, university to neighborhood, art gallery to website. "Democracy in everything" is favored for two essential reasons that combine the particular with the eternal: people know best how to organize and operate their own institutions, and radical democracy is necessary for the finest, ethical human qualities to be realized, for the human to emerge as a socially responsible yet creative and free individual. Take natural circumstances to begin with. Human beings are natural creatures bound into relations with the earth that originated them, cohabiting the environment with other organisms, dependent on the world's resources for the very possibility of continued existence. But now take the social: we are also utterly encultured, enthralled by social interaction and the constant fascination of language and expression. Social interaction occurs in reproductive institutions, such as the workplace, the school, the village, the university, the family, and the community, locales where life is made collectively and people must exist together. On the one hand, there is a structuring, necessary quality to social reproduction; on the other hand, necessity becomes enjoyable, indeed the source of pleasure, when subject to human creativity. The one underlies the other: work can satisfy exactly because it is necessary. This complex of necessary, yet potentially enjoyable, tasks and relationships connects natural environment and reproductive locale with radical democracies. For if social reproduction within environments is not subject to democratic control, but instead democracy is limited to the relatively superficial level of electing state representatives (under the constant barrage of media inducements), then how can it be claimed that society is, in any way, fundamentally, typically, democratic? And if democracy is interpreted as liberal and representative in form, rather than direct and participatory, how can it be claimed that people live actually democratic lives?

Hence the belief that democracy must entail control over the basic, essential, structuring activities of the life process. Democracy must be radical, reproductive, and participatory. From this alternative perspective, life-maintaining and life-expressing institutions are fundamentally characterized by cooperative effort among equal partners, "equal" in that all expend most of their lifetimes working to satisfy needs and remaking humankind. Beyond this lies an existential, locale-based equality between people living together in places, bound into networks through multiple social relations and intersecting life paths. Hence the emphasis by socialist feminism on production and reproduction as inseparable aspects of the making of existence. Hence a conception that includes gender as well as class relations, women's labor in the domestic and public spheres, child rearing and socialization, and the family, productive, and reproductive processes united again under new social relations. Hence a notion of the "economic" that includes all kinds of labor, not just the part badly rewarded through wages.

A truly democratic egalitarian society has to entail control over *all* life institutions by *all* their members as direct and equal participants. That is, all decisions about significant social practices must be democratically and directly made. Social and environmental relations would thus be subject to intense scrutiny by everyone directly involved. The democratic socialist idea is to direct institutional activities through collective discussion or "reasoning"—this involves clarifying assumptions, collectively structuring arguments, drawing connections between actions and possible consequences, evaluating the relative merits of consequences, and taking collective and individual responsibility for outcomes. In a critical modernist sense, this implies a conception of practical, embedded reason, the best reasonable people can do under prevailing conditions, rather than the achievement of rational perfection ("Reason") as with the Enlightenment or Hegel's idealism. The implication for collective action seems to be that worker-, member-, and community-controlled institutions should be organized by democratic planning—*democratic* to ensure that popular reasoning is expressed in social activities, and *planning* so that the probable consequences of actions, for the poorest people, for the environment, among other things, are known as collective decisions are made. In this, collective adherence and responsibility are gained through participation in decision making rather than through the imposition of laws; indeed, laws are admissions of social dysfunctionality.

When social relations, organized around these basic, structural activities, are interpreted in terms of equality of contribution, when decisions are made through the active participation of all members of society, an ethical system can emerge that emphasizes mutuality, in the sense of a deep responsibility to others, and to the environment. In such a cooperative, egalitarian, and democratic society the possibility exists that pragmatically rational, compassionate decisions can be made by ethical people whose commitment to each other, and to the society of which they are integral parts, extends forward in history and outward in space toward all other people, toward all other natural organisms, and to the world as a total system. Principles like these are worth the finest of intellectual and practical effort. In a phrase, development has to be radically reproductive and radically democratic.

Alternative Development

Let us now draw these ideas together to outline a truly alternative development, different from development practice as conventionally understood, yet drawing on the modern project of improving life by creating the material conditions for human contentedness and happiness. What can be extracted from developmentalism: What is worth saving? The idea, present even in liberal versions of development theory, of using production to satisfy needs in a reason*ed* environment, such as planning, where the consequences of action are discussed before action is taken. Specifically, that *development* means using production to meet the needs of the poorest people. Similarly, if we reexamine socialism, not as a monolith represented by the Soviet Union, not as a political dinosaur, but as a living tradition of critical thought, what is worth saving? The notion of *reproductive democracy*, that the people involved in an institution—the workplace, the university, or the family—should collectively control that institution. Specifically, that workers not only "participate" in management, or research, or whatever, that they *are* the managers, researchers, and so on. Putting the two notions together, *socialist development means transforming the conditions of reproduction under the control of directly democratic and egalitarian social relations so that the needs of the poorest people are met.* This is an argument for a critical, democratic, Marxist developmentalism that engages poststructural notions—for example, the analysis of discourse—learns from them, but continues to believe in structure, coherence, science, reason*ing*, and democracy in every sphere of life, and the use of productive resources to meet peoples' desperate needs.

Let us put the case succinctly: we want the crux of an alternative development to lie in the production of more goods to satisfy needs as part of a wider strategy of transforming power relations in society at large. Borrowing a term with deliberate sarcasm from the World Bank, development for us primarily means building "economic capacity" so that material life can be improved. Yet "economic" is broadly interpreted to mean all activities employing labor organized through social relations, whether productive in the existing, restricted sense, or socially reproductive in the feminist and radical democratic senses. The model of labor comes not from the globe-trotting executives, forever scheming how to make more money, but from mothers, peasants, and artisans whose work is connected with the direct reproduction of immediate life. Work is best when it involves sensuous interaction with natural materials, yet work is also useful and necessary for the people who do it and for those around them: this means bringing together processes of production and consumption even when separated by space, as with the notion of commodity chains (Hartwick 1998).

The second word in the above definition, "capacity," means not capitalist entrepreneurship, nor even just skills, but reproductive resources, that is, land, infrastructure, machines, fertilizers, and the like, devoted to increasing the production of food, housing, useful goods, and basic services like clinics, hospitals, schools, water mains, and toilets. Here we retain the notion of "economic growth" to mean not the expansion of the global economy in general, for the world already produces too much in dangerous ways, but growth of productive capacity in the hands of those people who need more so they can live. Furthermore, means of production have to be collectively owned, directly as cooperatives, partnerships, family enterprises, so that "development" does not continually re-create inequalities of income and power, and democratically controlled, again in direct, immediate ways, to ensure that "development" satisfies locally defined, but universally present, needs.

In the sense of critical modernism, the scientific and technical power of economic growth to underwrite development needs to be retained; but in the greater sense of democratic socialism, scientific, technical, and economic powers have to be placed in the hands of the people, directly and cooperatively, and not directed by state *or* market. In the sense of socialist feminism, development should combine, rather than separate, reproductive activities considered as a totality rather than split into hierarchical types. In the sense of utopian thinking, development has to be reconceptualized as a universal, liberating activity but, with the best of materialist poststructuralism, new imaginaries of development have to come from popular discourses, including the new social movements, but also the political ideas of the older, class-based organizations and even radical reactions to the Western Enlightenment; here we find Alatas's notion of universal knowledge from universal sources persuasive. In the sense of poststructuralism, existing discourses of development have to be ruthlessly deconstructed to reveal conceptual and political inadequacies rooted in the utter prejudices of absolute power; but in the sense of critical modernism, development has to be seen as a project employing reasoning in processes of collective improvement. Critical development-alism must be radical in the poststructural sense of changing the meaning of a corrupted term. But far more importantly, critical developmentalism, in the socialist sense, has to root material development in the transformation of society. Enormous resources are available for development, ranging from the $60 billions in aid that still flows from First World to Third World, to the thousands of people's movements organized to improve the lives of poor peoples: the first (aid) should go to the second (people's movements). Development remains a project deserving ethical respect, political support, and the best of intellectual imagination and practical activism. Let us rethink, restructure, and rework "development."

REFERENCES

Abdel-Malek, A. 1981. *Intellectual Creativity in Endogenous Cultures.* Tokyo: United Nations University.

Agarwal, B. 1991. *Structures of Patriarchy.* London: Zed Books.

Aglietta, M. 1979. *A Theory of Capitalist Regulation.* London: New Left Books.

Alatas, S. F. 1993. "On the Indigenization of Academic Discourse." *Alternatives* 18: 307–338.

Althusser, L. 1969. *For Marx.* Trans. B. Brewster. Harmondsworth, UK: Penguin.

Althusser, L., and E. Balibar. 1970. *Reading Capital.* Trans. B. Brewster. London: New Left Books.

Alvares, C. 1992. "Science." In Sachs (ed.), *The Development Dictionary:* 219–232.

Amin, S. 1976. *Unequal Development.* New York: Monthly Review Press.

Amin, S. 1989. *Eurocentrism.* New York: Monthly Review Press.

Anderson, B. 1983. *Imagined Communities.* London: Verso.

Apffel-Marglin, F., and S. Marglin, eds. 1990. *Dominating Knowledges: Development, Culture and Resistance.* Oxford, UK: Clarendon Press.

Apffel-Marglin, F., and S. Simon. 1994. "Feminist Orientalism and Development." In Harcourt (1994b: 26–45).

Arestis, P. 1996. "Post-Keynesian Economics: Towards Coherence." *Cambridge Journal of Economics* 20: 111–135.

Ashcroft B., G. Griffiths, and H. Tiffin, eds. 1989. *The Empire Writes Back: Theory and Practice in Post-Colonial Literatures.* London: Routledge.

Ashcroft B., G. Griffiths, and H. Tiffin, eds. 1995. *The Post-Colonial Studies Reader.* London: Routledge.

Ayres, C. E. 1957. "Institutional Economics: Discussion." *American Economic Review* 47: 26–27.

Balassa, B. 1981. *The Newly Industrializing Countries in the World Economy.* New York: Pergamon Press.

Bandarage, A. 1984. "Women in Development: Liberation, Marxism and Marxist Feminism." *Development and Change* 15: 495–515.

Banuri, T. 1990. "Development and the Politics of Knowledge: A Critical Interpretation of the Social Role of Modernization Theories in the Development of the Third World." In Apffel-Marglin and Marglin (1990: 29–72).

Baran, P. 1960. *The Political Economy of Growth*. New York: Monthly Review Press.

Baran, P., and P. Sweezy. 1966. *Monopoly Capital*. New York: Monthly Review Press.

Barnett, T. 1989. *Social and Economic Development*. New York: Guilford Press.

Barratt Brown, M. 1984. *Models in Political Economy*. Harmondsworth, UK: Penguin.

Baudet, H. 1965. *Paradise on Earth: Some Thoughts on European Images of Non-European Man*. New Haven, CT: Yale University Press.

Baudrillard, J. 1983. *Simulations*. Trans. P. Foss, P. Patton, and P. Beitchman. New York: Semiotexte.

Bauer, P. T. 1972. *Dissent on Development*. Cambridge, MA: Harvard University Press.

Bauer, P. T. 1981. *Equality, the Third World and Economic Delusion*. London: Methuen.

Becker, J. 1977. *Marxian Political Economy*. Cambridge, UK: Cambridge University Press.

Bentham, J. 1996. *An Introduction to the Principles of Morals and Legislation*. Oxford, UK: Clarendon Press.

Benton, T. 1984. *The Rise and Fall of Structural Marxism*. New York: St. Martin's Press.

Bernal, M. 1987. *Black Athena: The Afroasiatic Roots of Classical Civilization. Vol. 1: The Fabrication of Ancient Greece, 1785–1985*. New Brunswick, NJ: Rutgers University Press.

Best, S., and D. Kellner. 1991. *Postmodern Theory: Critical Interrogations*. New York: Guilford Press.

Bhabha, H. K. 1983. "The Other Question." *Screen* 24, 6: 18–35.

Bhabha, H. K. 1984. "Of Mimicry and Man: The Ambivalence of Colonial Discourse." *October* 28: 125–133.

Bhabha, H. K. 1986. The Other Question: Difference, Discrimination and the Discourse of Colonialism." In F. Barker et al. (eds.), *Literature, Politics and Theory*. London: Methuen: 148–172.

Bhabha, H. K. 1994. *The Location of Culture*. London: Routledge.

Bienefeld, M. 1981. "Dependence and the Newly Industrializing Countries (NICs): Towards a Reappraisal." In D. Seers (ed.), *Dependency Theory: A Critical Assessment*. London: Frances Pinter: 79–96.

Blaut, J. M. 1976. "Where Was Capitalism Born?" *Antipode* 8, 2: 1–11.

Blaut, J. M. 1994. "Robert Brenner in the Tunnel of Time." *Antipode* 26: 351–374.

Blomstrom, M., and B. Hettne. 1984. *Development Theory in Transition*. London: Zed Books.

Boggs, C. 1976. *Gramsci's Marxism*. London: Pluto Press.

Booth, D. 1985. "Marxism and Development Sociology: Interpreting the Impasse." *World Development* 13: 761–787.

Boserup, E. 1970. *Women's Role in Economic Development*. London: George Allen & Unwin.

Bowie, M. 1991. *Lacan*. Cambridge, MA: Harvard University Press.

Braudel, F. 1972. *The Mediterranean and the Mediterranean World in the Age of Phillip II*. Trans. S. Re. New York: Harper & Row.

Braudel, F. 1973. *Capitalism and Material Life, 1400–1800*. Trans. M. Kochen. New York: Harper & Row.

Brenner, R. 1977. "The Origins of Capitalist Development: A Critique of Neo-Smithian Marxism." *New Left Review* 104: 25–92.

Brohman, J. 1996a. "Postwar Development in the Asian NICs: Does the Neoliberal Model Fit Reality?" *Economic Geography* 72: 107–130.

Brohman, J. 1996b. *Popular Development: Rethinking the Theory and Practice of Development*. Oxford, UK: Blackwell.

Bunch, C., and R. Carillo. 1990. "Feminist Perspectives on Women in Development." In I. Tinker (ed.), *Persistent Inequalities*. Oxford, UK: Oxford University Press: 70–82.

Bunch, C., M. Dutt, and S. Fried. 1995. *Beijing 1995: A Global Referendum on the Human Rights of Women*. New Brunswick, NJ: Center for Women's Global Leadership.

Caldwell, M. 1977. *The Wealth of Some Nations*. London: Zed Press.

Cardoso, F. 1982. "Dependency and Development in Latin America." In H. Alavi and T. Shanin (eds.), *Introduction to the Sociology of Developing Societies*. New York: Monthly Review Press: 112–127.

Cardoso, F., and R. Faletto. 1979. *Dependency and Development*. Berkeley and Los Angeles: University of California Press.

Cassirer, E. 1951. *The Philosophy of the Enlightenment*. Princeton, NJ: Princeton University Press.

Chase-Dunn, C. 1989. *Global Formations: Structures of the Global Economy*. Cambridge, UK: Blackwell.

Chilcote, R. H. 1984. *Theories of Development and Underdevelopment*. Boulder, CO: Westview Press.

Chodorow, N. 1978. *The Reproduction of Mothering: Psychoanalysis and the Sociology of Gender*. Berkeley and Los Angeles: University of California Press.

Chowdry, G. 1995. "Engendering Development?" In Marchand and Parpart (1995: 26–41).

Cixous, H. 1980. "The Laugh of the Medusa." In S. E. Mark and I. de Courtivron (eds.), *New French Feminisms*. Amherst: University of Massachusetts Press: 245–264.

Clark, J. B. 1888. Capital and Its Earnings. *American Economic Association Quarterly* 3: 2.

Clark, M. 1990. *Nietzsche on Truth and Philosophy*. Cambridge, UK: Cambridge University Press.

Clark, J. 1991. *Democratizing Development: The Role of Voluntary Organizations*. West Hartford, CT: Kumarian Press.

Cohen, B. J. 1973. *The Question of Imperialism*. New York: Basic Books.

Cohen, G. A. 1978. *Karl Marx's Theory of History: A Defense*. Princeton, NJ: Princeton University Press.

Cohen, I. J. 1989. *Structuration Theory: Anthony Giddens and the Constitution of Social Life*. New York: St. Martin's Press.

Coleman, J. C. 1971. "The Development Syndrome: Differentiation–Equality–Capacity." In L. Binder et al. (eds.), *Crises and Sequences of Political Development*. Princeton, NJ: Princeton University Press.

Comaroff, J., and J. Comaroff. 1991. *Of Revelation and Revolution*. Chicago: University of Chicago Press.

Combahee River Collective. 1984. "A Black Feminist Statement." In A. M. Jaggar and P. S. Rothenberg (eds.), *Feminist Frameworks* New York: McGraw-Hill: 202–209.

Comte, A. 1988 ed. *Introduction to Positive Philosophy*. Indianapolis, IN: Hackett.

Cowen, M. P., and R. W. Shenton. 1996. *Doctrines of Development*. London: Routledge.

Cutler, A., B. Hindess, P. Hirst, and A. Hussain. 1977—1978. *Marx's "Capital" and Capitalism Today* (Vol. 2). London: Routledge & Kegan Paul.

Dalla Costa, M. 1973. "Women and the Subversion of the Community." In *The Power of Women and the Subversion of the Community*. Bristol, UK: Falling Wall Press: 19–54.

Dallmeyer, F. 1996. "Global Development? Voices from Delhi." *Alternatives* 21: 259–282.

Dasgupta, A. K. 1985. *Epochs of Economic Theory*. Oxford, UK: Blackwell.

de Certeau, M. 1984. *The Practice of Everyday Life*. Trans. S. Rendall. Berkeley and Los Angeles: University of California Press.

de Condorcet, M. 1972 ed. "Sketch for a Historical Picture of the Progress of the Human Mind." In L. M. Marsak (ed.), *The Enlightenment* New York: Wiley: 131–146.

deJanvry, A. 1981. *The Agrarian Question and Reformism in Latin America*. Baltimore: Johns Hopkins University Press.

Deleuze, G. 1983. *Nietzsche and Philosophy*. Trans. H. Tomlinson. New York: Columbia University Press.

Deleuze, G., and F. Guattari. 1987. *A Thousand Plateaus*. Trans. B. Massumi. Minneapolis: University of Minnesota Press.

Derrida, Jacques. 1971. "White Mythology." In *Margins of Philosophy*. Trans. A. Bass. Chicago: University of Chicago Press.

Di Stefano, C. 1990. "Dilemmas of Difference: Feminism, Modernity and Post-modernism." In L. Nicholson (ed.), *Feminism/Postmodernism*. New York: Routledge: 63–82.

Dirlik, A. 1994. "The Postcolonial Aura: Third World Criticism in the Age of Global Capitalism." *Critical Inquiry* 20: 328–356.

Domar, E. 1947 "Expansion and Employment." *American Economic Review* 37: 34–55.

Dorn, J. A., S. H. Hanke, and A. A. Walters, eds. 1998. *The Revolution in Development Economics*. Washington, DC: Cato Institute.

Dos Santos, T. 1970. "The Structure of Dependence." *American Economic Review* 60: 231–236.

Dreyfus, H. L., and P. Rabinow, 1983. *Michel Foucault: Beyond Structuralism and Hermeneutics.* Chicago: University of Chicago Press.

DuBois, M. 1991. "The Governance of the Third World: A Foucauldian Perspective on Power Relations in Development." *Alternatives* 16: 1–30.

Dugger, W. M. 1989. "Radical Institutionalism: Basic Concepts." In W. M. Dugger (ed.), *Radical Institutionalism: Contemporary Voices.* New York: Greenwood Press: 1–20.

Dunford, M., and D. Perrons. 1983. *The Arena of Capital.* New York: St. Martin's Press.

Edwards, M. 1989. "The Irrelevance of Development Studies." *Third World Quarterly* 11: 116–135.

Eisenstadt, S. N. 1973. "Social Change and Development." In S. N. Eisenstadt (ed.), *Readings in Social Evolution and Development.* Oxford, UK: Pergamon Press, 3–33.

Ekins, P., and M. Max-Neef, eds. 1986. *Real-Life Economics.* London: Routledge.

Emmanuel, A. 1972. *Unequal Exchange: A Study of the Imperialism of Trade.* New York: Monthly Review Press.

Engels, F. 1972. *The Origin of the Family, Private Property and the State.* New York: International Publishers.

Escobar, A. 1984–1985. "Discourse and Power in Development: Michel Foucault and the Relevance of His Work to the Third World." *Alternatives* 10: 377–400.

Escobar, A. 1988. "Power and Visibility: Development and the Invention and Management of the Third World." *Cultural Anthropology* 3: 428–443.

Escobar, A. 1992a. "Imagining a Post-Development Era? Critical Thought, Development and Social Movements." *Social Text* 31–32: 20–56.

Escobar, A. 1992b. "Culture, Economics, and Politics in Latin American Social Movements: Theory and Research." In A. Escobar and S. E. Alvarez (eds.), *The Making of Social Movements in Latin America.* Boulder, CO: Westview Press: 62–85.

Escobar, A. 1995. *Encountering Development: The Making and Unmaking of the Third World.* Princeton, NJ: Princeton University Press.

Esteva, G. 1987. "Regenerating People's Spaces." *Alternatives* 12: 125–152.

Esteva, G., and M. D. Prakash. 1997. "From Global Thinking to Local Thinking." In Rahnema with Bawtree (1997: 277–289).

Etienne, M., and E. Leacock, eds. 1980. *Women and Colonization.* New York: Praeger.

Evers, T. 1985. "Identity: The Hidden Side of New Social Movements in Latin America." In D. Slater (ed.), *New Social Movements and the State in Latin America.* Amsterdam: CEDLA: 43–71.

Fals Borda, O. 1988. *Knowledge and People's Power: Lessons with Peasants in Nicaragua, Mexico and Colombia.* New York: New Horizons Press.

Fannon, F. 1968. *The Wretched of the Earth.* New York: Grove Press.

Fannon, F. 1986. *Black Skin, White Masks*. London: Pluto Press.

Ferguson, A., and N. Folbre. 1981. "The Unhappy Marriage of Patriarchy and Capitalism." In L. Sargent (ed.), *Women and Revolution*. Boston: South End Press: 300–320.

Fitzgibbons, A. 1995. *Adam Smith's System of Liberty, Wealth and Virtue*. Oxford, UK: Clarendon Press.

Flax, J. 1990. "Postmodernism and Gender Relations in Feminist Theory." In L. J. Nicholson (ed.), *Feminism/Postmodernism*. New York: Routledge: 39–62.

Foucault, M. 1972. *The Archaeology of Knowledge*. Trans. A. M. Sheridan Smith. New York: Harper & Row.

Foucault, M. 1973. *The Order of Things*. New York: Vintage Books.

Foucault, M. 1980a. *Power/Knowledge: Selected Interviews and Other Writings*. Trans. C. Gordon. New York: Pantheon Books.

Foucault, M. 1980b. *History of Sexuality*. Trans. R. Hurley. New York: Vintage Books.

Frank, A. G. 1969a. *Latin America: Underdevelopment or Revolution?* New York: Monthly Review Press.

Frank, A. G. 1969b. *Capitalism and Underdevelopment in Latin America* New York: Monthly Review Press.

Frank, A. G. 1979. *Dependent Accumulation and Underdevelopment*. New York: Monthly Review Press.

Friedman, E. 1995. "Women's Human Rights: The Emergence of a Movement." In J. Peters and A. Wolper (eds.), *Women's Rights, Human Rights: International Feminist Perspectives*. New York: Routledge: 18–35.

Fukuyama, F. 1989. "The End of History?" *National Interest* 16: 3–18.

Furtado, C. 1963. *The Economic Growth of Brazil*. Berkeley and Los Angeles: University of California Press.

Galtung, J. 1978. *Toward Self-Reliance and Global Interdependence*. Ottawa: Canadian International Development Agency.

Gandhi, M. 1997. "The Quest for a Simple Life: My Idea of Swarej." In Rahnema with Bowtree (1997: 306–307).

Gates, H. L. 1991. "Critical Fanonism." *Critical Inquiry* 17: 457–470.

Gendzier, I. 1985. *Managing Political Change: Social Scientists and the Third World*. Boulder, CO: Westview Press.

Giddens, A. 1977. *Studies in Social and Political Theory*. New York: Basic Books.

Giddens, A. 1981. *A Contemporary Critique of Historical Materialism*. Berkeley and Los Angeles: University of California Press.

Giddens, A. 1984. *The Constitution of Society: Outline of a Theory of Structuration*. Berkeley and Los Angeles: University of California Press.

Godwin, W. 1946 ed. *Political Justice*. Ed. F. E. L. Priestly. Toronto: University of Toronto Press.

Goss, J. 1996. "Postcolonialism: Subverting Which Empire?" *Third World Quarterly* 17: 239–250.

Gould, P. 1964. "A Note on Research into the Diffusion of Development." *Journal of Modern African Studies* 2: 123–125.

Gouldner, A. 1970. *The Coming Crisis of Western Sociology.* New York: Basic Books.

Gramsci, A. 1971. *Selections from the Prison Notebooks of Antonio Gramsci.* Eds. Q. Hoare and G. N. Smith. New York: International Publishers.

Gudeman, S., and A. Rivera. 1992. "Remodelling the House of Economics: Culture and Innovation." *American Ethnologist* 19: 141–154.

Guha, R. 1983. *Elementary Aspects of Peasant Insurgency in Colonial India.* Delhi, India: Oxford University Press.

Guha, R. 1988. "The Prose of Counter-Insurgency." In R. Guha and G. Spivak (eds.), *Subaltern Studies* (Vol. 6). Delhi, India: Oxford University Press: 37–44.

Guha, R., and G. Spivak, eds. 1988. *Selected Subaltern Studies.* Delhi, India: Oxford University Press.

Hagen, E. 1962. *On the Theory of Social Change.* Homewood, IL: Dorsey Press.

Hagerstrand, T. 1952. *The Propagation of Innovation Waves.* Lund Studies in Geography, Series B, No. 4. Lund, Sweden: C. W. K. Gleerup.

Hamilton, P. 1983. *Talcott Parsons.* London: Tavistock.

Haney, L. H. 1949. *History of Economic Thought.* New York: Macmillan.

Haraway, D. 1988. "Situated Knowledges: The Science Question in Feminism and the Privilege of Partial Perspective." *Feminist Studies* 14: 575–599.

Haraway, D. 1991. *Simians, Cyborgs and Women: The Reinvention of Nature.* New York: Routledge.

Harcourt, W. 1994a. "Negotiating Positions in the Sustainable Development Debate." In Harcourt (1994b: 11–25).

Harcourt, W., ed. 1994b. *Feminist Perspectives on Sustainable Development.* London: Zed Books.

Harding, S. 1986. *The Science Question in Feminism.* Ithaca, NY: Cornell University Press.

Harding, S. 1990. "Feminism, Science, and the Anti-Enlightenment Critiques." In Nicholson (1990: 83–106).

Harris, N. 1986. *The End of the Third World.* Harmondsworth, UK: Penguin.

Harrod, R. F. 1939. "An Essay in Dynamic Theory." *Economic Journal* 49: 14–33.

Hart-Landsberg, M., and P. Burkett. 1998. "Contradictions of Capitalist Industrialization in East Asia: A Critique of 'Flying Geese' Theories of Development." *Economic Geography* 74: 87–110.

Hartmann, H. 1984. "The Unhappy Marriage of Marxism and Feminism: Towards a More Progressive Union." In L. Sargent (ed.), *Women and Revolution.* Boston: South End Press:

Hartsock, N. 1985. *Money, Sex and Power.* Boston: Northeastern University Press.

Hartwick, E. 1998. "Geographies of Consumption: A Commodity Chain Analysis." *Society and Space* 16: 423–437.

Harvey, D. 1982. *The Limits to Capital.* Oxford, UK: Blackwell.

Hecksher, E. F. 1935. *Mercantilism* (2 vols.). London: Unwin Hyman.

Hegel, G. W. F. 1967 ed. *The Phenomenology of Mind.* Trans. J. B. Baillie. New York: Harper.

Heidegger, M. 1962. *Being and Time*. Trans. J. Macquarrie and E. Robinson. New York: Harper & Row.

Heidegger, M. 1977. "Letter on Humanism." In D. F. Krell (ed.), *Martin Heidegger: Basic Writings*. London: Routledge & Kegan Paul: 197–242.

Heilbroner, R. L. 1986. *The Worldly Philosophers* (6th ed.). New York: Simon & Schuster.

Higgins, B. 1968. *Economic Development: Principles, Problems and Policies*. New York: Norton.

Higgot, R. 1983. *Political Development Theory: The Contemporary Debate*. New York: St. Martin's Press.

Hindess, B., and P. Hirst. 1975. *Pre-Capitalist Modes of Production*. London: Routledge & Kegan Paul.

Hindess, B., and P. Hirst. 1977. *Mode of Production and Social Formation: An Autocritique of Pre-Capitalist Modes of Production*. London: Macmillan.

Hirsch, J. 1978. "The State Apparatus and Social Reproduction." In J. Holloway and S. Picciotto (eds.), *State and Capital: A Marxist Debate*. London: Edward Arnold: 57–107.

Hirschman, A. 1958. *The Strategy of Economic Development*. New Haven, CT: Yale University Press.

Hirshman, M. 1995. "Women and Development: A Critique." In Marchand and Papert (1995: 42–55).

Hobson, J. A. 1902. *Imperialism: A Study*. London: Allen & Unwin.

Hofstadter, R. 1955. *Social Darwinism in American Thought*. Boston: Beacon Press.

Holland, M. 1998. "World Bank Book (Shh!)" *Nation* 226, 10: 4–5.

hooks, b. 1984. *Feminist Theory: From Margin to Center*. Boston: South End Press.

Horkheimer, M., and T. Adorno. 1991. *Dialectic of Enlightenment*. Trans. J. Cumming. New York: Continuum.

Hoselitz, B. 1960. *Sociological Aspects of Economic Growth*. Glencoe, IL: Free Press.

Hulme, P. 1986. *Colonial Encounters: Europe and the Native Caribbean, 1692–1797*. London: Methuen.

Hume, D. 1987 ed. *Essays, Moral, Political and Literary*. Indianapolis: University of Indiana Press.

Husserl, E. 1970. *The Crisis of European Sciences and Transcendental Phenomenology: An Introduction to Phenomenological Philosophy*. Trans. D. Carr. Evanston, IL: Northwestern University Press.

Hutchison, T. W. 1953. *A Review of Economic Doctrines, 1870–1929*. Oxford, UK: Clarendon Press.

Illich, I. 1997. "Development as Planned Poverty." In Rahnema with Bawtree (1995: 94–102).

Inkeles, A., and D. H. Smith. 1974. *Becoming Modern: Individual Change in Six Developing Countries*. Cambridge, MA: Harvard University Press.

Innes, S. 1995. *Creating the Commonwealth: The Economic Culture of Puritan New England*. New York: Norton.

Insel, A. 1993. "La part du don: Essai d'evaluation." In M. Mauss, *Ce que veut dire: Don et interet*. Paris: Decouverte: 221–234.

Irigaray, L. 1985. *This Sex Which Is Not One*. Ithaca, NY: Cornell University Press.

Jackman, R. W. 1984. "Dependence on Foreign Investment and Economic Growth in the Third World." In M. A. Seligson (ed.), *The Gap between Rich and Poor: Contending Perspectives on the Political Economy of Development*. Boulder, CO: Westview Press: 211–223.

Jagger, A. 1983. *Feminist Politics and Human Nature*. Totowa, NJ: Rowman & Littlefield.

James, P. 1997. "Postdependency? The Third World in an Era of Globalism and Late Capitalism." *Alternatives* 22: 205–226.

Jaquette, J. 1990. "Women and Modernization Theory: A Decade of Feminist Criticism." *World Politics* 34: 267–284.

Jevons, W. S. 1911 ed. *The Theory of Political Economy*. London: Macmillan.

Johnson, E. S., and H. G. Johnson. 1978. *The Shadow of Keynes: Understanding Keynes, Cambridge and Keynesian Economics*. Oxford, UK: Blackwell.

Johnson, H. G. 1971. "The Keynesian Revolution and the Monetarist Counter-Revolution." *Papers and Proceedings, American Economic Association* 61: 1–14.

Johnson, P. 1994. *Feminism as Radical Humanism*. Boulder, CO: Westview Press.

Kabeer, N. 1994. *Reversed Realities: Gender Hierarchies in Development Thought*. London: Verso.

Keynes, J. M. 1936. *The General Theory of Employment, Interest and Money*. New York: Harcourt Brace.

Kiely, R. 1998. "Neo Liberalism Revised? A Critical Account of World Bank Concepts of Good Governance and Market Friendly Intervention." *Capital and Class* 64: 63–88.

Kojm, C., ed. 1984. *The Problem of International Debt*. New York: Wilson.

Kothari, R. 1989. *Rethinking Development: In Search of Humane Alternatives*. New York: New Horizons.

Kristeva, J. 1980. *Desire in Language: A Semiotic Approach to Literature and Art*. Oxford, UK: Blackwell.

Kuznets, S. 1953. *Economic Change*. New York: Norton.

Laclau, E., and C. Mouffe. 1985. *Hegemony and Socialist Strategy: Towards a Radical Democratic Politics*. London: Verso.

Lal, D. 1980. *A Liberal International Economic Order*. Essays in International Finance, No. 139. Princeton, NJ: Princeton University Press.

Lal, D. 1983. *The Poverty of Development Economics*. London: Institute of Economic Affairs.

Latouche, S. 1993. *In the Wake of the Affluent Society: An Exploration of Post-Development*. London: Zed Books.

Leborgne, D., and A. Lipietz. 1988. "New Technologies, New Modes of Regulation: Some Spatial Implications." *Society and Space* 6: 263–280.

Leibenstein, H. 1957. *Economic Backwardness and Economic Growth*. New York: Wiley.

Lefort, C. 1978. "Marx: From One Vision of History to Another" *Social Research* 45, 4.

Lekachman, R. 1959. *A History of Economic Ideas* New York: Harper & Row.

Lekachman, R. 1966. *The Age of Keynes.* New York: Random House.

Lenin, V. I. 1975 ed. *Imperialism, the Highest Stage of Capitalism.* Peking: Foreign Language Press.

Lerner, D. 1958. *The Passing of Traditional Society: Modernizing the Middle East.* New York: Free Press.

Lévi-Strauss, C. 1966. *The Savage Mind.* Chicago: University of Chicago Press.

Lewis, W. D. 1955. *The Theory of Economic Growth.* Homewood, IL: Irwing.

Lipietz, A. 1985. *The Enchanted World.* London: Verso.

Lipietz, A. 1986. "New Tendencies in the International Division of Labor: Regimes of Accumulation and Modes of Regulation." In A. Scott and M. Storper (eds.), *Production, Work, Territory.* Boston: Allen & Unwin: 16–40.

Lipietz, A. 1987. *Mirages and Miracles.* London: Verso.

List, F. 1909 ed. *The National System of Political Economy.* London: Longmans.

Little, I. M. D. 1982. *Economic Development: Theory, Policy and International Relations.* New York: Basic Books.

Lloyd, G. 1984. *Man of Reason: "Male" and "Female." In Western Philosophy.* Minneapolis: University of Minnesota Press.

Logan, I. B., and K. Mengisteab. 1993. "IMF–World Bank Adjustment and Structural Transformation in Sub-Saharan Africa." *Economic Geography* 69: 1–24.

Long, D. G. 1977. *Bentham on Liberty: Jeremy Bentham's Idea of Liberty in Relation to His Utilitarianism.* Toronto: University of Toronto Press.

Long, N. 1975. "Structural Dependency, Modes of Production and Economic Brokerage in Peru." In I. Oxaal, A. Barnett, and D. Booth (eds.), *Beyond the Sociology of Development.* London: Routledge & Kegan Paul:

Lorde, A. 1981. "The Master's Tools Will Never Dismantle the Master's House." In C. Morroga and G. Anzaldua (eds.), *The Bridge Called Me Back: Writings by Radical Women of Color.* Watertown, MA: Persaphone Press: 98–101.

Luxembourg, R. 1951 ed. *The Accumulation of Capital.* London: Routledge & Kegan Paul.

Lyotard, J-F. 1984. *The Postmodern Condition.* Trans. G. Bennington and B. Massumi. Minneapolis: University of Minnesota Press.

MacCabe, C. 1987. "Foreword." In G. Spivak, *In Other Worlds: Essays in Cultural Politics.* New York: Methuen: ix–xix.

Macpherson, C. B. 1962. *The Political Theory of Possessive Individualism.* Oxford, UK: Clarendon Press.

Malthus, T. R. 1933 ed. *Essay on Population.* New York: Everyman.

Marchand, M. H., and J. L. Parpart, eds. 1995. *Feminism/Postmodernism/Development.* London: Routledge.

Marshall, A. 1920. *Principles of Economics.* London: Macmillan.

Marx, K. 1970. "Preface." In *A Contribution to the Critique of Political Economy.* Moscow: Progress Publishers: 19–23.

Marx, K. 1973. *Grundrisse: Introduction to the Critique of Political Economy.* Trans. M. Nicolaus. Harmondsworth, UK: Penguin.

Marx, K. 1976. *Capital* (Vol. 1). Harmondsworth, UK: Penguin.

Marx, K. 1983. *Capital* (Vol. 3). Harmondsworth, UK: Penguin.

Marx, K., and F. Engels. 1981 ed. *The German Ideology.* New York: International Publishers.

Mazlish, B. 1991. "The Breakdown of Connections and Modern Development." *World Development* 19: 31–44.

McClelland, D. C. 1961. *The Achieving Society.* Princeton, NJ: Van Nostrand.

McClelland, D. C., and D. G. Winter. 1971. *Motivating Economic Achievement.* New York: Free Press.

McGrane, B. 1989. *Beyond Anthropology: Society and the Other.* New York: Columbia University Press.

McNamara, R. S. 1981. *The McNamara Years at the World Bank* Baltimore: Johns Hopkins University Press.

Meier, G., ed. 1984. *Leading Issues in Development Economics* (4th ed.). New York: Oxford University Press.

Melucci, A. 1988. "Getting Involved: Identity and Mobilization in Social Movements." In H. Kriesi, S. Tarrow, and B. Vui (eds.), *International Social Movements Research* (Vol 1). London: JAI Press:

Merchant, C. 1980. *The Death of Nature.* San Francisco: Harper & Row.

Mies, M. 1986. *Patriarchy and Accumulation on a World Scale* London: Zed Books.

Miles, A. 1996. *Integrative Feminisms: Building Global Visions, 1960s–1990s.* New York: Routledge.

Mill, J. S. 1909 ed. *Principles of Political Economy.* London: Longmans.

Minh-ha, T. T. 1989. *Woman, Native, Other: Writing Postcoloniality and Feminism.* Bloomington: Indiana University Press.

Mitchell, J. 1966. "Women, the Longest Revolution." *New Left Review* 40: 11–37.

Mitchell, T. 1988. *Colonising Egypt.* Cambridge, UK: Cambridge University Press.

Moggridge, D. E. 1980. *The Collected Works of John Maynard Keynes* (2 vols.). London: Macmillan.

Mohanty, C. 1991a. "Cartographies of Struggle: Third World Women and the Politics of Feminism." In C. T. Mohanty, A. Russo, and L. Torres (eds.), *Third World Women and the Politics of Feminism.* Bloomington: Indiana University Press: 1–49.

Mohanty, C. 1991b. "Under Western Eyes: Feminist Scholarship and Colonial Discourses." In C. Mohanty, A. Russo, and L. Torres (eds.), *Third World Women and the Politics of Feminism.* Bloomington: Indiana University Press: 51–80.

Mommsen, W. J. 1980. *Theories of Imperialism.* Chicago: University of Chicago Press.

Moser, C. 1993. *Gender Planning and Development.* New York: Routledge.

Mueller, A. 1987. *Peasants and Professionals: The Social Organization of*

Women in Development Knowledge. PhD diss., Department of Education, University of Toronto.

Myrdal, G. 1984. "Trade as a Mechanism of International Inequality." In Meier (1984: 498–503).

Nandy, A. 1983. *The Intimate Enemy: Loss and Recovery of Self under Colonialism*. Delhi, India: Oxford University Press.

Nandy, A. 1987. *Tradition, Tyranny and Utopias*. Delhi, India: Oxford University Press.

Newman, P. C. 1952. *The Development of Economic Thought*. New York: Prentice-Hall.

Nicholson, L., ed. 1990. *Feminism/Postmodernism*. New York: Routledge.

Nietzsche, F. 1968 ed. *The Will to Power*. Trans. W. Kaufmann and R. J. Hollingdale. New York: Random House.

North, D. C. 1990. "Institutions and a Transaction–Cost Theory of Exchange." In J. E. Alt and K. A. Shepsle (eds.), *Perspectives on Positive Political Economy*. Cambridge, UK: Cambridge University Press: 182–194.

North, D. C. 1995. "The New Institutional Economics and Third World Development." In J. Harris, J. Hunter, and C. M. Lewis (eds.), *The New Institutional Economics and Third World Development*. London: Routledge: 17–26.

O'Conner, M., and R. Arnoux. 1993. "Translators' Introduction." In Latouche (1993: 1–20).

Ollman, B. 1976. *Alienation: Marx's Conception of Man in Capitalist Society*. Cambridge, UK: Cambridge University Press.

Overbeek, H. 1990. *Global Capitalism and National Decline: The Thatcher Decade in Perspective*. London: Unwin Hyman.

Overbeek, H. ed. 1993. *Restructuring Hegemony in the Global Political Economy: The Rise of Transnational Neo-Liberalism in the 1980s*. London: Routledge.

Palma, G. 1978. "Dependency: A Formal Theory of Underdevelopment or a Methodology for the Analysis of Concrete Situations of Underdevelopment?" *World Development* 6: 881–924.

Palma, G. 1981. "Dependency and Development: A Critical Overview." In D. Seers (ed.), *Dependency Theory: A Critical Assessment*. London: Frances Pinter: 20–78.

Parpart, J. L. 1995. "Deconstructing the Development Expert." In Marchand and Parpart (1995: 221–243).

Parpart J. L., and M. H. Marchand. 1995. "Exploding the Canon: An Introduction/Conclusion." In Marchand and Parpart (1995: 1–22).

Parsons, T. 1948. *The Structure of Social Action*. New York: McGraw-Hill.

Parsons, T. 1960. *Structure and Process in Modern Societies*. Glencoe, IL: Free Press.

Parsons, T. 1961. "Some Considerations on the Theory of Social Change." *Rural Sociology* 26: 219–239.

Parsons, T. 1966. *Societies: Evolutionary and Comparative Perspectives*. Englewood Cliffs, NJ: Prentice-Hall.

Parsons, T. 1971a. *The Social System*. Glencoe, IL: Free Press.

Parsons, T. 1971b. *The System of Modern Societies*. Englewood Cliffs, NJ: Prentice-Hall.

Parsons, T., and E. Shils. 1951. *Towards a General Theory of Action*. Cambridge, MA: Harvard University Press.

Parsons, T., and N. J. Smelser. 1956. *Economy and Society*. London: Routledge & Kegan Paul.

Payer, C. 1982. *The World Bank: A Critical Analysis*. New York: Monthly Review Press.

Peet, R. 1985. "The Social Origins of Environmental Determinism." *Annals of the Association of American Geographers* 75: 309–333.

Peet, R. 1996. "A Sign Taken for History: Daniel Shays' Memorial in Petersham, Massachusetts." *Annals of the Association of American Geographers* 86: 21–43.

Peet, R. 1998. *Modern Geographical Thought*. Oxford, UK: Blackwell.

Peet, R., and M. Watts. 1996. *Liberation Ecologies*. London: Routledge.

Pezzullo, C. 1982. *Women and Development: Guidelines for Programme and Project Planning*. Santiago, Chile: United Nations Economic Commission for Latin America and the Caribbean.

Philo, C. 1992. "Foucault's Geography." *Society and Space* 10: 137–161.

Pieterese J., and B. Parekha, eds. 1995. *The Decolonization of Imagination: Culture, Knowledge and Power*. London: Zed Books.

Piore, M., and C. Sabel. 1984. *The Second Industrial Divide*. New York: Basic Books.

Poggi, G. 1983. *Calvinism and the Capitalist Spirit: Max Weber's Protestant Ethic*. Amherst: University of Massachusetts Press.

Polanyi, K. 1944. *The Great Transformation*. Boston: Beacon Press.

Post, K. 1978. *Arise Ye Starvlings*. The Hague: Martin Nijhoff.

Prakash, G. 1994. "Subaltern Studies as Postcolonial Criticism." *American Historical Review* 99: 1475–1490.

Prebisch, R. 1972. *International Economics and Development*. New York: Academic Press.

Rahnema, M. 1990. "Participatory Action Theory: The 'Last Temptation of Saint' Development." *Alternatives* 15: 199–226.

Rahnema, M. 1997. "Towards Post-Development: Searching for Signposts, a New Language and New Paradigms." In Rahnema with Bawtree (1997: 377–403).

Rahnema, M., with V. Bawtree, eds. 1997. *The Postdevelopment Reader*. London: Zed Books.

Rand, A. 1957. *Atlas Shrugged*. New York: Random House.

Rathgeber, E. M. 1990. "WID, WAD, GAD: Trends in Research and Practice." *Journal of Developing Areas* 24: 489–502.

Republic of South Africa. 1996. *Growth, Employment and Redistribution: A Macroeconomic Strategy*. Pretoria: Department of Finance, Republic of South Africa.

Rey, P. O. 1973. *Les alliances de classes*. Paris: Maspero.

Ricardo, D. 1817. *The Principles of Political Economy and Taxation*. London: John Muffay.

Rich, A. 1986. *Blood, Bread and Poetry: Selected Prose, 1979–1985*. New York: Norton.

Riddell, J. B. 1970. *The Spatial Dynamics of Modernization in Sierra Leone*. Evanston, IL: Northwestern University Press.

Rist, G. 1997. *The History of Development: From Western Origins to Global Faith*. London: Zed Books.

Ritzer, G. 1992. *Contemporary Sociological Theory*. New York: McGraw-Hill.

Rocheleau, D., B. Thomas-Slayter, and E. Wangari, eds. 1996. *Feminist Political Ecology: Global Issues and Local Experiences*. London: Routledge.

Roches, G. 1975. *Talcott Parsons and American Sociology*. New York: Barnes & Noble.

Rodney, W. 1974. *How Europe Underdeveloped Africa*. Washington, DC: Howard University Press.

Rogers, B. 1980. *The Domestication of Women: Discrimination in Developing Societies*. London: Tavistock.

Roll, E. 1942. *A History of Economic Thought*. New York: Prentice-Hall.

Rosenstein-Rodan, P. 1943. "Problems of Industrialization of Eastern and South-Eastern Europe." *Economic Journal* 53: 205–216.

Rostow, W. W. 1960. *The Stages of Economic Growth: A Non-Communist Manifesto*. Cambridge, UK: Cambridge University Press.

Roth, G., and W. Schluchter. 1979. *Max Weber's Vision of History: Ethics and Methods*. Bekeley and Los Angeles: University of California Press.

Roussakis, E. N. 1968. *Friedrich List, the Zollverein, and the Uniting of Europe*. Bruges, Belgium: College of Europe.

Sachs, J. 1991. *The Economic Transformation of Eastern Europe: The Case of Poland*. Memphis, TN: P.K. Seidman Foundation.

Sachs, W., ed. 1992. *The Development Dictionary: A Guide to Knowledge as Power*. London: Zed Books.

Sachs, W. 1997. "The Need for the Home Perspective." In Rahnema with Bawtree (1997: 290–300).

Said, E. W. 1979. *Orientalism*. London: Routledge & Kegan Paul.

Said, E. 1989. "Representing the Colonized: Anthropology's Interlocutors." *Critical Inquiry* 15: 205–225.

Samuels, W. J. 1995. "The Present State of Institutional Economics." *Cambridge Journal of Economics* 19: 569–590.

Samuelson, P. 1980. *Economics* (11th ed.). New York: McGraw-Hill.

Savage, S. 1981. *The Theories of Talcott Parsons: The Social Relations of Action*. New York: St. Martin's Press.

Schluchter, W. 1981. *The Rise of Western Rationalism: Max Weber's Developmental History*. Berkeley and Los Angeles: University of California Press.

Schultz, T. W. 1964. *Transforming Traditional Agriculture*. New Haven, CT: Yale University Press.

Schumpeter, J. 1934. *The Theory of Economic Development*. Cambridge, MA: Harvard University Press.

Schumpeter, J. 1952. *The Sociology of Imperialism*. New York: Kelly.

Scott, A. 1988. "Flexible Production Systems and Regional Development: The

Rise of New Industrial Spaces in North America and Western Europe." *International Journal of Urban and Regional Research* 12: 171–186.

Scott, A., and M. Storper, eds. 1986. *Production, Work, Territory.* Boston: Allen & Unwin.

Scott, C. V. 1995. *Gender and Development: Rethinking Modernization and Dependency Theory.* Boulder, CO: Lynne Reiner.

Scott, J. 1985. *Weapons of the Weak: Everyday Forms of Peasant Resistance.* New Haven, CT: Yale University Press.

Scott, J. 1990. *Domination and the Arts of Resistance: Hidden Transcripts.* New Haven, CT: Yale University Press.

Seers, D. 1962. "A Theory of Inflation and Growth in Under-Developed Countries Based on the Experience in Latin America." *Oxford Economic Papers* 14: 173–195.

Seers, D. 1983. *The Political Economy of Nationalism.* Oxford, UK: Oxford University Press.

Semple, E. C. 1903. *American History and its Geographic Conditions.* Boston: Houghton Mifflin.

Semple, E. C. 1911. *Influences of Geographic Environment on the Basis of Ratzel's System of Anthropo-Geography.* New York: Russell & Russell.

Sen, G., and C. Grown. 1987. *Development Crises and Alternative Visions.* New York: Monthly Review Press.

Shanin, T. 1997. "The Idea of Progress." In Rahnema with Bawtree (1997: 65–72).

Shannon, T. R. 1989. *An Introduction to the World-System Perspective.* Boulder, CO: Westview Press.

Shi, D. 1997. "The Searchers after the Simple Life." In Rahnema with Bawtree (1997: 308–310).

Shionoya, Y. 1997. *Schumpeter and the Idea of Social Science.* Cambridge, UK: Cambridge University Press.

Shiva, V. 1989. *Staying Alive.* London: Zed Books.

Shohat, E. 1992. "Notes on the Post-Colonial." *Social Text* 31–32: 99–113.

Singer, H. 1992. "Lessons of Post-War Development Experience: 1945–88." In S. Sharma (ed.), *Development Policy.* New York: St. Martin's Press: 35–80.

Skinner, A. S. 1992. "Political Economy: Adam Smith and His Predecessors." In P. Jones and A. S. Skinner (eds.), *Adam Smith Reviewed.* Edinburgh: Edinburgh University Press: 217–42.

Slater, D. 1992. "Theories of Development and Politics of the Post-Modern—Exploring a Border Zone." *Development and Change* 3: 283–319.

Slater, D. 1993. "The Geopolitical Imagination and the Enframing of Development Theory." *Transactions* (Institute of British Geographers) 18: 419–437.

Smith, A. 1937 ed. *The Wealth of Nations.* New York: Modern Library.

Smith, A. 1976 ed. *The Theory of Moral Sentiments.* Oxford, UK: Oxford University Press.

Smith, D. 1990. *The Conceptual Practices of Power.* Boston: Northeastern University Press.

Snyder, M. 1995. *Transforming Development: Women, Poverty and Politics.* London: Intermediate Technology.

Soja, E. W. 1968. *The Geography of Modernization in Kenya: A Spatial Analysis of Social, Economic and Political Change.* Syracuse, NY: Syracuse: University Press.

Solow, R. 1970. *Growth Theory: An Exposition.* New York: Oxford University Press.

Sorensen, T., ed. 1988. *"Let the Word Go Forth": The Speeches, Statements, and Writings of John F. Kennedy.* New York: Delacorte Press.

Spencer, H. 1882. *The Principles of Sociology.* New York: Appleton.

Spivak, G. C. 1987. *In Other Worlds: Essays in Cultural Politics.* New York: Routledge.

Spivak, G. C. 1988. "Can the Subaltern Speak?." In C. Nelson and L. Grossberg (eds.), *Marxism and the Interpretation of Culture.* Urbana: University of Illinois Press: 271–313.

Spybey, T. 1992. *Social Change, Development and Dependency.* Cambridge, MA: Polity Press.

Streeten, P. 1995. "Foreword." In ul Haq (1995: vii–xvi).

Sunkel, O. 1972. "Big Business and Dependencia." *Foreign Affairs* 50: 517–531.

Szentes, T. 1976. *The Political Economy of Underdevelopment* (3rd ed.). Budapest: Akademia Kiado.

Taussig, M. 1987. *Shaminism, Colonialism and the Wild Man.* Chicago: University of Chicago Press.

Taylor, J. G. 1979. *From Modernization to Modes of Production.* London: Macmillan.

Tilman, R. 1992. *Thorstein Veblen and His Critics, 1891–1963.* Princeton, NJ: Princeton University Press.

Timpanaro, S. 1975. *On Materialism.* London: New Left Books.

Todaro, M. 1971. *Development Planning: Models and Methods.* Nairobi, Kenya: Oxford University Press.

Todorov, T. 1984. *The Conquest of America: The Question of the Other.* New York: Harper & Row.

Touraine, A. 1981. *The Voice and the Eye.* New York: Cambridge University Press.

Touraine, A. 1988. *The Return of the Actor.* Minneapolis: University of Minnesota Press.

Toye, J. 1987. *Dilemmas of Development: Reflections on the Counter-Revolution in Development Theory and Policy.* Oxford, UK: Blackwell.

Tribe, K. 1988. "Friedrich List and the Critique of 'Cosmopolitical Economy.' " *Manchester School* 61: 17–36.

ul Haq, M. 1995. *Reflections on Human Development.* New York: Oxford University Press.

United Nations Development Program. 1991. *Human Development Report.* New York: United Nations Development Program.

United Nations Development Program. 1998. *Human Development Report.* New York: United Nations Development Program.

Vandergeist, P., and F. Buttel. 1988. "Marx, Weber, and Development Sociology: Beyond the Impasse." *World Development* 16: 683–695.

Veblen, T. 1912. *The Theory of the Leisure Class: An Economic Study of Institutions.* New York: Macmillan Co.

Vico, G. B. 1984 ed. *The New Science of Giambattista Vico.* Trans. T. G. Bergin and M. H. Fisch. Ithaca, NY: Cornell University Press.

Visvanathan, N. 1997. "Introduction to Part I." In Visvanathan et al. (1997: 17–32).

Visvanathan, N., et al., eds. 1997. *The Women, Gender and Development Reader.* London: Zed Books.

Vogel, L. 1983. *Marxism and the Oppression of Women.* London: Pluto Press.

von Hayek, F. 1956. *The Road to Serfdom.* Chicago: University of Chicago Press.

von Hornick, P.W. 1961. "Austria Over All If She Only Will" (1684). In K. W. Kapp and L. L. Kapp, *History of Economic Thought: A Book of Readings.* New York: Barnes & Noble: 47–62.

von Thünen, J. H. 1966. *von Thünen's Isolated State.* Oxford, UK: Oxford University Press.

Wallerstein, I. 1974. *The Modern World System* (Vol. 1). New York: Academic Press.

Wallerstein, I. 1979. *The Capitalist World Economy.* New York: Cambridge University Press.

Watts, M. 1983. *Silent Violence: Food, Famine and Peasantry in Northern Nigeria.* Berkeley and Los Angeles: University of California Press.

Weber, M. 1958 ed. *The Protestant Ethic and the Spirit of Capitalism.* Trans. T. Parsons. New York: Scribner's.

Weber, M. 1978. *Max Weber: Selections in Translation.* Ed. W. G. Runciman. Trans. E. Matthews. Cambridge, UK: Cambridge University Press.

Weeks, J. 1981. *Capital and Exploitation.* London: Edward Arnold.

Weeks, P. 1990. "Post-Colonial Challenges to Grand Theory." *Human Organization* 49, 3: 236–244.

Williamson, J., ed. 1990. *Latin American Adjustment: How Much Has Happened?* Washington, DC: Institute for International Economics.

Williamson, J. 1997. "The Washington Consensus Revisited." In L. Emmerij (ed.), *Economic and Social Development into the 21st Century.* Washington, DC: Inter-American Development Bank.

Williamson, O. E. 1985. *The Economic Institutions of Capitalism: Firms, Markets, Relational Contracting.* New York: Free Press.

World Bank. 1978. *World Development Report.* New York: Oxford University Press.

World Bank. 1981. *Accelerated Development in Sub-Saharan Africa: An Agenda for Action.* Washington, DC: World Bank.

World Bank. 1983. *World Development Report.* New York: Oxford University Press.

World Bank. 1984. *World Development Report.* New York: Oxford University Press.

World Bank. 1985. *World Development Report.* New York: Oxford University Press.

World Bank. 1987. *World Development Report.* New York: Oxford University Press.

World Bank. 1989. *World Development Report.* New York: Oxford University Press.

World Bank. 1990. *World Development Report.* New York: Oxford University Press.

World Bank. 1997. *World Development Report.* New York: Oxford University Press.

World Bank. 1998. *East Asia: The Road to Recovery.* Washington, DC: World Bank.

Young, K. 1992. *Gender and Development Reader.* Ottawa: Canadian Council for International Cooperation.

Young, K. 1993. *Planning Development with Women.* New York: St. Martin's Press.

Young, R. 1990. *White Mythologies: Writing History and the West.* London: Routledge.

Zeitlin, I. M. 1972. *Capitalism and Imperialism: An Introduction to Neo-Marxian Concepts.* Chicago: Markham.

INDEX